Toussaint Louverture

Toussaint Louverture

A Biography

MADISON SMARTT BELL

PANTHEON BOOKS   NEW YORK

ISBN-13: 978-0-375-42337-6

Book design by Soonyoung Kwon
Printed in the United States of America
Book Club Edition

Aux grands marrons!

Yves Benot
Gérard Barthélemy
Michel Rolph Trouillot

Toussaint Louverture, placed in the midst of rebel slaves from the beginning of the revolution of Saint Domingue, thwarted by the Spanish and the English, attached to the French, attacked by everyone, and believing himself deceived by the whole world, had early felt the necessity of making himself impenetrable. While his age served him well in this regard, nature had also done much for him . . . One never knew what he was doing, if he was leaving, if he was staying; where he was going or whence he came.[1]

—Général Pamphile de Lacroix

Does anyone think that men who have enjoyed the benefits of freedom would look on calmly while it is stripped from them? They bore their chains as long as they knew no better way of life than slavery. But today when they have left it, if they had a thousand lives they would sacrifice them all rather than to be again reduced to slavery . . . We knew how to face danger to win our liberty; we will know how to face death to keep it.[2]

—Toussaint Louverture

Contents

Acknowledgments

My thanks to Laurent Dubois, Jacques de Cauna, Albert Valdman, and David Geggus for their extraordinarily generous help in straightening me out on numerous specific points . . . but these scholars are not to be held responsible for the conclusions I then drew. I thank Marcel Dorigny, Laënnec Hurbon, Jane Landers, and Alyssa Sepinwall for their aid and comfort. *Grand merci et chapeau bas* to Fabrice Hérard and Philippe Pichot for a very educational visit to the Fort de Joux.

Toussaint Louverture

Introduction

As the leader of the only successful slave revolution in recorded history, and as the founder of the only independent black state in the Western Hemisphere ever to be created by former slaves, François Dominique Toussaint Louverture can fairly be called the highest-achieving African-American hero of all time. And yet, two hundred years after his death in prison and the declaration of independence of Haiti, the nation whose birth he made possible, he remains one of the least known and most poorly understood among those heroes. In the United States, at least until recently, the fame of Toussaint Louverture has not spread far beyond the black community (which was very well aware of him and his actions for two or three generations before slavery ended here). Neither Toussaint's astounding career nor the successful struggle for Haitian independence figures very prominently in standard history textbooks—despite, or perhaps because of, their critical importance from the time they began in the late eighteenth century to the time of our own Civil War.

In his own country, Toussaint Louverture is honored very highly indeed—but not unequivocally. In the pantheon of Haitian national heroes, Toussaint is just slightly diminished by the label "Precursor" of liberty and nationhood for the revolutionary slaves who took over the French colony of Saint Domingue. The title "Liberator" is reserved for

Jean-Jacques Dessalines, the general who took Toussaint's place in the revolutionary war, who presided over Haiti's declaration of independence from France, and soon after crowned himself emperor. It's true enough that Dessalines was the first man across the finish line in the race for liberty in Haiti. But without Toussaint's catalytic role, it's unlikely that Dessalines or anyone else would have known how or where to enter that race.

Today's Haiti, known until 1804 as French Saint Domingue, occupies the western third of the island of Hispaniola, or "Little Spain"—the name that Christopher Columbus gave it when he first arrived in 1492. The 1.3 million Taino Indians who already lived there called their homeland Ayiti, which means "mountainous place." Most of the Indians were peaceable Arawaks, though a community of more warlike Caribs had settled, comparatively recently, on an eastern promontory, in what is today the Dominican Republic.

Hispaniola was not the first landfall in the New World for Columbus's expedition, but it was the first place where he built a settlement on land, beginning with timber from one of his three ships, the *Santa Maria,* which had foundered in the Baie d'Acul, on Haiti's northwest coast. After their long, cramped voyage of uncertain destination, Columbus's sailors and soldiers may well have felt that they had blundered into paradise, especially since in the beginning the Arawaks received them as gods descended from the sky. Food grew on trees and the living was easy. The awestruck Arawaks were friendly, their women agreeably willing. The Spaniards were fascinated, among other things, by the pure gold ornaments these natives wore.

Columbus left one of his crews in these pleasant conditions and sailed back to Spain to report his success and to gather more men and material to exploit it. By the time he returned, in 1493, the Arawak-Spanish honeymoon had come to an ugly end. Exasperated by the abduction and rape of Arawak women, the cacique Caonabo, one of five chiefs who ruled the five kingdoms into which the Arawaks had divided the island, had launched a retaliation; the fort called La Navidad was razed and a handful of the Spaniards were slain.

This second time, Columbus arrived in Hispaniola with seventeen ships and two hundred men, including four priests. His patrons, King Ferdinand and Queen Isabella of Spain, had instructed him to convert the Indians to Christianity, and to acquire for Spain the considerable quantity of gold which their jewelry suggested they must possess. The hostilities which had broken out during Columbus's absence provided a pretext to conduct these operations by force. According to royal orders, the Arawaks were compelled to accept Christ as their savior and to labor in the mines of Cibao to extract and surrender the gold which they themselves had used only for ornament, not for money. Thirty years later, this program had reduced a native population of well over a million to something between five and ten thousand, all of whom would eventually disappear, leaving next to no trace that they had ever existed. It was one of the most vast and successful examples of genocide recorded in human history.

Columbus's second expedition also included a Spaniard named Bartolomé de Las Casas, who during his first days in Hispaniola comported himself as a conquistador, and enjoyed his own team of Indian slaves. In 1506 he returned to Spain, where he took holy orders; by 1511 he had been ordained as a Dominican priest. Back in Hispaniola, with the cooperation of a few others in the Dominican order, he began to struggle, fervently if futilely, against the cruel and fatal mistreatment of the Indians.

The Spanish throne, church, and military justified the enslavement of the Indians on the grounds that they were idolatrous and barbarous, the latter point proved by their alleged practice of cannibalism (though it seems that few if any of Hispaniola's Indians ever were cannibals). An argument was borrowed from Aristotle to the effect that such benighted beings were naturally meant to be slaves. The counterarguments used by Las Casas had much in common not only with the idea of natural and universal human rights which would later drive the American, French, and Haitian revolutions, but also with the liberation theology which, a full five centuries down the road, would help bring Father Jean-Bertrand Aristide to leadership in Haiti. Las Casas believed that the Indians were as fully endowed with reason as the Europeans enslaving them, and that the so-called evangelical mission merely masked the Spanish greed for gold.

By 1517, Las Casas could see that Indian civilization and the whole Indian race were in real and imminent danger of extermination. He joined a handful of others in suggesting that the indigenous people of Hispaniola, who died like flies in conditions of slavery, might successfully be replaced by African slaves, who seemed better able to tolerate that situation. Though often blamed for it, Las Casas did not single-handedly invent the African slave trade, which the Portuguese had already begun; he was not the only one to conceive of bringing African slaves to European New World colonies, though he was one of the first. He lived long enough to recognize that the substitution of African slaves would not save Hispaniola's Indians after all, and before the end of his career he had become as much an advocate for the human rights of the African slaves as for those of the Indians. But the spirit of African slavery had been loosed from its bottle; it would take over three centuries, and many bloody wars, to put it to rest.

Haitian Vodou, which has its deepest roots in the religions of the several tribes of Africa's west coast, also makes use of a great deal of Catholic symbolism, many of the fundamentals of charismatic Christianity, and at least a few beliefs and practices of Hispaniola's indigenous Indians, some of whom did survive long enough to interact with the African-born slaves—especially in the mountain retreats of the runaway slaves who were called *marrons,* or maroons. Vodou lays a great importance on the idea of *kalfou,* or crossroads. There is understood to be a great crossroads between the world of the living and the other world inhabited by the spirits of the dead, which is considered to be quite near to our own, though invisible. Traffic through this crossroads defines a great deal of Vodouisant religious practice: spirits of the ancestors, amalgamated into more universal spirits called *lwa,* pass through to enter the world of the living and make their needs and wishes known.

In more practical terms, quantities of time and distance in Haiti are more likely to be recognized and understood in terms of intersections, rather than the lines between them. Historically, the island of Hispaniola is a tremendously important *kalfou*—the crossroads where Europeans, Native Americans, and Africans came together for the first time. The fundamental pattern of their relationship all over the Western Hemisphere—dispossession and extermination of the Indians by the Europeans, who go on to exploit the seized territory with African slave labor—was set for the first time here.

Though the Spaniards opened the channel to the New World for the African slave trade, they never really made full use of it. The conquistadors were much more interested in pure gold than in the riches that could be wrung from a labor-intensive plantation economy. Sugar production in Hispaniola did begin under Spanish rule, but by the end of the sixteenth century most of the conquistadors had moved on to the looting of gold-rich Indian empires on the South American continent. The plantation economy of Hispaniola (by this time more commonly called Santo Domingo, after its capital city in the southeast) was stagnant, and even the importation of slaves had slowed to a trickle. The continuous hard labor of growing cane and processing sugar was mostly abandoned in favor of cattle ranching.

The early Spanish voyagers in the New World had the habit of releasing a few domestic animals—goats, pigs, or cattle—on every island where they made landfall. The practice was an investment in the future: when they next visited one of these islands, months or years later, meat would be available on the hoof. In the seventeenth century there was enough wild livestock in the western third of Hispaniola (an area only sparsely settled by the Spanish) to support a group of European hunters called "buccaneers" after the fire pit, or *boucan,* over which they smoked their meat. At the same time, the island of Tortuga, just off Hispaniola, had become a permanent base for the *flibustiers,* who during Europe's frequent wars were licensed by the French government to capture enemy ships as prizes, and during peacetime captured any ships they could, as pure piracy. Despite frequent attempts, the Spaniards were unable to uproot either of these two groups.

In the Windward Islands, to Hispaniola's southeast, the French had had colonies at Martinique and Guadeloupe since 1635. In 1697 a French commander appeared in western Hispaniola, by then a de facto French colony, though unrecognized by law or treaty, to recruit from the buccaneer and *flibustier* communities for a raid on Cartagena, a prosperous Spanish port on the coast of present-day Colombia. The smashing success of this expedition was an important factor in the cession of western Hispaniola by the Spanish in the Treaty of Ryswick later the same year. The colony of French Saint Domingue now officially existed.

Once legally sanctioned, the French colonists began to turn from buccaneering and piracy toward a plantation economy, reviving the sugar production which the Spanish had let drift into dereliction. About one hundred new sugar plantations were founded in the four-year period from 1700 to 1704, and the importation of African slaves to work them increased proportionately.

Pirate and buccaneer communities were notoriously short of women, and most of the colonists who began to immigrate to the new French Saint Domingue did not bring their families with them. Their idea was not to put down permanent roots in Saint Domingue (in contrast to the British colonies on the North American continent) but to make a quick killing in the lucrative sugar trade, then return to Paris to enjoy the money. Legend has it that, in response to the request of the colonial government for white women immigrants, a boatload of prostitutes was swept from the streets of Paris and shipped to Saint Domingue. Some of these ladies, faute de mieux, became matriarchs of the first families of the colony.

Under these conditions, cohabitation of Frenchmen with African slave women was more or less inevitable. By 1789, 30,000 persons of mixed European-African ancestry were counted in Saint Domingue, as compared with a white population of 40,000. These mixed-blood people were sometimes called "mulattoes," a less-than-polite term derived from the French word for "mule," or more courteously described as "colored people": gens de couleur. Under the British slave system, which the United States inherited, a person with as much as a sixteenth part of African blood (notably, one step further than the naked eye can detect) was defined as black and thus subject to slavery. The French system, by contrast, recognized the gens de couleur as a third race. As the American abolitionist Wendell Phillips put it, "unlike us, the French slaveholder never forgot his child by a bondwoman. He gave him everything but his name."[1]

Some mulattoes remained in slavery, but more were freed by their fathers and became property and slave owners themselves. By 1789, the population of African slaves was estimated at 500,000 or more. A decade following the American Revolution, and just as the French Revolution began, the slaves of Saint Domingue outnumbered the white master class by at least twelve to one, and they outnumbered the combined white and colored population by at least seven to one.

Most of the wealthiest sugar planters had become absentee owners, living in France on income produced by slaves governed by professional plantation managers on site. Owners of not-quite-so-profitable plantations of indigo, cotton, or (increasingly) coffee were more likely to live in the colony, with their white families, mixed-blood families, or often enough some uneasy combination of both. These plantation owners, the cream of colonial society, were commonly called *grands blancs,* or "big whites." Even before the whole situation was polarized by the French Revolution, there was a degree of class tension between this group and the "little whites," or *petits blancs,* a population of merchants, artisans, sailors, international transients, and fortune seekers who mostly lived in the rapidly expanding cities and towns along the coast. The entire white community was united by fervent racism and by a mutual investment in the slave system (most *petits blancs* hoped and intended to evolve into *grands blancs*), but divided by differences of economic status and interest.

The free *gens de couleur* were socially and politically excluded by the whites (their parents) and at the same time given very considerable educational and economic support. The luckiest had been sent to France for their schooling (the home government, wary of trends that might lead to an independence movement in the colony, forbade the establishment of colleges for anyone in Saint Domingue) and owned plantations and slaves themselves. Others belonged to the artisan and petty merchant class. Colored women included a famous community of courtesans; mistresses to the most powerful white men of the colony, they were renowned for their grace, beauty, charm, and finely honed professional skill. Most *gens de couleur,* whatever their walk of life, counted relatives among both the African slaves and the European slave masters.

The *gens de couleur* outnumbered the whites in two of Saint Domingue's three provinces, and were an economic force to be reckoned throughout the colony, but regardless of their status within their group, they were all subject to the same vicious racial discrimination. As of 1789, the colored people had no political rights whatsoever, and were subject to numerous humiliating little rules. Their surnames, usually derived from white parentage, were required to carry the phrase *le dit*—a derisive "the so-called." Colored men could not carry arms in town and were forbidden to mingle with whites in situations like church or the theater. A dress code existed for both sexes, though it was much relaxed for colored women following a strike by the notorious courtesans.

At the same time, colored men were a large majority in all branches of colonial military service. In the latter half of the eighteenth century, service in the militias and the *maréchaussée* (a sort of police force that devoted much time to the capture of runaway slaves) was seen as onerous by the whites of Saint Domingue, who assiduously sought to evade it. But the military was embraced by the *gens de couleur*. For freedmen it was a way of earning respect; for others (including some slaves of undiluted African blood) it was a pathway to freedom. Though not uncommon, the freeing of slaves was frowned on by the government and discouraged by a manumission tax of between five hundred and two thousand colonial livres—a very substantial sum, payable by the slave owner. Those who served in special military missions (including support of the American Revolution at the battle of Savannah in 1779) could earn a waiver of this tax, and the *maréchaussée* offered such waivers even in peacetime. An unintended and unexamined consequence of these practices was that much of the defense of the colony was placed in the hands of a race and class which the whites of Saint Domingue were determined to oppress.

The labor-intensive plantation system of French Saint Domingue required extraordinary growth of the slave population, mainly through importation rather than new births. As many as thirty thousand new slaves arrived from Africa every year. Some slaves were able to earn their freedom, through military service, as with the *gens de couleur,* or the exercise of some particular skill which might pay down their price to their masters. In the records of the time, free blacks are hard to distinguish from free *gens de couleur;* their legal status was the same, though their social situation was not, and often the two groups are amalgamated under the designation *affranchis,* or freedmen.

Conditions for Saint Domingue's slaves were unusually harsh. The colony's geography encouraged escape. At the edge of every cane field was likely to be found the first of a seemingly infinite series of mountains, covered with near-impenetrable jungle, with rain forest at the greatest heights. It was easy enough to snatch up one's cane-cutting machete and bolt, difficult to be recaptured. The colony distinguished between *petit marronage,* where a slave might go AWOL for just a few days to visit neighboring plantations, carry out personal business, or just enjoy a taste of freedom, and *grand marronage,* where escape was permanent, or intended to be. The number and size of maroon communities in the mountains have been disputed by late-twentieth-century scholarship, but certainly there were more than a few of them. Some were quite sizable, and some, like the large group at Bahoruco, southeast of the capital of Port-au-Prince, had their independence and freedom formally recognized by the colonial government. In the beginning, some maroon groups joined Hispaniola's last surviving few Arawaks, and though the Indian bloodline was soon invisibly submerged in the African, some Indian religious and cultural practices were absorbed by the maroons. Meanwhile, the demand to recapture runaway slaves, and the need for defense against bands of maroon raiders who sometimes pillaged outlying plantations, required both the maroons and the *maréchaussée* to develop a certain expertise at jungle warfare.

The American Declaration of Independence began with the famously resonant claim of natural human rights to "life, liberty, and the pursuit of happiness." Everyone tacitly understood, however, that these rights belonged to white men, only. Thomas Jefferson believed that the right to vote should be limited to significant property holders—the North American equivalent of Saint Domingue's class of *grands blancs.* Those whom the French system recognized as *gens de couleur* were in the North American colonies considered to be (for legal purposes at least) as black as any African, and most of them were slaves. Slavery was not an issue in the American Revolution, many of whose political and military leaders, like Jefferson and Washington, came from Virginia's slave-holding planter class.

Though it almost immediately started evolving into a democratizing force which would be vastly influential all over the world, the American Revolution (never mind the liberation ideology it proclaimed) began for all practical purposes as a tax revolt. This revolution had no intention to disrupt any aspect of the existing colonial class structure. Its motive was to break free of the severe economic constraints imposed by the relationship of the North American colonies to their parent country, Great Britain.

The success of the American Revolution as a tax revolt found at least a few admiring eyes among the proprietors of French Saint Domingue. France imposed a trade monopoly (called the *exclusif*) on all goods produced in the colony, as well as on most goods purchased there. Saint Domingue's producers of sugar, coffee, cotton, and indigo could have traded much more advantageously in a free market that admitted Britain, the newborn United States, and all the large and small European colonies of the surrounding islands. Between 1776 and 1789, an American-style revolutionary spirit breathed among the *grands blancs* of Saint Domingue, but it would soon be overtaken by other and much more drastic events.

The French Revolution, which erupted in the heart of the homeland rather than in some distant colony, was from the start a genuine class revolution. The lower echelons of French society—what became known as the Third Estate—were determined to reverse or annihilate the old orders of precedence, privilege, and power that emanated from the throne, the aristocracy, and the clergy, and within the first two years of their movement they went a very long way toward doing just that. The French Revolution proclaimed "Liberty, Equality, and Brotherhood" as natural human rights, and while it was generally, tacitly understood that only white men were invited to enjoy them, this assumption was openly challenged, at the seat of the French home government, by representatives of Saint Domingue's *gens de couleur*.

In the colony of Saint Domingue, response to the outbreak of the

French Revolution split predictably along class lines. The *grands blancs* were apt to be royalist and reactionary, while the *petits blancs* embraced the revolution and were quick to form Jacobin political clubs in the style of those popular in Paris. Some in the *grand blanc* party fantasized about making the colony a protectorate of royalist Britain, or even making it an independent redoubt of the ancien régime and a refuge for émigré noblemen fleeing revolutionary France. The quarrel between these two tiny white factions grew so intense that they forgot all about the slumbering forces in the much larger population that surrounded them on every side.

In the first phases of the French Revolution there was absolutely no thought of letting the colony go or of changing anything significant about the way it operated. At this time Saint Domingue was the single richest European colony in the whole Western Hemisphere. Port-au-Prince, the capital and seat of government, was a relatively modest settlement, but Cap Français, the cultural capital on the north coast, was the size of eighteenth-century Boston, with a beauty and grandeur that made it known as the "Jewel of the Antilles." The sugar and coffee of Saint Domingue had not only enriched the colony's own planters, but vastly increased the prosperity of the French nation as a whole. Moreover, as revolutionary France saw its home economy disrupted and as it found itself at war with practically all the surrounding European powers, Saint Domingue was almost the only element in the whole national economy that still produced income and generally functioned as it was supposed to. Therefore the slave system in the colony, along with its systematic discrimination against colored and black freedmen, was considered to be a necessary, if evil, exception to the libertarian and egalitarian ideology which drove the revolution at home.

The French capital, meanwhile, had taken measures to discourage an independence movement. Children of colonists were required to seek their higher education in France, so that their ties to the homeland would be tightened during their formative years. The administration of Saint Domingue was divided between a military governor and a civilian intendant, placed in a situation of natural rivalry where each would serve as a check on the other; both reported, independently, to Paris. Intended to hamper colonial revolt, this deliberately engineered conflict between the civilian and the military authority actually did a great deal to destabilize the colony during the last ten years of the eighteenth century.

Conservative representatives of the colonies in Paris negotiated for Saint Domingue and the other colonial slaveholding regimes to be governed by exceptional laws that excluded the leveling terms of documents like the new French Constitution and the Declaration of the Rights of Man. At the same time, however, representatives of the free *gens de couleur* were lobbying for the right to vote in Saint Domingue, with the support of liberals in the home government, like the Abbé Grégoire. In 1790, what became known as the "decree of March 8" actually did extend the vote to free colored men, but in sufficiently ambiguous terms that the white government in Saint Domingue felt comfortable ignoring it.

In October 1790, an *homme de couleur* named Vincent Ogé returned from France to Saint Domingue and raised an armed rebellion in Dondon, a town in the mountains east of Cap Français. With his second in command, Jean-Baptiste Chavannes, and a couple of hundred other supporters, he captured the nearby town of Grande Rivière and from there sent an ultimatum to Cap Français, demanding that the provisions of the decree of March 8 be honored for all free men of color. Other such risings sprang up here and there across the country, but after some skirmishing the rebellion was crushed. Ogé and Chavannes were tortured to death in a public square in Le Cap: broken on the wheel, dismembered, their severed heads mounted on pikes as a warning. A season of equally ugly reprisals against the mulatto population followed.

To the last, Ogé insisted that he had nothing against slavery and had never had any intention to incite the slaves of Saint Domingue to join his rebellion—though some of his co-conspirators felt differently about the latter point. Certainly the Ogé revolt would have had a much better chance of success with even a fraction of the great mass of black slaves behind it, but Ogé was probably sincere in renouncing that idea; most free *gens de couleur* were as thoroughly invested in the slave system as the whites. The failure to enlist the slaves in the mulatto rebellion of 1790 was certainly a strategic mistake, though not so severe as the mistake made by the whites. What was ultimately fatal to the whites of Saint Domingue was their obstinate refusal to make common cause with the free *gens de couleur,* whom they themselves had engendered.

In the midst of all these disruptive events, the slave population of Saint Domingue was growing by leaps and bounds, though not because of reproductive success—far from it. For various reasons, abuse of the slaves on the French sugar plantations was extraordinarily severe—much more so than in the African diaspora as whole. The production of sugar requires the milling and refining as well as the cultivation and harvesting of cane, creating a temptation to work slave crews both day and night. The Code Noir of 1685, issued in the name of the king of France, set minimum standards for the treatment of slaves, but was more often honored in the breach than in the observance. The prevalence of absentee ownership exacerbated abuse, for the on-site managers were wont to overwork the slaves to extract an extra profit for themselves and to embezzle funds and provisions meant for the slaves' support. Observers in both the seventeenth and the eighteenth centuries agree that more than a third of newly imported slaves died within the first few years of their arrival in Saint Domingue.

Many planters thought it best to keep their slaves intimidated by punishments of extraordinary cruelty. Flogging was universal. Amputation of an arm or a leg was a common punishment for attempted escape; thieves might have their hands cut off. A slave who ate fruit or sugarcane in the field would be forced to work with his or her head locked in a tin cage. Some slaves were thrown alive into ovens, others buried neck-deep in the ground and left to be tormented by mosquitoes and biting ants. Still others had their anuses packed with gunpowder and exploded—a sport called "making a nigger jump."

With life such a misery, suicide, abortion, and infanticide were shockingly common among the slaves, though these too were severely punished—even the bodies of suicides were mutilated so that they would be disfigured in the afterlife, for the whites had an inkling of the blacks' belief that death was a route to a metaphysical Africa. Even for slaves who made no attempt on their own lives, life expectancy was extremely short, thanks to overwork, malnutrition, and general abuse.

Women's resistance to bringing children into the world of slavery was widespread.

Thus a huge annual importation of slaves from Africa was required to maintain a stable workforce in the colony. Between 1784 and 1790 a total of 220,000 slaves were brought in. One unintended consequence of this situation was that two-thirds of the more than half a million slaves in the colony had been born free in Africa—and nearly half of the whole slave population had been deprived of freedom within the past ten years. Therefore the atmosphere in Saint Domingue was infinitely more volatile than in other slave regimes like the United States, where by the end of the eighteenth century the majority of slaves had been born into servitude. Moreover, the example of *marronage* was ever present to the slaves of Saint Domingue. While the maroon groups were not large enough to threaten the stability of the colony on their own, the idea of them was revolutionary in the slave communities—all the more so if exaggerated—and the idea was constantly refreshed by *petits marrons* who came and went from their plantations, sometimes, it seemed, almost at will.

From 1789 on, the whites of Saint Domingue were so caught up in their own class conflict that they were careless of what they said in earshot of their slaves. Even if they had been more circumspect, it would have been very difficult to keep news of the Ogé rebellion and of the revolutionary ideology sweeping over France from the slave population. Though literacy among slaves was severely discouraged, some slaves could and certainly did read the newspapers. The fevered political discussions of the whites were bound to be overhead by mistresses, household slaves, and the black overseers and managers called *commandeurs*. And indeed, the whites were at least sometimes aware of their risk. They knew they were sitting on a powder keg, and that there were open flames nearby, but none of them seemed to know what to do to prevent the increasingly inevitable explosion.

Though the written record does not say much about it, it's safe to assume that this whole situation was being quietly and carefully observed by a man then known as Toussaint Bréda, his surname taken from Bréda Plantation, out on the fertile Northern Plain not far from

Cap Français, where he had spent much of his life as a slave and as a manager of slaves. Toussaint claimed to be over fifty in 1789—a remarkable age for a black in Saint Domingue, where thanks to exhaustion, overwork, and abuse, most slaves died much younger. He had not only survived, but conserved all his faculties; events of the next few years would prove his health, intelligence, and vigor to be absolutely extraordinary.

ONE

Opening the Gate

On August 29, 1793, a curious proclamation emerged from Camp Turel, one of numerous small fortified positions in the mountain range that runs from Gonaïves on Saint Domingue's west coast eastward to the Central Plateau and the Spanish frontier, and which had been occupied, since 1791, mostly by groups of revolting slaves, but sometimes by French soldiers and militiamen who were trying to suppress the revolt. The proclamation was a brief one:

Brothers and Friends,

I am Toussaint Louverture; perhaps my name has made itself known to you. I have undertaken vengeance. I want Liberty and Equality to reign in Saint Domingue. I am working to make that happen. Unite yourselves to us, brothers, and fight with us for the same cause.

Your very humble and obedient servant,

(Signed)
Toussaint Louverture.
General of the armies of the king, for the public good.[1]

Probably this proclamation was not the first time that the man formerly known as Toussaint Bréda had used the new surname Louverture, since it assumes that the name may already be known to his audience—but if it is not the very first time he entered this new identity into the written record, it is the first time he deliberately announced it to the general public.

Not by coincidence, August 29 was also the date that Léger Félicité Sonthonax, commissioner and chief representative of the French government then in Saint Domingue, proclaimed the abolition of slavery in the colony. The newly minted Toussaint Louverture was then officially part of the Spanish army; Spain was at war with France, and the colonists of Spanish Santo Domingo had adopted the rebel slaves of the French colony as auxiliaries to their own military. Thus, in the close of his proclamation, Toussaint was probably referring to the king of Spain, though his clustering of the words "liberty," "equality," and "brothers" is an intentional echo of the most familiar phrase of the French Revolution, *"liberté, égalité, fraternité."* Moreover, and somewhat confusingly, the rebel slaves of Saint Domingue had been claiming loyalty to the king of France almost from the moment of their first rising.

Since the fall of 1791, Toussaint had been in the mountains with the revolting slaves, though before 1793 his role was not obviously prominent. The proclamation of Camp Turel was his first deliberate effort to call attention to himself and the part he intended to play. Though Toussaint had been fighting a guerrilla war against the French for nearly two years, the timing of the proclamation suggests that he must have known in advance that Sonthonax would abolish slavery and when he was going to do it. What he meant to convey, in his lines and between them, was that Toussaint Louverture, a black man born into slavery in the colony, was the true apostle of liberty here—not the white commissioner Sonthonax, who had only recently arrived from France.

Toussaint Bréda had been a trusted retainer on Bréda Plantation, near Haut du Cap, and only a short distance from the port of Cap Français. He served as coachman for Bréda's French manager, Bayon de Libertat—an important role, since coachmen often carried messages for their masters, alone and on their own responsibility. In his additional role of *commandeur,* Toussaint enjoyed considerable authority over the majority of more ordinary slaves on the plantation. Such *commandeurs* were responsible for organizing and directing work gangs and often had other managerial duties. Surprisingly, they were allowed to carry swords, as an emblem of their authority and perhaps as a practical tool of enforcement as well.

Nocturnal gatherings of Saint Domingue's slaves were prohibited in theory, but often tolerated in practice, as a means of defusing tensions that might otherwise be released in the rebellion which all the French colonists had excellent reason to fear. Commonly called "calenda," these gatherings featured drumming and dancing and sometimes competitive stick-fighting and were officially regarded by the French as innocuous peasant dances—though some observers did report that rituals drawn from African religion were performed on these occasions.

On the night of August 14, 1791, an assembly of *commandeurs* took place in a wooded area called Bois Caïman, or Crocodile Forest, part of the Lenormand de Mézy Plantation in Morne Rouge, on the border of the richest cane-growing area in all Saint Domingue, the Northern Plain. The *commandeurs* came from all the important plantations of the Northern Plain and the foothills surrounding it: Limbé, Quartier Morin, Petite Anse, Port Margot, and Limonade. Their purpose, confessed to the French colonists by a couple of conspirators captured several days later, was to plan an enormous insurrection that would lay waste to the entire Northern Department of Saint Domingue and annihilate the white population.

This practical purpose of the meeting at Bois Caïman was set down on paper by European reporters, soon after the fact; Haitian oral tradition holds, with equal conviction, that the most important event that took place there was a huge Vodou ceremony. In real time, it had taken a century of slavery in Saint Domingue to consolidate the religions of various African tribes (along with a dusting of the Catholicism to which all slaves were theoretically supposed to be converted) into a single religion which all the slaves could share. The legend of Bois Caïman makes this transformation happen in one apocalyptic day.

Vodou practitioners believe that the souls of the dead do not depart. Instead they go into a parallel universe invisible to the living, but quite nearby—and not impossible to reach. Ceremonial observance begins with opening the gateways between the visible and the invisible worlds. When the passage is open, spirits constituted from the vast reservoir of spiritual energy into which the souls of the dead have pooled begin to pass through it into the world of the living. These spirits, called either *lwa* or *zanj,* cover the range of personalities of any polytheistic pantheon, or may as easily be identified with the archetypes of the collective unconscious. Aided by hypnotic chanting and drumming, the *lwa* take possession of the bodies of their human believers and servants, suppressing the individual consciousness of the people they "mount" and often endowing them with superhuman powers for the duration of the ride. Tradition has it that the angriest, most warlike spirits appeared at Bois Caïman: Ogoun Ferraille, Ezili Gé Rouj. The *lwa* lent their power to the rebellion being planned; a black pig was sacrificed to seal the compact.

Toussaint Bréda belonged to the class of *commandeurs* who presented themselves as leaders of the insurrection, but whether he attended the meeting at Bois Caïman has never been known for sure. Almost certainly, given his position of trust and authority among both blacks and whites, among slaves and free, he would have been well aware of which way the winds were blowing and that an insurrection was being planned. As for the Vodou element of the meeting, Toussaint's ostentatiously devout Catholicism might have kept him away from any African, pagan rite.* On the other hand, from the 1700s until now, many if not most blacks in Haiti have practiced Vodou and Catholicism simultaneously with next to no discomfort or sense of paradox in the combination. In fact, the two practices are often seen as different aspects of the same religion.

---

*An old priest in the Cul de Sac plain argued (years after the insurrection had bloomed into revolution, Toussaint had been deported to France, and the independence of Haiti had been declared) that Toussaint's absence from the early phases of the insurrection was explained by the fact the Arada *lwa,* water spirits who were his ancestral protectors and guides, forbade him to associate with the angry, fiery, Petro *lwa* invoked at Bois Caïman to lend the heat of their rage to the destruction of the slave-master colonists. To this day, some explain Haiti's difficulty in ending its cycles of political violence by the fact that the revolution was originally founded on fire instead of water.

If Toussaint was present at Bois Caïman, he remained invisibly in the background. A slave named Boukman Dutty presided; he had been sold, as a troublemaker, from Jamaica. Most likely his offense was sorcery. Legend claims that he was one of the comparatively few Muslim slaves in the West Indies and that his name is a slight French distortion of the English "Bookman," which implies that he knew how to read. Other *commandeurs* known to have been present are Jean-François Papillon, Georges Biassou, and Jeannot Billet; these three and Boukman himself were the most prominent leaders in the first weeks of the insurrection, which broke out with explosive violence on the night of August 22.

By dawn of August 23, the whole Northern Plain was devastated, the cane fields and sugar refineries ablaze. The disaster was first announced to Cap Français by the arrival of a rolling cloud of black smoke, out of which the first battered refugees emerged. Any whites who could not escape to the fortified towns of the coast were slaughtered, some sawed in half between planks, others strung up on steel hooks by their jawbones, still others simply hacked to pieces or burned alive in their houses. Haitian historians have argued that the reports of fetuses cut from the womb and of infants impaled and carried on pikes amount to no more than French propaganda, but such atrocities were also reported during white French reprisals on the *gens de couleur* in the aftermath of the Ogé rebellion. Murderous assaults on the newborn and unborn occur the world over as signals of genocidal intent. The August 1791 uprising was among other things the first engagement in a three-way genocidal race war in which each of Saint Domingue's three races—the white, the black, and the *gens de couleur*—would do its absolute worst to exterminate the other two.

No one has ever been able to say for certain just where Toussaint Bréda was during this initial tumult. If he did have a hand in the August insurrection, he kept it very well hidden. In the midst of the bloody, fiery vengeance that the rebel slaves were taking on their masters, some slaves remained loyally on their plantations and did their best to protect the white families there. Apparently Toussaint remained quietly at

Bréda Plantation for at least one month after the rebellion first erupted in late August. Curiously, the river of fire and blood flowing over the Northern Plain to lap against the hastily bolstered fortifications of Le Cap seems to have parted around Bréda, leaving it more or less intact. Still more curiously, only 22 of Bréda's 318 slaves decamped in the early days of the rebellion. The rest stayed—with Toussaint—to protect the plantation and its white mistress, Madame de Libertat.

In 1799 a letter appeared in the French newspaper *Le Moniteur,* describing Toussaint's conduct during the turbulence of 1791. Though unsigned, it could hardly have been written by anyone other than Bréda's manager, Bayon de Libertat.

> Eight days before the insurrection on the Le Cap plain, some blacks of the neighboring plantation set fire to four fields of cane . . . I was at that moment on my plantation seven leagues distant from Le Cap; Toussaint and the commandeur Bruno, invariably attached to the interests of their masters, succeeded in stopping the fire without any other help than that of the blacks of the plantation. When I arrived the next evening, all the scorched cane had been cut and pressed, and they were just finishing cooking the sugar which had been extracted from it. Toussaint came before me with a pained expression and said, "We have had an accident, but don't alarm yourself, the loss is not serious; I wanted to spare you the sight of it when you arrived, but you have come too soon." I leave it to the reader to weigh these words.
>
> Toussaint displayed an inexpressible joy to see me constantly in the midst of the blacks, giving them my orders to arouse their vigilance and their courage—and this at a time when it was enough to be white to be massacred.[2]

Toussaint's ability to keep order and conduct business as usual, in the midst of the anarchy that had engulfed the surrounding region, seems altogether extraordinary. But sometime in the fall of 1791, he left Bréda, crossed the ash-strewn ruins of the Northern Plain, and went up into the mountains of Grande Rivière, where he joined a band of rebel slaves led by Biassou. At first he served Biassou as a secretary; later he was given the title of *médecin général,* or general doctor. At Bréda Plantation and the surrounding area, Toussaint had the reputation of an excellent veterinarian, especially for horses, and he was also recognized as a *doktè fey*—literally "leaf doctor." Along with substantial skill in African/Creole herbal medicine, he seems to have had some instruction in European doctoring.

If Toussaint did any fighting when he first joined Biassou, he was not much noticed as a leader; no white observers picked him out of the fray. However, a couple of his surviving letters suggest that he already had more authority among the rebels than he wanted to be known outside that group. To Biassou he writes on October 4, 1791:

My dear friend,

I have received your letter with pleasure; I cannot agree to your rendezvous; we are not able to leave our camp, for both of us to travel to meet the Spaniard. If this Spaniard has something to communicate to me, he has only to get himself to my camp; as for myself, I don't have time to appear; I wish you the most perfect health and am for life your friend.[3]

Though Toussaint modestly signs this letter "Médecin Général," at a time when Jean-François and Biassou had declared themselves "Généralissime" and the like, there is no sign that he was under Biassou's orders—on the contrary, the message seems to pass between equals. Later on, when relations between the rebel slaves and the military of Spanish Santo Domingo had become more official, Toussaint would explain himself more fully to the Spanish colonial governor: "I reported and accounted for my operations to General Biassou, not at all because I considered myself to be his subordinate, but for love of the good, being familiar with his impetuous, muddle-headed, thoughtless character, likely to do more harm than good, as he demonstrated under all circumstances."[4]

Toussaint wrote to Biassou again on October 15, 1791, referring obscurely to what seems to have been a planned attack on the outskirts of Cap Français, if not on the town itself. The letter implies, though lightly, that Biassou may have been pushed too far in this direction by the rebels' Spanish contacts; in the event, the attack did not take place.

My Very Dear Friend,

After the requests which I have just made to the Spaniard, and as I am waiting day by day for the things which I asked for, I beg you to wait until we should be in better shape before we undertake what you have had the friendliness to write me about. I would very much like to go for it, but I would like to have, on all the plantations, enough crowbars to roll rocks down from the mountains of Haut du Cap, to hinder them [the enemy] from approaching us, for I believe there is no other way, unless we expose our people to butchery. I beg you to make certain that you will have the spy you have sent explain very well the location of the powder magazine of Haut du Cap, so that we can succeed in seizing the powder; my good friend, you can see from the above that I am taking every precaution in this affair; and you may say as much to Boukman; as for Jean-François he can always keep going on carriage rides with the ladies, and he has not even done me the honor to write me a word for several days. I am even astounded by that. If you need rum, I will send it to you whenever you want, but be careful how you manage it; you know that you must not give them [the rank and file of the rebel slaves] so much that they are deranged by it. Send me some carts, for I need them to haul wood to build cabins at La Tannerie to house my people.[5]

Though this letter is also signed "Médecin Général," it is noticeably devoid of medical concerns (apart from the judicious ration of rum). In both tone and content it shows Toussaint, behind the scenes of the revolt, to be confident of an authority comparable to that of the recognized chiefs: Boukman, Biassou, and Jean-François. Not only is he in regular communication with the top leaders of the rebellion, but he is also enough their equal that he can make sport of one in a letter to another. He has considerable supplies under his control and an interest and ability to procure more. Already he has begun to fortify his camp at La Tannerie, an important post at the bottom of the gorge of Grand Gilles, which protected the approaches to Dondon above and the passes to the Black Mountains and the Central Plateau beyond, and which would be the theater of important engagements in the months to come.

Moreover, this letter provides an interesting glimpse of the military situation of the rebel slaves in the fall of 1791. The leaders lacked firearms and powder—in the beginning they had only what they could capture from the whites—and they had very few men skilled in the use of musket or cannon. By October, the Spanish had begun to furnish some munitions, but the opaque references in Toussaint's letter suggest that this supply line was not very reliable.

In the beginning, when the rebels had been able to overwhelm better armed and trained opponents by the sheer force of their numbers (but with a terrible loss of life), Toussaint had stayed well out of it. At the time the letter was written, he had begun to develop a strategy to prevent his underarmed and still poorly trained men from confronting the fire of organized European troops at close quarters. Instead, the mass of rebel slaves would hurl down boulders from the bluffs—out of range of muskets and field artillery—while the best-organized strike teams raided the arsenals for powder and guns. Even at this early stage, Toussaint was beginning his famous practice of raiding the enemy for arms and ammunition. There was hardly anywhere else for him to get them.

Further hints of Toussaint's evolving role among the rebel slaves occur in a series of letters written by Biassou to the Abbé Guillaume Sylvestre Delahaye, parish priest of Dondon, who had been captured when this small mountain town was overrun by Jeannot on August 27, 1791.

Jeannot, notorious for torturing and murdering the white prisoners in his hands, was savage enough to shock the other rebel leaders, but the Abbé Delahaye seemed to enjoy special treatment—though confined to the Dondon parish house, he was apparently unmolested, and even promised money for saying masses when Jeannot demanded it (though it does not appear that he was ever actually paid).

Many whites already suspected Delahaye of abolitionist tendencies. Now he came under suspicion of active collaboration with the rebel slaves during the long period he spent in or near their camps. He hotly denied these accusations after he returned to the white-controlled area—at a time when other priests were being executed for the same sort of collaboration of which he was accused. Other white prisoners grouped Delahaye with a handful of priests who were actively encouraging the slave insurrection, and Biassou once wrote to request his help in drafting laws to govern the men in his command (there is no evidence that Delahaye ever responded).

Both Jeannot and Biassou showed Delahaye special consideration, the latter writing to him on October 28, 1792, that "M. le Maréchal Toussaint" had put an end to certain unspecified "hostilities" bothersome to Delahaye, and had ordered Delahaye's domestic servants (i.e., his slaves) to return to work at the Dondon parish house. The same letter reports that Toussaint had ordered a Señor García, presumably a white Spaniard, to be put in irons for insolence to Delahaye, which suggests that his authority had grown quite considerable. By the end of October, at least, Toussaint had been promoted from *médecin général* to *maréchal;* some six weeks later, on December 18, Biassou mentioned in another letter to Delahaye that "Toussaint is recognized to be general of the army."[6]

By November 1791, the military situation had drifted into a kind of standoff. In the beginning, Boukman had been the principal leader of attacks on the whites and their property that more resembled enormous riots than any sort of organized military campaign. Boukman was himself a *houngan,* or Vodou priest, as Biassou and many of the other early leaders of the revolt were reputed to be, and according to contemporary white observers, many of the men who followed them into wild charges were probably possessed by their *lwa* when they attacked. Some waved bull's tails to fan away bullets; others would simply wrap themselves around cannon mouths so that the men behind them could advance in safety.

At first these jihadlike onslaughts had been very successful. As Muslim soldiers believe that death in battle guarantees them Paradise, so the rebel slave warriors saw death as the fastest road to Ginen anba dlo. The defenses of the whites scattered over the Northern Plain were frail, and the rebel slaves needed just a few days to drive the survivors to refuge in Cap Français. The first few sorties by the town's defenders were also overwhelmed by the frenzy of the rebel attacks—these were men who seemed to care nothing for death, and though many of them were slaughtered by organized fire, the sheer force of their numbers was still enough to rout the white military. As the weeks wore on, though, the rebels began to notice their casualties. Accordingly, their tactics changed. "They did not expose themselves en masse with the former fury," wrote Des Fosses, a French combatant, "they formed groups, hiding in thickets before falling on their enemy. They even withdrew swiftly into the undergrowth. We were dealing with an enemy who, instead of making a concerted attack on the colors, was disposed in small groups so that they were able to surround or wipe out isolated or small detachments. It was a new type of warfare, more dangerous because it was unknown." Unknown at least to European soldiery, who in the eighteenth century had a confirmed habit of confronting each other on open ground in tightly composed squares. The guerrilla tactics so bewildering to the French troops were common in African wars of the period (in which many of Saint Domingue's slaves had first been captured), and also very well adapted to Haiti's mountainous jungle terrain. Toussaint's letter of October 15 suggests that he may well have had an influence on the tactical change.

In November, Boukman was killed in a battle with the regular French army on the plain near Acul. The whites, still more or less besieged, impaled his head on a stake on the public square of Cap Français with a sign reading "The head of Boukman, leader of the rebels."[7] When news of Boukman's death reached Grande Rivière, there was a spontaneous lunge to slaughter all the white prisoners there in reprisal. However, cooler heads prevailed, if by a narrow margin.

When the rebels first overran the Northern Plain, they had swept many prisoners from the plantations and taken them into their camps around Grande Rivière. The more temperate leaders saw the value of the white captives as hostages, but for others they were tempting victims for torture and rape. The not-so-temperate leader Jeannot had control of a good many prisoners, and amused himself by torturing a few of them to death every day. Finally, the other rebel leaders decided he had gone too far. Jeannot was apparently lighting a fire to roast the remaining white captives alive when a party led by Jean-François arrived, put Jeannot through some sort of hasty court-martial, and executed him just as summarily.

The white prisoners were not set free after Jeannot's execution, but they were no longer egregiously mistreated. Procurator Gros, one of Jeannot's surviving captives who'd been a legal functionary before the rebellion, was drafted as Jean-François's secretary. Much correspondence needed to be done, for the surviving rebel leaders were preparing to negotiate terms with the whites.

In France, the revolution had been hurtling forward for two years. The feudal privileges of the aristocracy and the clergy had been abolished early on. In late June 1791, Louis XVI and his family were captured at Varennes while attempting to flee the country and brought back to Paris as prisoners in all but name. Procurator Gros, still a prisoner of the rebels in the territory they controlled around Dondon, Vallière, and Grande Rivière, was startled at just how well his captors seemed to be informed of these events in Europe and how interested they seemed to be in the fate of the French monarchy.

The slave insurrection in French Saint Domingue was alarming to British slavery-based colonies in the Caribbean, especially in nearby Jamaica. The idea that French Jacobin ideology could provoke revolt among African slaves was unthinkably awful—and yet it had happened just next door. At the same time, as England verged upon war with France, the chaos in France's heretofore most prosperous colony presented an interesting point of vulnerability. Philibert-François Rouxel de Blanchelande, the military governor of French Saint Domingue, appealed to both his British and his Spanish neighbors for help; the British kept mum, while the Spanish Santo Domingans were already giving covert support to the rebel slaves camped near their border with the French colony. Toussaint, before joining Biassou, had taken his wife and children to sanctuary in the region of Saint Raphael and Saint Michel on the Central Plateau, which was then in Spanish territory, though no great distance from the rebel camps on the French side.

For the slave states of the southern United States, the insurrection in Saint Domingue was their worst nightmare made real. The tabloid newspapers were full of horror stories, some exaggerated or fabricated outright for propaganda purposes, but many of them true enough. The panoramic destruction of the plantations of the Northern Plain was practically impossible to exaggerate. In Charleston and other slave-trading ports, there was a move to stop importation of West Indian blacks. But aside from the very real concern that the rebellious contagion might spread from Saint Domingue to the plantations of the American South, the greatest U.S. interest in Saint Domingue was trade. Despite the monopolistic French trade policy, Saint Domingue was already a significant trade partner for the United States, thanks to a few small relaxations of the French *exclusif* and still more to widespread, vigorous smuggling. And for the duration of the American Revolution, trade with the United States had been legalized by the French.

There were fifty American merchantmen in the Cap Français harbor when the insurrection first broke out on the Northern Plain, so it was not long before the United States began to receive frantic requests for supplies and military aid from the besieged French colonists. The official response was hesitant at first. The fledgling United States was short of cash and wary of being drawn into bewildering French internal conflicts. Two years of strife among Saint Domingue's *blancs* had not gone unnoticed by American tradesmen in the ports. In general, American officials and diplomats were having a hard time formulating a coherent attitude toward events in France and her colonies— understandably, since the most drastic differences between the American and the French revolutions had not yet become obvious. But

despite some ambivalence of the U.S. government, unofficial shipments to Saint Domingue soon hit a high enough level to make the
French representative in the United States worry that the French
exclusif might be completely shattered.

A one-way voyage from France to Saint Domingue took six weeks, more
or less, depending on the weather. Reaction of the home government to
events in the colony could never be rapidly expressed. On May 15, 1791,
the French National Assembly had passed a hotly contested piece of
legislation which granted civil rights and the vote to *gens de couleur*
born of free parents. In July, the colored men in Saint Domingue's
Western Department, the area surrounding Port-au-Prince, raised a
clamor for enforcement of the new law. Denied, they then raised an
armed rebellion commanded by Louis-Jacques Beauvais, who like so
many leaders of the Haitian Revolution was a veteran of the siege of
Savannah during the American Revolutionary War. In late August and
early September, as the fires of the black rebellion were sweeping the
Northern Department, Beauvais's troops won a couple of engagements
with French troops and colonial militias.

   In the meantime, a clash between royalist *grands blancs* and revolutionary *petits blancs* in Port-au-Prince had ended with the slaying of the
Chevalier de Mauduit, the ranking regular army officer there. His royalist partisans retreated to the village of Croix des Bouquets, a few miles
inland from the capital. By then, news of the huge slave rebellion to
the north had begun to filter through the mountains that separated the
Cap Français region from Port-au-Prince. At Croix des Bouquets, the
grands blancs suddenly thought it best to recognize their colored relatives as equals. A mutual defense pact was struck—the Concordat of
Croix des Bouquets—by whose terms the whites recognized the law of
May 15, with its extension of civil rights to mulattoes. In the Southern
Department, on the long jawbone of Hispaniola's southwest peninsula,
similar arrangements were made between the *grands blancs* and the *gens
de couleur,* who after all shared not only a blood tie but also a vital interest in the plantation system and the slave system on which it depended.
The success of these pacts was partly explained by the fact that the *gens*

de couleur were proportionally more numerous in the Western and Southern departments than in the north—they were still outnumbered by the black slaves but not by such a crushing margin.

Word of the slave rebellion in the Northern Department and the general unrest in the Western Department had not yet reached Paris when on September 24, 1791, the National Assembly passed yet another law. This one abrogated all the terms of the decree of May 15 and threw the question of mulatto civil rights back to the white colonists. Three civil commissioners—Edmond de Saint-Léger, Frédéric Ignace de Mirbeck, and Philippe Roume de Saint Laurent—were quickly dispatched to deliver the new decree to Saint Domingue. They also brought news of a general amnesty declared by the National Assembly for "acts of revolution." Of course the amnesty was meant to settle conflicts among whites, but the black rebel leaders in the Northern Department were quick to claim a share in it.

In fact, the rebel leaders had made efforts to open negotiations before the commissioners ever arrived, writing to Governor Blanchelande, and to the Chevalier de Tousard, a senior officer of the Régiment du Cap; the latter responded, "Do not believe that the whites . . . would lower themselves so far as to receive conditions dictated and demanded of them by their rebel slaves."[8] Unconditional surrender of the rebels was the only solution that the whites would even consider, though they were in no position at all to enforce it. However, after all the damage the whites on the Northern Plain had suffered, emotions among the survivors inevitably ran high. The commissioners (who did not know the full extent of the disaster before they arrived in Cap Français on November 22) did their best to calm them, though with small success. Unfortunately, the Colonial Assembly took the position that the commissioners should not be involved in negotiations with the rebel slaves at all, since the commissioners themselves had just delivered a decree from the home government giving the assembly an overarching authority to decide "the fate of the slaves."[9] This controversy over jurisdiction crippled all the commission's efforts to resolve the crisis.

Freeing the slaves of Saint Domingue was not the original goal of the rebellion in the north. According to the rhetoric of the political segment of the meeting at Bois Caïman, the slaves were to revolt not for their freedom but to demand an end to whipping and other abuses, to gain three free days per week, and to win enforcement of some other provisions of the official Code Noir which were generally ignored by plantation owners. Throughout the summer of 1791, rumors had circulated through the whole colony's slave population that King Louis XVI had already granted the three free days but that the slave masters of Saint Domingue had refused to implement his order. This rumor inspired a plot for rebellion in the area of Les Cayes in the Southern Department, which was discovered and snuffed out some weeks before the mass insurrection exploded in the north.

The slaves who gathered at Bois Caïman were given to understand that King Louis XVI wished them well and had created the Code Noir for their benefit, but that he himself was being held hostage by evil white men who surrounded him (a distorted but not entirely groundless view of what was actually going on in France). This understanding explains, at least in part, why so many bands of rebel slaves used royalist flags and insignia and declared that they were fighting for the king.

Perhaps a hundred thousand slaves had risen in arms in August, but on December 4, the leaders (including Jean-François, Biassou, and by this time Toussaint) offered to return them peaceably to the plantations in return for abolition of the whip, one extra free day per week, and freedom for a mere three hundred people—a very small number which was later reduced to around fifty. By Gros's account, "the negro Toussaint à Bréda" was instrumental in persuading Biassou to accept the smaller number; without him "the conference would have ended without success."[10]

Impervious to the diplomatic efforts of Mirbeck, Roume, and Saint-Léger, the Colonial Assembly rejected this proposal in such contemptuous terms that Biassou, when he got the message, flew into a rage and wanted to kill all the white prisoners without delay. According to Gros, only Toussaint's quick and eloquent intercession saved him and the rest from an ugly death; "braving all dangers, he tried to save us, were himself to be the victim of the monster's rage."[11] Another white captive, M. la Roque, saw Toussaint report the breakdown of the deal to Jean-François: "Toussaint à Bréda . . . told him, with tears in his eyes, that all was lost, that the twenty-some prisoners that had come from the different camps would no longer be going to Le Cap, and that war had again been decided."[12]

The rebel leaders had not only sent emissaries to the Colonial Assembly but had also directly approached military leaders like Tousard, and had begun to make direct contact with the commissioners recently arrived from France. As the commissioners were much more concilia-tory than the Colonial Assembly, the rebel leaders preferred to deal with them—despite the fact that the assembly had formally forbidden the commissioners to treat with the rebel slaves.

Soon after the collapse of the original deal to exchange the white prisoners for a limited number of liberties, a new meeting with the commissioners was arranged for December 21 on Saint Michel Plan-tation. Again, the discord on the white side took its toll: as the two parties approached each other, M. Bullet, who had been master of Jean-François, rushed out and struck him in the face. But Commissioner Saint-Léger went after Jean-François, who had quickly retreated to the midst of his men, and persuaded him to swallow the insult and return to the conversation. Tradition has it that Jean-François was so impressed with Saint-Léger's approach that he knelt at the white man's feet.

On the strength of this parlay, the white prisoners finally were released. This time they were gathered at the camp of La Tannerie; from there Toussaint himself would escort them safely into Le Cap. By the end of December Toussaint had dug himself in deep at La Tannerie, which Gros describes as one of the two most seriously fortified camps under rebel control, equipped with cannon and surrounded by ditches and pitfall traps "which could wound a lot of our people."[13]

"What was our surprise," Gros goes on, "when once we arrived at La Tannerie, we saw the blacks gather and fall upon us with saber in hand, threatening to send only our heads to Le Cap, and cursing the peace and their generals."[14] Again it was only thanks to Toussaint's intervention that a wholesale slaughter of the prisoners was prevented.

Toussaint's more cynical observers find this episode suspicious. How likely was it that he could be attacked in this way by his own men in his own best stronghold without any inkling it was going to happen?

In the future, Toussaint would become notorious for secretly instigating violent popular uprisings which only his authority could subdue. And perhaps he wanted to make sure that the white prisoners would remember that he, Toussaint, had been their savior on the very day of their release. However, it is at least as likely that the attack at La Tannerie was a spontaneous response to the discovery, on the part of the mass of insurgent slaves, that their leaders meant to send them all back to the fields for the pittance of fifty liberties. That would have given them good enough reason to curse both the peace and their own generals.

Whatever had sparked it, the attack was deflected, and Toussaint led the prisoners out of the mountains, "across the countryside hostile to the whites," reports Roger Dorsinville, "and the streets of Le Cap, hostile to himself, all the way to the seat of the Assembly. He was seen, apparently tranquil behind his mask, traversing these stormy double lines."[15] He rode at the head of 150 cavalry dragoons—a show of organized force which must have been startlingly impressive to the whites of Le Cap, and more than sufficient to guarantee Toussaint's safe passage in and out of town. Once the prisoners had been returned, Toussaint had hoped to negotiate a complete peace settlement, but the assembly refused even to receive him, sending out a note instead: "Continue to give proofs of your repentance . . . Address yourself to the commissioners."[16]

The last fillip must have been derisory, since the assembly had undercut the commission at every turn and derailed every settlement the commissioners could arrange. Whether Toussaint had tears of frustration in his eyes when he left Le Cap that day has not been recorded; more likely he remained impassive, as Dorsinville described him on the way in. Certainly he understood very well that the whites' inability to agree among themselves had ruined their last chance to reach a peaceful settlement with the blacks.

During the weeks of talks with the whites, the rebel slaves had maintained a sort of cease-fire. By Gros's account, Biassou meted out serious punishments to any of his men who went raiding in white-controlled territory during that period. But once the assembly's contemptuous attitude derailed the negotiations, the Northern Department was back at war. By mid-January 1792, Jean-François and his men were on the offensive, capturing the district of Ouanaminthe on the Spanish frontier, while Biassou made a daring night raid on l'Hôpital des Pères de la Charité on the edge of Cap Français itself, rescuing his mother, who was a slave there, and slaughtering the patients on his way out. To reach this hospital (where he himself had formerly been a slave), Biassou had flanked the outer defenses of Le Cap, briefly occupying Fort Belair, which protected the southern approach to the town along the road from Haut du Cap. He could most likely have captured or destroyed the entire town, if the goal of his raid had been less limited.

Jean-François had intimated to Gros that he felt himself to be almost a captive of the great mass of rebel slaves he was ostensibly leading. Of course, Jean-François could anticipate that Gros would report to the Colonial Assembly upon his release and so may have been simply hedging his bets. However, it does seem somewhat doubtful that he and the other leaders really could have delivered their followers back into slavery, especially on such disadvantageous terms as those being discussed in December 1791. An eyewitness reports that when the amnesty offer of September 24 was read in Biassou's camp, Toussaint followed it with such a persuasive speech that the rebel slaves in his audience were moved to declare themselves ready to return to work that very day, if he asked them to. At most other times, however, their mood was very much more intransigent.

The original purpose of the revolt in the north was not to end slavery for the majority of the slaves, but simply to improve its conditions. Soon enough, though, the stream of events they had started carried them far beyond that limited goal. In the last days of September, when white troops routed an encampment of insurgent slaves from Galliflet Plantation on the Northern Plain, they found a letter addressed to "Monsieur le général and the citizens of Le Cap," dated September 4, 1791, and signed by Jean-François. "Come down to where we are," the missive exhorts its audience,

> and see this land which we have watered with our sweat—or what shall I say: with our blood; these edifices we have raised

in the hope of a just compensation; have we received it? No, Monsieur Général; the king, the universe have bemoaned our fate, and have broken the chains which we were dragging, while we, humble victims, were ready to bear anything, we never wanted to leave our masters: what shall I say: I deceive myself, those who should have been fathers to us, after God, were tyrants, monsters unworthy of the fruit of our labors . . . No, it is too late; God who fights for the innocent is our guide; he will never abandon us, thus our device: Victory or death.

The letter goes on to demand that all the white colonists evacuate the Northern Department and Le Cap itself; they might depart unmolested if they left the country to the former slaves—"we are only after our dear liberty." The letter concludes by swearing a third time "to win or to die for liberty."[17]

This letter was never sent, however, unless leaving it to be found in the routed camp could be considered a way of both sending it and not. And hard-pressed as the white colonists might have been in 1791, they were a long way from considering evacuation of the north. By the summer of 1792, the goals of the rebel leaders were changing again, in the direction of conciliation and settlement.

That spring, when it had become clear that the members of the first commission were having no success at all in resolving the crisis in Saint Domingue, the French National Assembly also decided to change tactics. French legislators were inclined to believe, without much other basis than the colonists' propaganda, that the *gens de couleur* were behind all the disturbances in the colony, not only those in which they themselves took part but also the hugely destructive slave rebellion in the Northern Department. No one was quite ready to believe that the black slaves could have organized and carried it out all on their own. This suspicion was reinforced by Procurator Gros after his release; he had enjoyed a privileged view of the rebel organization and insisted that it was manipulated by *hommes de couleur* and by free blacks—two racially and socially different groups which were easy to confuse and commingle on paper. So the comte de Guiton, addressing the National Assembly, was referring mostly to the mulattoes when he said, "We are without the means to resist them. Their progress is frightening. So we will have to treat with them; nothing is more immediate than this necessity."[18]

On April 4, 1792, the National Assembly, increasingly radicalized and now influenced by an organization called Les Amis des Noirs, a French society advocating mulatto rights and with strong abolitionist leanings, passed a law guaranteeing civil and political rights to all free men, regardless of their race, or parentage, or status at birth. Still more alarming to Saint Domingue's white colonists was the term that all elected bodies formed without the participation of voters recognized by the law of April 4 were void and must be dissolved, pending new elections. Saint Domingue's Colonial Assembly accepted the new law as regards the rights of free men of color, but quickly decreed, on the 12th of May, that slavery would be perpetual in the colony.

On the strength of the law of April 4, Governor Blanchelande toured the Western and Southern departments, where he had some success in reconciling the confederations of *grands blancs* and *gens de couleur* that occupied most of the countryside with the *petits blancs* who had occupied Port-au-Prince and the other port towns, often with the support of sailors from ships in the harbor; these sailors were more and more inclined to identify themselves with the Jacobin revolutionaries in France. Meanwhile, the Northern Plain and the mountains surrounding it remained very much a no-go area for colonials of any faction. What the rebel slaves were actually doing up there, no one could know for certain. But they had at least temporarily eliminated slavery in a large swath of territory, creating a sort of free zone that included Dondon, Grande Rivière, Vallière, and the border town of Ouanaminthe on the Massacre River, and they had a wide open line of communication with Spanish Santo Domingo.

In July 1792, a wonderfully eloquent letter emerged from this quarter, addressed by the "Chiefs of the Revolt" to the General Assembly and the national commissioners (though the latter, except for Roume, had given up and gone back to France):

Gentlemen,

Those who have the honor to present you with these Memoirs are a class of men whom up to the present you have failed to recognize as like unto you, and whom you have covered in opprobrium by heaping upon them the ignominy attached to their unfortunate lot. These are men who don't know how to choose big words, but who are going to show you and all the world the justice of their cause; finally, they are those whom you call your slaves and who claim the rights to which all men may aspire.

For too long, Gentlemen, by way of abuses which one can never too strongly accuse to have taken place because our lack of understanding and our ignorance—for a very long time, I say, we have been victims of your greed and your avarice. Under the blows of your barbarous whip we have accumulated for you the treasures you enjoy in this colony; the human race has suffered to see with what barbarity you have treated men like yourself—yes, men—over whom you have no other right except that you are stronger and more barbaric than we; you've engaged in [slave] traffic, you have sold men for horses, and even that is the least of your shortcomings in the eyes of humanity; our lives depend on your caprice, and when it's a question of amusing yourselves it falls on a man like us [*sic*] who most often is guilty of no other crime than to be under your orders.

We are black, it is true, but tell us, Gentlemen, you who are so judicious, what is the law that says that the black man must belong to and be the property of the white man? Certainly you will not be able to make us see where that exists, if it is not in your imagination—always ready to form new [phantasms] so long as they are to your advantage. Yes, Gentlemen, we are free like you, and it is only by your avarice and our ignorance that anyone is still held in slavery up to this day, and we can neither see nor find the right which you pretend to have over us, nor anything that could prove it to us, set down on the earth like you, all being children of the same father created in the same image. We are your equals then, by natural right, and if nature pleases itself to diversify colors within the human race, it is not a crime to be born black nor an advantage to be white. If the abuses in the Colony have gone on for several years, that was before the fortunate revolution which has taken place in the Motherland, which has opened for us the road which our courage and labor will enable us to ascend, to arrive at the temple of Liberty, like those brave Frenchmen who are our models and whom all the universe is contemplating.

For too long we have borne your chains without thinking of shaking them off, but any authority which is not founded on virtue and humanity and which only tends to subject one's fellowman to slavery, must come to an end, and that end is yours. You Gentlemen who pretend to subject us to slavery—have you not sworn to uphold the French Constitution of which you are members? What does it say, this respectable Constitution?—what is the fundamental law?; have you forgotten that you have formally vowed the declaration of the rights of man which says that men are born free, equal in their rights; that the natural rights include liberty, property, security and resistance to oppression? So then, as you cannot deny what you have sworn, we are within our rights, and you ought to recognize yourselves as perjurers; by your decrees you recognize that all men are free, but you want to maintain servitude for four hundred and eighty thousand individuals who allow you to enjoy all that you possess; by your creatures you offer us only to give liberty to our chiefs; but it is still one of your maxims of politics that is to say that those who have been the half of our work would be delivered by us to be your victims. No, we prefer a thousand deaths to acting that way toward our own kind. And you want to accord us the benefits which are due to us, they must also shower onto all of our brothers . . .

Gentlemen, in very few words you have seen our way of

thinking—it is unanimous and it is after consulting everyone to whom we are connected in the same cause that we present to you our demands, as follows.

First: General Liberty for all men detained in slavery.

Second: General amnesty for the past.

Third: The guarantee of these articles by the Spanish Government.

Fourth: the three articles above are the basis and the sole means to be able to have a peace which would be respected by the two parties, and only after the approbation that would be made in the name of the Colony and approved by M. the Lieutenant Général and the National Civil Commissioners to present it to the King, and to the National Assembly. If like us, you desire that the articles above be accepted, we will commit ourselves to the following: first, to lay down our arms; second that each of us will return to the plantation to which he belongs and resume his work on condition of a wage which will be set by the year for each Cultivator who will begin to work for a fixed term.

Here, Gentlemen, is the request of men who are like you, and here is their final resolution: they are resolved to live free or die.

We have the honor to be, Gentlemen, your very humble and obedient servants.

(Signed)
Biassou, Jean-François, Belair[19]

Between this letter and the one signed by Jean-François in September 1791 falls the failed negotiation with the members of the first commission. Only a few months before, the leaders of the revolt had been quite ready to sell their brethren back into slavery in return for a handful of liberties to be shared among themselves. Now it must be liberty for all or death, a demand expressed in similar terms to those of the September '91 letter, and founded on the idea of a natural human right to freedom. That notion had first been derived, by both the American and the French revolutions, from the writings of Jean-Jacques Rousseau.

When the revolt first erupted out of Bois Caïman, most of the slaves who took part understood it to be a protest against the conditions of slavery. As of the writing of this letter, the rebellion now focused its attack on the entire institution of slavery—and did so in extraordinarily sophisticated terms for a gang of supposedly ignorant, illiterate, and generally uncivilized blacks. The authors show a detailed knowledge of the rhetoric of both the American and the French revolutions, and a familiarity with specific documents of the latter, like the Constitution and the Declaration of the Rights of Man. Their grasp of the abstract principles is very firm and they are astute and accurate in applying those principles to their own situation. Moreover, the practical clauses at the end of the letter show a thorough knowledge of the various levels of the French governmental system, at both the colonial and the national level: the writers had a clear idea of what it would take to make such an agreement stick.

Who wrote it? The white colonists of Saint Domingue dismissed it as the work of white or mulatto conspirators and instigators, which the uneducated blacks could never have written themselves; they must have merely signed it, perhaps without even understanding the content. At this time, the white colonists were, somewhat understandably, in a very paranoid and cynical state. They also had a near-pathological tendency to underestimate their black adversaries.

Most likely the letter was the product of a committee, and much of its phrasing may have been the work of other hands than those that signed it. All the black leaders (whether or not they could read and write themselves) made use of secretaries, often captured clerks like Procurator Gros. There were also the priests who had entered the rebel slave encampments, notably the Abbé Delahaye, who did have an interest in improving the lot of the slaves. It has long been assumed that Delahaye and other priests in the rebel-ruled free zone played a large part in composing such missives. Under interrogation by the French in 1793, Delahaye reluctantly admitted to having helped draft a few of them.

At the same time it really does seem that the letter expresses the point of view, the fears, and the hope of the vast majority of rebel slaves who could not read or write but nevertheless had become aware of their leaders' earlier scheme to sell them down the river. One senses that this demand for liberty for all, not just a few, must have been composed with their full knowledge and dispatched with their approval. That point is underlined by the statement that the authors' "way of thinking" has been formed by "consulting everyone to whom we are connected in the same cause."

Of the three signatories, Jean-François and Biassou were by then recognized as the two most formidable leaders of the black revolt. Charles Belair, who was Toussaint's nephew by blood or adoption, was a child of fourteen in 1792. Given his tender age and the relationship, some suspect that Belair's name was used as a screen and that Toussaint was really the third author of the document. Though pure speculation, the idea is intriguing nonetheless. Toussaint had signed other missives that were sent to the whites earlier—but those messages were a lot more moderate than this one. During this early period of the revolution, Toussaint seemed to be doing everything in his power to pass completely unnoticed. If he was noticed, by an observer like Gros, he was always playing a mediatory role—displaying his willingness and his ability to temporize between violently opposed factions.

The letter of July 1792 describes very clearly almost all the points of policy which Toussaint Louverture would fight to achieve over the next decade. Jean-François and Biassou would both be trafficking in slaves themselves before they were done. Toussaint, from this day forward, was always committed to general liberty. The idea of restoring the plantations with free, wage-earning labor was one he pursued to the very end. And the principle of natural human rights was bedrock to which he would always return. That black slaves were laying claim to the natural rights which white Frenchmen had declared for themselves is the most radical aspect of the document. The black leaders, and especially Toussaint, understood very well that in order to justify the institution of slavery, the white slave masters needed to define black men as something less than human. The black men would fight, and many would die, to annihilate that definition.

. . .

Given that the 1792 letter was addressed as an appeal to the French Colonial and National assemblies, the requirement that it be ratified by the Spanish government seems a little peculiar. But for some time before the letter was written, the rebel slaves in the Northern Department had a much healthier relationship with the Spanish colonists on the eastern two-thirds of the island than with the French to the west. Jean-François and Biassou had established themselves in the mountains along the Spanish border. Ouanaminthe, which they controlled, was a border town with its Spanish sister Dajabón just across the Massacre River, related like Ciudad Juárez to El Paso. These positions also gave the rebel slaves access to the grassy savannah of what is now Haiti's Central Plateau, then a sparsely populated Spanish possession. There the black warriors could find beef on the hoof, and perhaps fresh horses; it was also the area Toussaint thought safest for his wife and children in the fall of 1791.

Both Toussaint's first letters to Biassou and the report of Procurator Gros offer evidence that the Spanish were supplying arms and ammunition to the insurgent slaves from an early date. Gros, whose memoir is practically the only eyewitness account of what went on in the rebel camps around Grande Rivière, believed that the whole slave rebellion had been instigated by Spanish and probably French royalists, using the mulattoes as pawns. It must be remembered that Gros's pamphlet was published as a piece of propaganda; the first edition, printed when Gros was a refugee in Baltimore, puts an English translation first, with the French original in small print in the back. Gros was trying to make a particular case to the anglophone community where he had been dropped. Given these conditions, his analysis is best taken with a pinch of salt, but there were some mulatto leaders taking part in the northern rebellion (a man named Candy was the most notorious) and three *hommes de couleur* (Desprez, Manzeau, and Aubert) had signed the December 1791 peace proposal, along with Jean-François, Biassou, and Toussaint.

On January 21, 1793, Louis XVI was guillotined in France. Within the next few weeks France found itself at war with England, Holland, and Spain, and the latter conflict could now express itself openly across the border between French Saint Domingue and Spanish Santo Domingo. The white colonial response to the passionate letter sent by the black rebels in July 1792 could be summarized thus: "We did not fetch half a million savage slaves off the coast of Africa to bring them to the colony as French citizens."[20] Early in 1793, the warriors led by Jean-François and Biassou were incorporated into the Spanish army as auxiliaries; their presence in the French colony now constituted an invasion, and they were joined by a few Spanish troops and officers. Both Biassou and Jean-François were elevated to the rank of general in the Spanish service and copiously, gaudily decorated by Spanish officialdom.

At this point Jean-François and Biassou had divided the free zone into two spheres of influence, with Jean-François claiming Ouanaminthe, Vallière, much of Grande Rivière, and the area along the Spanish border. Biassou established a headquarters and a sort of government at Grand Boucan, on the heights above Grande Rivière, identified by Gros as one of the two best fortified posts in the free zone (the other being La Tannerie, where Toussaint was based). Biassou's command extended from La Tannerie in the gorge of Dondon along the mountainous border of the Northern Plain all the way through Ennery and Limbé to Port Français on the north Atlantic coast, a point only a few miles west of Cap Français itself. The western extension of this line meant that Le Cap could be isolated, surrounded, and attacked from all sides; Biassou had used those positions as a base for the raid that rescued his mother from l'Hôpital des Pères.

Toussaint, who was not quite yet Toussaint Louverture, remained nominally subordinate to Biassou, but quietly began to develop a certain autonomy. Not only did he command at La Tannerie, he was also involved in the western end of Biassou's line, and he took a particular interest in maintaining a string of small posts called the Cordon de l'Ouest, which ran from Gonaïves on the west coast across the mountains through Plaisance and Marmelade to Dondon, at the pass to the Central Plateau. Upon the first outbreak of rebellion in the north, Governor Blanchelande had tried to occupy this line and use it as a cordon sanitaire to keep the insurrection from spilling over into the west. This measure was roughly half-successful, though white occupation of these mountain posts was always hotly contested by the rebel blacks.

Gonaïves, though smaller than Cap Français or Port-au-Prince, was a significant seaport. Toussaint understood its strategic worth very well, and he also grasped the importance of the line through the mountains that connected Gonaïves to the island's inaccessible interior—and also to the town of Saint Raphaël on the Central Plateau, where he had stationed his wife and children, just across the Spanish frontier from Dondon. When he joined the Spanish army in 1793, Toussaint had already begun to accumulate troops who really were answerable only to him; they were attracted because Toussaint ran a more orderly camp than Jean-François or Biassou. A few French regular army officers, unhappy with the revolutionary trends in their barracks, had drifted into Toussaint's region, and he used them to train his black soldiers in European military discipline and in the European style of war. Most likely based at La Tannerie, these troops also patrolled the Cordon de l'Ouest and sometimes ranged as far as Port Français.

On September 18, 1792, a new civil commission had arrived in Cap Français. Again, there were three commissioners: Jean-Antoine Ailhaud, Etienne Polverel, and Léger Félicité Sonthonax. Their mission was to enforce the law of April 4, which not only gave the right to vote to all free persons of whatever race but required that all elected bodies in Saint Domingue be dissolved and replaced by new ones chosen by this racially expanded electorate. The new commissioners were empowered to overrule and even disband any and all colonial assemblies, and to deport anyone who disputed their authority for trial and judgment in France. Sonthonax, especially, would make heavy use of the power of deportation.

Both Sonthonax (a lawyer by profession) and Polverel were protégés of Jacques Brissot, a rising power in the French Revolutionary government who was also a fervent abolitionist and member of Les Amis des Noirs. Brissot had sponsored Sonthonax and Polverel in the Jacobin Club of Paris. The commissioners soon started similar clubs in the towns of Saint Domingue, where they proved to be magnetically attractive to the *petits blancs*. The overthrow of the hereditary French nobility was well under way by the time the Second Commission set sail from Rochefort; Sonthonax soon began to denounce the *grands blancs* of Saint Domingue as *aristocrats de la peau,* or aristocrats of the skin. During Sonthonax's first tour of duty in the colony, many in this class would be deported, including Governor Blanchelande and his replacement, General Desparbès.

Though abolitionist in their personal sentiments, Sonthonax and Polverel had no authority to abolish slavery in Saint Domingue, and the home government did not intend them to do any such thing. Moreover, they brought no significant military force to back up any of their policies, and most of the army units already in the colony were of a much more conservative, if not outright royalist, disposition. The commissioners' official policy was to recognize no race or class differences in the colony other than the difference between free men and slaves. In the beginning, Sonthonax was in no rush to end slavery. He believed, and wrote to Brissot, that to free the slaves abruptly would "undoubtedly lead to the massacre of all the whites."[21] But leveling social differences between *blancs* and *gens de couleur* turned out to be a very stormy business.

In October 1792, Polverel went to Port-au-Prince to supervise the Western Department. Ailhaud, who had failed to adapt to either the meteorological or the political climate of Saint Domingue, started on a similar mission to the Southern Department but somehow ended up back in France. Thanks to the slow communications in the colony, Sonthonax was left to act unilaterally in Cap Français. His pressure to integrate colored officers into the all-white Régiment du Cap provoked a firefight between the two groups on the main parade ground of the town, but with the help of a more progressive officer, Etienne Laveaux, Sonthonax won back enough military support to regain control.

Laveaux turned out to be a very capable commander. Under his leadership, French troops began to take back segments of the devastated Northern Plain, driving the insurgent blacks into the mountains. But in 1793, when the rebel slaves became Spanish auxiliaries, these gains began to be eroded. Moreover, the presence of a Spanish-sponsored black army along the Cordon de l'Ouest interfered with communications between Cap Français and the north of Saint Domingue with Port-au-Prince and the Western and Southern departments. To further worry the beleaguered commissioners, a British invasion of the colony, abetted and encouraged by *grand blanc* plantation owners, was looking more and more likely.

From the first, Sonthonax and Polverel were regarded with the deepest suspicion by *grand blanc* landowners and members of the government. After all, the new commissioners had a mandate to dissolve any colonial assemblies elected before the law of April 4 was enacted, and they were prompt in carrying it out. The ensuing power vacuum in the structure of government lent credence to a charge made against the commissioners in a letter that circulated among conservative colonists in 1792:

> Do not doubt it, Gentlemen, I am sure of it, the work has all been readied in the National Assembly, and it will be proclaimed as soon as the commissioners have seized control of all the authorities . . . The scheme of this assembly is to free all the negroes in all the French colonies, then to use these first freedmen to pursue the freeing [of all the slaves] in all the foreign colonies, and so to carry revolt, followed by independence, all over the New World . . . Repel, Gentlemen, repel these blood-drunk tigers![22]

Though this message was false in its details, its gist was not without a certain plausibility. The French Revolution was very much interested in propagating itself outside the borders of France, and for that reason it was on the brink of war with most of the rest of Europe. Radical extremism in France had already become unnerving to the United States; the French Revolution could no longer be understood as a reenactment of the American Revolution on European soil.

The notion of using the black revolutionaries of Saint Domingue to overthrow slavery in other West Indian colonies and even on the North American continent would become significant later, but if it had already occurred to the members of the French National Assembly it was nowhere near being part of their program. At this point, the majority in the assembly was too pragmatic to consider disrupting the slave system of its colonies, for the economic price would have been too great. Given the revolutionary turmoil at home, the West Indian colonies in general and Saint Domingue in particular were practically the last functioning elements in the economy of the whole French empire (provided that healthy economic function could be restored in Saint Domingue). It is not cheap for a nation to wage war on all its borders at once. Far from abolishing slavery, the object of the Second Commission was to bring an end to the slave rebellion and put the insurgent blacks back to work. That was easier said than done.

Sonthonax, especially, seems to have been an ambitious man, but although technically the commissioners could "seize control of all the authorities," their grasp on real power was very weak. In theory the commission was the highest civil authority in the colony, and the deportation of men like Desparbès and Blanchelande left them without a competitive leader on the military side, but with the Colonial assemblies abolished by the law of April 4 and following the precipitous departure of Ailhaud, the commission amounted to just two men, widely separated by geography and out of communication for long periods.

The military forces in the colony were a threadbare patchwork of militias and regular army units which included, for example, a sizable contingent of Irish mercenaries stationed at the tip of the northwest peninsula, at Môle Saint-Nicolas. The military had been strained by armed rebellions all over the colony, not only the huge one in the north, and their loyalty to representatives of the French Revolutionary government was questionable. The *petits blancs* who'd taken control of many of the bigger towns like Port-au-Prince had been quick to declare for the revolution and to join the Jacobin clubs—maneuvers which got them out from under the heel of the *grands blancs*. But the *petits blancs* hated the *gens de couleur* even worse than they hated the *grands blancs,* so the commissioners' program of appointing colored men to public posts and inserting them into the officer corps (in the case of Sonthonax a very aggressive program) soon eroded the popularity they had enjoyed when they first arrived. Both commissioners knew they were walking on eggshells with every step they took.

In their regions divided from each other by the Cordon de l'Ouest, Polverel and Sonthonax were so busy trying to manage the volatile tensions among the *grands blancs,* the *petits blancs,* and the *gens de couleur* in the urban centers that they had little time or opportunity to do much about the masses of insurgent slaves in the countryside. Operations led by Laveaux on the Northern Plain had at first been successful. The huge but ill-disciplined bands of Jean-François and Biassou folded quickly before organized European assault—the blacks had learned that they would lose confrontations with massed troops in open country. For a short time the French military had hopes that these two insurgent chiefs might be captured.

Tougher resistance came in the mountainous terrain between the lowlands and Dondon, and Laveaux had a couple of very hard battles to fight at Morne Pelée and La Tannerie. Toussaint commanded the insurgent blacks in these two engagements, making himself known to the French for the first time as a significant military leader. He had spent much time and energy on the fortification of La Tannerie, and was not dislodged from it easily. When Laveaux finally won the position in January 1793, he found seventeen cannon there, including a couple of twenty-four-pounders.

By mid-February, Sonthonax had begun to suspect that military force would not be sufficient to solve the problem of the slave insurrection, but large areas of the Northern Plain had been secured by Laveaux's campaign, and some colonists felt safe enough to return to the cinders of their plantations. Sonthonax decided to rejoin Polverel in the Western Department. His brother commissioner had been grievously overloaded since Ailhaud's departure, trying to govern the west and the south at the same time, across unmanageable distances.

During the commissioners' joint tour, the *petits blancs* of Port-au-Prince started an open rebellion against them; the preference the commissioners showed the *gens de couleur* had moved this faction toward the counterrevolutionary camp. On April 12, 1793, Sonthonax and Polverel (who had established their base at Saint Marc, the next significant port up the coast) launched a combined assault by land and sea to subdue the revolt. The ship from which they directed the attack was hit several times by cannon on shore; a fire that resulted was finally put out. Since war had been declared between England and France as of February 1, the commissioners also feared that the arrival of a British fleet might interrupt their conquest of the colonial capital, but it did not come.

Following the success of their operation at Port-au-Prince, the commissioners were able to regain control of the Western Department and most of the Southern. On May 15, the town of Jacmel on the southern coast admitted them without much struggle. But counterrevolutionary activity held out at Jérémie, on the tip of the southern peninsula otherwise known as the Grande Anse. An expedition against Jérémie led by André Rigaud, a colored goldsmith and experienced militiaman whom the commissioners had promoted to the rank of general, failed to subdue the rebellion there. In fact the counterrevolutionaries on the Grande Anse had now opened communications with sympathizers in Cap Français. Sonthonax and Polverel rushed back there, arriving on the 10th of June.

For decades, the home government in France had intentionally divided the administration of Saint Domingue against itself. Power was shared, or contested, between a military governor and a civilian intendant. From the point of view of average white colonists, the main activity of the governor was to inconvenience them with militia service requirements, while the only thing the intendant did was burden them with taxes and obnoxious restraints on trade. Therefore both officials were normally detested by the citizens they governed, and since their spheres of authority were apt to collide, they did not like each other much either. Paris fostered animosity between governor and intendant, with the thought that so long as they were at odds, each would prevent the other from nurturing any sort of independence movement of the sort that had recently cost England its American colonies.

The powers of the Second Commission superseded those of the intendant, and soon after his arrival Sonthonax had deported Governor Blanchelande. But on May 7, while the commissioners were frantically trying to restore their authority in the west and the south, a new governor landed at Cap Français: Thomas François Galbaud. Sent out from France to replace Blanchelande, Galbaud was himself a Creole, born in Port-au-Prince, and he owned property in the colony. He had achieved the rank of general in the regular French army, and he was thought to be loyal to the revolution; however, counterrevolutionary colonists in Paris believed that he would take their part in Saint Domingue, and had lobbied for his appointment to the governor's post. Though Galbaud's orders subordinated him to the authority of the commissioners, his status as the colony's military commander in chief allowed the owners of plantations and slaves to hope that he would become a rallying point for their interests.[23] In the volatile situation of Saint Domingue in 1793, the tension which the home government had long nurtured between the civil and military powers in the colony proved a recipe for disaster.

Galbaud found the city government of Le Cap in the hands of the *gens de couleur* Sonthonax had appointed, and he was not pleased. The governor's presence and the commissioners' absence brought white counterrevolutionaries flocking to the town. By the time Sonthonax and Polverel arrived on June 10, tension between mulattoes and whites was close to a flash point. Between the commissioners and the new governor, whatever diplomacy was attempted failed. On June 13, Polverel and Sonthonax ordered Galbaud and his party aboard the *Normandy* for deportation to France.

The move turned out to be a rash one. The many deportations already ordered by Sonthonax had roused resentment of the commission at all levels of white society. The ships in Le Cap harbor were packed with deportees who had not yet set sail, and crewed by sailors who sympathized with the *petit blanc* class that had so recently been in rebellion. Confined on board the anchored ships were some five hundred planters who in the words of one observer "had done no wrong except to be white and above all to be landowners." To add injury to insult, the commissioners had just confiscated their harvests of sugar and coffee to pay for foodstuffs imported from the United States and England. The sailors in the fleet, meanwhile, were irked by the commissioners' order that none of them could be on shore after nightfall. Sometime during the evening of June 19, a delegation from these two groups approached Galbaud and suggested he do something about it.

On the morning of June 20, Galbaud led two thousand of these men in a landing by force. Colored troops defended the commissioners with real fervor, but on the second day of fighting, Sonthonax and Polverel were forced to flee to Haut du Cap; by coincidence they established a headquarters at Bréda Plantation, where Toussaint Louverture had been a slave.

That same day, as a last resort, the commissioners released a proclamation which read, in part: "We declare that the will of the French Republic and of its delegates is to give freedom to all the Negro warriors who will fight for the Republic under the orders of the civil commissioners, against Spain or other enemies, whether internal or external . . . All the slaves declared free by the delegates of the Republic will be equal to all free men—they will enjoy all the rights belonging to French citizens."[24]

This message was carried to the rebel slaves camped outside Le Cap by the mulatto officer Antoine Chanlatte, accompanied by Ginioux and Galineux Degusy, "two white adventurers still more frenzied than he."[25] The first to receive it were Pierrot and Macaya, whose bands of insurgents occupied the territory beyond Haut du Cap and also had encampments on the heights of Morne du Cap, the steep mountain which dominated Cap Français. Toussaint himself was camped near Pierrot's band, at Port Français on the far side of the mountain from the town; it is likely he received the same proffer as the other two leaders but if so he took no overt action.

It was the bands of Pierrot and Macaya, ten thousand strong, who stormed Le Cap late in the day of June 21. Galbaud and his faction fled to their ships. When they sailed they brought with them most of the whites who had taken their part—the remnants of the *grand blanc* landowners and the *petit blanc* counterrevolutionaries (including Procurator Gros); this huge flotilla of refugees eventually landed in Baltimore. Though ready enough to sack the town, the rebel slaves did not seem particularly responsive to the orders of the civil commissioners or anyone else. Some fires had apparently already started while Galbaud was nominally in charge of the town. During the huge onslaught of the insurgent slaves, the fires spread uncontrollably. By the time the ten thousand blacks had carried their loot back into the hills, and Sonthonax and Polverel reoccupied Cap Français, five-sixths of the Jewel of the Antilles had been destroyed.

The commissioners were back in control of the colony, but at a crippling cost. Again they separated, Polverel returning to Port-au-Prince. Olivier Delpech, who'd been sent to replace Ailhaud, took up the reins of administration in the south. Both Polverel and Sonthonax continued to circulate their proclamation of June 21, hoping to win over the black insurgents with the promise of freedom in return for military service. But, frustratingly, Jean-François and Biassou, when approached on behalf of the commissioners by the Abbé Delahaye, kept protesting their fealty to the idea of royalty in general and (now that the king of France had been executed) to the king of Spain in particular. Macaya, who'd helped the commissioners repel Galbaud, now returned to the rebel camp, declaring: "I am the subject of three kings; of the king of the Congo, master of all the blacks; of the King of France, who represents my father; of the king of Spain, who represents my father. These three kings are the descendants of those who, led by a star, came to adore God made Man."[26]

Toussaint, whose importance as a commander had been recognized by the French since his engagements with Laveaux, replied that "the blacks wanted to serve under a king and the Spanish king offered him his protection."[27] In the course of this negotiation, Toussaint persuaded the French commander Allemand (who was supposed to win him over to the commission and the republic) to surrender to him the camp of La Tannerie with all its weapons and ammunition. This turn of events, deeply disconcerting to the French as it once again cut off Dondon from Le Cap, is one of the first examples of Toussaint's remarkable skill in winning bloodless victories.

During the months of internal struggle between the *gens de couleur* and the various white factions, Spain's black auxiliaries had had time to recover and regroup. Again they posed a serious threat to the French republic, especially in the north. The commissioners' limited proffer of freedom for military service had not proved effective. More and more it seemed that universal emancipation of Saint Domingue's slaves might be the only solution—although at this point it would be no more than formal recognition of the fact that the slaves had succeeded in freeing themselves. Many of the whites remaining in Le Cap now backed the idea of emancipation; on August 15, fifteen thousand people voted in its favor, and on August 29, Sonthonax proclaimed it. Whether the French home government would endorse the abolition of slavery (which went far beyond the powers the commissioners had been granted) remained to be seen. For the moment, there was no one nearby to tell Sonthonax he couldn't do it.

Toussaint had probably been as busy as Sonthonax and Polverel during the summer of 1793, though he left fewer traces in the white man's record books. But the battles he fought at Morne Pelée and La Tannerie proved what a redoubtable combatant he could be. At Morne Pelée, Toussaint had a vigorous sword fight with the Chevalier d'Assas, finally retreating, with a sword cut on his arm, to his second and most important line of defense at La Tannerie. Though Laveaux finally drove him out of that position too, Toussaint, with a force of just six hundred men, was able to cover the retreat of Jean-François's and Biassou's much larger groups into the mountains beyond Dondon. The small unit under his direct command now included men who would be important members of his officer cadre in the future: Jean-Jacques Dessalines, the teenaged Charles Belair, and another of Toussaint's adoptive nephews, known only as Moyse.

Soon Toussaint would become notorious for his rapid movements: no one could ever be certain just where he was, and often he seemed to be in several different places at the same time. Morne Pelée and La Tannerie are a considerable distance, over very difficult terrain, from the western end of the Cordon de l'Ouest, an area in which Toussaint was extremely active. A French colonist complained in a letter to the Spanish authorities about "several useless little posts that Toussaint Louverture has established, supposedly to protect travelers, while his agents who occupy them commit robberies and assassinations every day—thus the complaints and murmurs of all the inhabitants and plantation owners. Toussaint profits from the outcry of the inhabitants to denounce them as suspects, he kidnaps and arms all the slaves from their plantations; he announces to these wretches that they will be free if they are willing to assassinate the whites."[28]

By the time this letter was written Toussaint had already issued his own proclamation from Camp Turel. He who eighteen months before would have put the slaves back into harness in exchange for fifty liberties was now and henceforward completely, fervently committed to liberty for all the blacks of Saint Domingue.

As if to cast off his former self, Toussaint à Bréda, he had chosen and announced his new name. The origin of the appellation "Louverture"—or "the opening"—has been much discussed. Some suggest that it comes from a small gap Toussaint is supposed to have had between his two front teeth. Others claim it derives from Polverel's reaction to Toussaint's string of lightning attacks in 1793 and 1794—"That man makes an opening everywhere."

Yet it is clear enough from the record that Toussaint selected the name Louverture for himself, and with particular purposes. Like many Haitian rhetoricians who would follow him, he was a master manipulator of layers of meaning. The name Louverture has a Vodouisant resonance: a reference to Legba, the spirit of gates and of crossroads, a rough equivalent of Hermes in the Greek pantheon. In the conflation of Vodou with the Catholic cult of the saints, Legba is identified with images of Saint Peter, holding his key to Heaven's gate. Practically all Vodou ceremonies begin with a version of this song: "Attibon Legba, open the way for me." It is Legba's special power and special role to open the gateway between the world of the living and the world of *Les Invisibles, Les Morts, et Les Mystères.*

Toussaint was outwardly an extremely devout Catholic, and late in his career he set out to repress Vodou, which only means he may have been the first (but far from the last) Haitian ruler to forbid Vodou publicly while at the same time secretly practicing it. The association of his surname with Legba lent a spiritual power to the essential message of the proclamation from Camp Turel: that Toussaint Louverture alone was master of the crossroads of liberty for the former slaves of Saint Domingue. At the moment that Sonthonax announced emancipation, it was critical for Toussaint to distinguish himself from the Frenchman and to do whatever he could to place himself at the head of the men who would henceforth be known as the *nouveaux libres,* or newly free.

This maneuver was all the more important since Toussaint himself was actually an *ancien libre.* When the Haitian Revolution broke out in 1791, Toussaint was a free man, and had been free for at least fifteen years. He had been an owner of slaves himself, though he did not want anyone to remember it.

TWO

Before the Storm

The second son of Toussaint's legal marriage, Isaac Louverture, wrote two memoirs concerning his father. The first is an anecdotal account of events, most of which Isaac personally witnessed, during the invasion of Toussaint's Saint Domingue by Napoleon Bonaparte's army. The second, though less complete and more fragmentary than the other, is almost the only source available on Toussaint's ancestry and his childhood. The memoir which Toussaint himself wrote during his final imprisonment is wonderfully vague on these matters. Though it is a sort of autobiography, Toussaint's memoir was meant as a legal brief for a military trial which never took place, and so cannot safely be taken at its full and apparent face value.

What becomes obvious from his memoir, his correspondence, his proclamations and public addresses, his more casual statements that have survived in memory, and even from the way he told a tale of himself through his actions, is that Toussaint Louverture always shaped and controlled his own story—the narrative which presented him as a character—with great deliberation, care, and ingenuity. His awareness of the importance of his public image, and that it could be fashioned without a very strict regard for the truth, is one of the several peculiarly modern qualities that put him centuries ahead of his time.

Isaac Louverture had been sent to school in France in his early teens. He returned to Saint Domingue in 1802, essentially as a hostage of the army sent by Napoleon Bonaparte to subdue what Bonaparte had decided to regard as a rebellion against the authority of what was swiftly becoming his government in France. Isaac's reunion with Toussaint was brief, and it is unlikely that he had any opportunity to speak to his father again after both were arrested later that year. Though Toussaint was deported from Saint Domingue on the same ship as his wife Suzanne and his three legitimate sons, he was allowed no contact with them during the voyage and in France he was imprisoned in a province far from his family. Isaac never returned to the island of his birth, so his notes on Toussaint's life before Napoleon's invasion depend on his own childhood memories, and probably those of his mother, who finished her days in Agen, near him. Thus it is possible that elements of his story are apocryphal.

By Isaac's report, Toussaint was the grandson of an African king named Gaou-Guinou, of the Arada "warrior nation."[1] Intertribal African wars were a constant source of supply for the slave trade. Gaou-Guinou's second son (also and somewhat confusingly known as Gaou-Guinou) was captured in one of these and sold to traders who shipped him to Saint Domingue, apparently along with numerous warriors of his tribe. The colonial writer Moreau Saint-Méry describes the Aradas, who came from Africa's Gold Coast and whose reddish yellow skin tone often caused them to be mistaken for mulattoes in Saint Domingue, as well-known for both intelligence and ferocity.

The unfortunate African prince and his tribesmen ended up on Bréda Plantation, near the village called Haut du Cap, just a few miles southeast of Cap Français (and a few more miles northwest of Bois Caïman). "Far from his native land," writes Isaac, in the flowery French style of the early nineteenth century, "the second son of Gaou-Guinou no longer heard . . . the fierce and terrible songs of the warriors of his nation, in which they celebrated the valor of their king and of his ancestors; but he had held on to their memory. In his captivity he met some of his own who, subjects like himself in another hemisphere, recognized him for their prince, and paid him homage, and saluted him after the fashion of their country. Humanity and good intentions softened misfortune in the establishment of the comte de Noé. He [the African prince] enjoyed total liberty on the lands of his protector. He had five blacks to cultivate a portion of land which was assigned to him. The Catholic religion became his own; he married a beautiful and virtuous woman of his country. Both of them died almost at the same time, leaving five male children, of whom the youngest, who resembled his ancestor,* received the name of Gaou, and three daughters. The oldest of the five male children was Toussaint-Louverture, less illustrious for the rank his ancestors held in Africa than for himself."[2]

This romantic tale strains credibility without absolutely defying it. Though it seems unlikely that a slave owner would be foolhardy enough to leave an African war chief more or less at liberty among a group of men who had quite recently been his soldiers, the history of the last days of colonial Saint Domingue is rich with examples of similarly self-destructive behavior. More recent research supports the idea that Toussaint's father was indeed the son of the junior Gaou-Guinou, who was shipped to Saint Domingue with his first wife, Affiba, and two children. The Arada prince was baptized with the name of Hyppolite and survived, though blind, until 1804. François Dominique Toussaint—Louverture-to-be—was the child of Hyppolite's second marriage to a woman named Pauline, which produced four daughters and three sons besides Toussaint: Jean, Paul, and Pierre, all of whom would later adopt the name of Louverture.

There is, however, one difficulty with this version of Toussaint's origins: he does not appear in the property lists of the comte de Noé, nor in those of Monsieur de Bréda, the uncle from whom Noé inherited Bréda Plantation in 1786 and who was the actual owner of the property during Toussaint's childhood and youth.

No written record of Toussaint's birth has ever been found either, and he contradicts himself (and others) concerning the date. His name suggests strongly that he was born on All Saints' Day, but does nothing to tell us the year. A letter he addressed to the French Directory in 1797 declares that he had "arrived at the age of 50 years when the French Revolution, which changed my destiny as it changed that of the whole

---

*Apparently Gaou-Guinou is the ancestor intended.

world, had just begun."[3] This statement yields a birth date of 1739, yet according to Isaac Louverture, Toussaint was born in 1746, whereas a couple of other early biographers offer 1743, and in 1802 Toussaint himself, a prisoner in France, gave his age as fifty-eight, which supposes yet another birth date of 1745. In the absence of written records it is likely that he himself could only guess at the year of his birth, within this roughly seven-year spread, but it is clear enough that he was either in his late forties or early fifties when destiny changed everything for him.

He had lived much, much longer than the average slave in Saint Domingue—against expectation, for he was born a frail and sickly child and legend has it he was not expected to survive. Perhaps he owed his early nickname, Fatras-Baton (Throwaway-Stick), to this childhood frailty. But all slaves too old, unhealthy, or injured to work were marked as *fatras* (trash) on the lists of slaves on Bréda Plantation. Toussaint had the care of his father (who actually outlived him) once he was old and blind, and the name Fatras-Baton might also have implied that he was in charge of all the infirm slaves at Bréda.

According to Isaac's notes, Toussaint was educated by his godfather, Pierre Baptiste, who had a good knowledge of French, some knowledge of Latin, and "even some notions of geometry."[4] Baptiste, who by Isaac's description was most likely a freedman, got his own education from someone whom Isaac terms a "missionary," and who very probably was a Jesuit priest. It seems almost certain that Toussaint learned to read and write during his childhood or early youth, though in later life he liked to say that he had taught himself these skills when already in his forties, thus very shortly before the revolution began.

A legal document to which Toussaint was a party in the 1770s is signed by someone else in his stead, suggesting that Toussaint could not write his own name at that date. But this suggestion might very well have been a ruse. The white colonists of Saint Domingue frowned on literacy among their slaves, fearing the dangerous ideas that might be introduced, and there is evidence that the slaves themselves saw reading and writing as rebellious if not revolutionary acts—which it would have been most advisable to practice in secret. Another story, perhaps apocryphal, holds that Toussaint was beaten bloody by a colonist who saw him reading a book on the main street of Haut du Cap, and that

Toussaint wore the bloodstained coat until, in the early days of the revolution, he found his assailant again and killed him.

Almost all of Toussaint's correspondence was dictated to secretaries. A few surviving letters written from prison in his own hand reveal that he was able to write in French, rather than the much more common Creole patois in which slaves communicated with their masters and among themselves, though his spelling was strictly phonetic. He seems to have read Epictetus, the Stoic philosopher who had himself once been a slave. In public addresses he made at the height of his power, he occasionally referred to Machiavelli, and his career indicates that he had mastered many fundamentals of *The Prince,* whether or not he learned them from the book.

If he had not read all of the Abbé Raynal's *Histoire des deux Indes,* he certainly had read the notorious passage in which the radical priest predicts a violent end to slavery: "All that the negroes lack is a leader courageous enough to carry them to vengeance and carnage. Where is he, this great man, that nature owes to its vexed, oppressed, tormented children? Where is he? He will appear, do not doubt it. He will show himself and will raise the sacred banner of liberty. This venerable leader will gather around him his comrades in misfortune. More impetuous than the torrents, they will leave everywhere ineffaceable traces of their just anger."[5]

In Isaac's version, Toussaint was born on Bréda Plantation. During his youth, the plantation had among its team of French managers a man named Béagé. In his maturity, Toussaint would be renowned for his self-control; he distinguished himself from the other rebel leaders by a more temperate disposition and a much cooler head. Still, at the age of eighteen he lost his temper with Béagé in an argument about a horse, and went so far as to strike him. Such events were almost unheard-of: any slave who forgot himself so far as to hit a white man was liable to punishment by death, and more than likely a very slow and painful death. Apparently in this rare case the unusually humanitarian program which Isaac credits the comte de Noé with installing at Bréda was respected by the manager. If Toussaint's rash action had any consequences, they were not permanent or fatal.

From an early age, Toussaint had been put in charge of much of Bréda's livestock. It was a logical assignment for a slave too small and frail to be of much service in the cane fields; moreover, Toussaint seems to have had an inborn talent for working with animals, which his masters encouraged him to develop. With something like a natural jockey's build, Toussaint would become famous as a horseman—even Frenchmen who sneered at his style admitted there was no horse he could not handle. He also became an expert horse trainer and had considerable skill as a vet. When Bayon de Libertat took over the management of Bréda in 1772, Toussaint emerged as the new steward's coachman and probably his most trusted black subordinate. "Having fathomed the character of Toussaint," the manager recalled in 1799, "I entrusted to him the principal branch of my management, and the care of the livestock. Never was my confidence in him disappointed."[6]

It was difficult for slaves to marry in colonial Saint Domingue, as the Code Noir made it illegal for a married couple and their children to be separated by a sale. Perhaps for that reason, Toussaint married rather late in life, when he was over forty. However, his life before his marriage did not lack for romance. Though he was never a handsome man, Toussaint's unusual skills, intelligence, and status as a *commandeur* and trusted personal servant of Bréda's manager seem to have made him attractive enough to women that he was able to father eight *enfants naturels* outside the confines of wedlock: four sons (Jean-Pierre, Didine Gustave, Benjamin, and Rainville) and four daughters (Martine, Marie-Noël, Rose, and Zizine).

Toussaint's wife, Suzanne Simon Baptiste, was mother to a ten-month-old son named Placide at the time of their marriage in 1782. By some accounts, this infant's father was a mulatto named Séraphin Clère. Placide was light-skinned, and once identified himself in a legal document as a *griffe* (one of sixty-four officially recognized permutations of combined European and African blood). However, Toussaint acknowledged paternity of Placide when he married Suzanne, at which point his capacity to father children out of wedlock had already been thoroughly proved. Placide's skin tone might well have been accounted for by Toussaint's Arada heritage. And Toussaint's relationship to

Placide was markedly closer than what he had with the two younger children of his marriage, Isaac and Saint-Jean; in 1802 Placide joined Toussaint's army in resisting the Napoleonic invasion, while Isaac declared himself incapable of taking up arms against the French. Later on, during their exile in France, the issue of paternity soured the relationship between the two (half?) brothers, and Isaac tried legal means to prevent Placide from using the Louverture name. Portraits of Isaac and Placide (almost certainly drawn from life) show a marked resemblance between Isaac and the most credible portraits of Toussaint Louverture, while the Placide-Toussaint resemblance is slight to nonexistent. On the other hand, when Toussaint enumerated all of his eleven children to the interrogator Caffarelli in the prison of the Fort de Joux, he pointedly included Placide among his three legitimate sons.

The four dots enclosed by the last extravagant loop of the signature which Toussaint deployed for the first time in his proclamation from Camp Turel indicate that he was a Freemason, and of a very high degree; all his subsequent signatures also include this symbol. Toussaint's name is not to be found in the membership list of any Masonic lodge; yet those lists do include the names of many of his protégés—men who were officers in his army and would figure prominently in future governments of Haiti, not only his brother Paul Louverture and his nephew Charles Belair but also many white men who were close to him. The implication is that the ever-secretive Toussaint occluded his own name from the membership rolls while discreetly using the Masonic temple structure to reinforce the position of his closest associates—whose presence there strongly suggests that Toussaint's sponsorship was very influential.

Freemasonry has preserved its essential secrets from its origins up until the present day. During the eighteenth century it was established in Saint Domingue by French colonists, but even in the colonial period the Masonic lodges included (surprisingly) some free blacks and *gens de couleur* as well as whites. Toussaint's membership in the organization would have furnished him a relationship—on exceptionally equal terms—with some of the most powerful white men in the colony. Via this network, he and other leaders of the first insurrection are supposed to have been in contact with significant figures among the *grands blancs* before the great rising of the slaves in August 1791.

Toussaint's presence is implied between the lines of the Masonic records, and also in those of two hospitals originally founded by the Fathers of Charity, a Jesuit order, in the region of Cap Français. One of these, sometimes called the Providence Hospital, was located on the high ground of Le Cap, near the military barracks and the Champ de Mars: the other was on the heights outside of town, above the road which leads to Haut du Cap. The sympathy of the Jesuit priests with the slaves and free blacks was alarming enough to the colonial authorities that the order was formally forbidden to operate in Saint Domingue by an edict of 1763; the Jesuits' landholdings and other property, including slaves, were confiscated. These hospitals continued to operate after 1763 (thirty years later, Biassou raided one of them to rescue his mother), though they were no longer officially connected to the Jesuits.

Both before and after the expulsion of the Jesuits from Saint Domingue, these hospitals were much frequented by free blacks, including Toussaint Bréda (and probably also his godfather Baptiste). Haitian historian Père Cabon asserts that Toussaint was a slave at "the Hospital of the Fathers in Le Cap." In a 1779 letter to the Abbé Grégoire in France, Père Constantin of Luxembourg claims to have known Toussaint before his rise to fame and power: "a negro, slave at the hospital of the Fathers of Charity, where he served me at table when I went there to dine."[7]

It is possible, though not very likely, that Toussaint Louverture was a slave of the Jesuits before he turned up on Bréda Plantation, to which he conceivably could have been sold when the Jesuits were expelled in 1763, or even at a later date. Not all the Jesuits actually left the colony that year; one of them, the Abbé Leclerc, hung on in quasi hiding on a plantation formerly owned by the Fathers of Charity in the region of Haut du Cap. An early biographer reports that Toussaint was a slave on this plantation, which burned in 1772—the very year Bayon de Libertat took over the management of Bréda.

Whether or not he was ever actually owned by the Jesuits, it seems very likely that Toussaint was in a position to imbibe their influence during his youth (he was somewhere between eighteen and twenty-four at the time of their expulsion) and that they had a hand in his education. (One cynic commented that Toussaint spent enough time with the Jesuits to absorb the duplicity and hypocrisy of which the order was often accused, along with their erudition.) The Jesuits were diligent in religious instruction not only for their own slaves but also for those on nearby plantations, including Bréda, and that is the likely source for the Catholic devotion which Toussaint so constantly displayed as he rose to power. And it seems certain that Toussaint was sometimes employed at either or both of the Jesuit-founded hospitals, which used some slaves and free blacks as nurses, with between ten and twenty-five patients in their care; some blacks also assisted in surgery. Toussaint very likely served in such a role, as well as waiting on visiting clerics at meals. This situation was propitious for augmenting his considerable knowledge of African-based herbal medicine with European medical lore of the period. Toussaint's ability in both styles of treatment goes a long way to explain why "Médecin Général" became his first title among the rebel slaves in 1791. Georges Biassou's family belonged to the Jesuit hospital system, so it's there that his acquaintance with Toussaint most likely began.

As in the Masonic lodge and the Jesuit hospitals, Toussaint's invisible presence is felt in the extensive correspondence between the manager Bayon de Libertat and the absentee proprietor of Bréda Plantation, Monsieur de Bréda. In these letters, Bayon frequently mentions his preference for Arada slaves, whom he believed to be unusually capable and trustworthy, and recommends that the owner purchase more members of this tribe. Here again, Toussaint, though unnamed, is suggested by Bayon's descriptions. These letters, combined with the anomalous fact that Toussaint cannot be identified on the rolls of slaves belonging to Bréda Plantation, suggest an alternative to the story of his origin recounted by Isaac Louverture.

Isaac's description of Gaou-Guinou/Hyppolite's status at Bréda is consistent with a condition called *liberté de savane,* according to which a slave would be freed for all practical purposes, but without an official manumission document and thus without the owner's being obliged to pay the prohibitive manumission tax. If his father had been freed in this manner, then Toussaint would never have been listed on the rolls of slaves at Bréda. General François Marie Périchou de Kerverseau, a French officer who wrote a hostile but incisive study of the black leader at the height of his power, claimed (somewhat spitefully) that Toussaint had never known slavery in anything but name.

And yet, in 1878, Bayon de Libertat's widow wrote to Placide Louverture's daughter Rose: "You must have heard your parents speak about the family of Bayon, in which Monsieur your father was born. Monsieur Bayon, recognizing the intellectual qualities of Monsieur votre père, had him raised like his own son."[8]

In the early 1770s, Bayon de Libertat sold a plantation with eighty-six slaves in order to make the move to Haut du Cap, but he kept a few of his slaves from the place he gave up and brought them with him to Bréda. In a letter to Bréda's owner, who had offered him the services of one of his coachmen, de Libertat wrote, "I have no need of his help, I have coachmen of my own."[9]

The previous manager of Bréda Plantation, a Monsieur Gilly, died at his post in 1772, and in his last testament he recommended to the owner in Paris that his godson, Bayon de Libertat, take over the management of this property and another plantation owned by Monsieur de Bréda a few miles off near the town of Plaine du Nord. It was a valuable concession: not only were the two plantations rich in sugarcane, but the one at Haut du Cap included a pottery works which produced tiles, bricks, and vessels sought after by planters all over the region, for the clay used in the manufacture was of a nonporous type that did not react with sugar, but "favored the cares of the refiner and even seemed to embellish his work."[10] More than one jealous observer had an eye on the job which Gilly had vacated and Bayon had assumed.

Bayon's first year at Bréda was difficult. A severe drought brought on illness among the livestock; many animals were lost. In February 1773, a windstorm damaged many of the plantation's buildings. And although Bayon seems to have been a good friend of the late M. Gilly, he found a good deal of fault with his predecessor's management. According to Bayon's first letters back to France, Gilly had done little more than barely keep things going. Bayon himself was for growth and development; he wanted to increase the slave labor force (in part through more births on the plantation), to plant more staples for the slaves to live on, and to make other substantial improvements. Monsieur de Bréda (whose own letters are lost) must have complained about the expense entailed, for on August 6, 1773, Bayon wrote to complain of a "lack of Confidence"; moreover, the owner's remarks had wounded Bayon's "delicacy." Abruptly, Bayon turned over Bréda Plantation to a Sieur Delribal, writing tartly to Monsieur de Bréda: "It's up to you to give your Confidence to whoever seems good to you; you have made a beautiful choice. It remains to be Known just how your plantations will be managed."[11]

Delribal's tenure at Bréda was catastrophic. Livestock there continued to die, most likely of drought-related disease which was widespread in the region, but the new manager suspected poisoning. Fear of poisoning was a kind of neurosis among the planter class, nurtured by the fact that every so often a poison plot really did exist, like the one organized by Macandal, a notorious maroon leader, in 1757. This conspiracy, which had the destruction of the whole white population as its goal, was foiled just before it was launched, and Macandal was captured and burned at the stake. Its specter, however, remained vividly present to the minds of men like Delribal.

Bayon thought his rival's suspicions absurd, writing to the owner on August 18, "There is no one but the Sieur Delribal, alone, who pretends that it's poison . . . He has said he is Convinced of it by the testimony of the herdsmen, whom he has put to torture; finally Louis, a creole, the only one of your negroes who understands the bandaging of animals, was put in a dungeon of the prison in Le Cap; Despair moved him to Cut His Throat with a broken bottle; this unfortunate did not die on the spot, though we doubt that he will survive; another of your negroes was brought to the same extremity on your plantation; finally whatever reasonable negroes are there have been reduced to the greatest despair."[12]

The Toussaint who would become Louverture is suggested in these lines—by his absence. By all accounts, he had acquired a famous skill in veterinary medicine by 1773. But apparently he was not one of

Monsieur de Bréda's Negroes; more likely he had left Bréda Plantation with his master, Bayon, with whom he would later return.

The "reasonable" Negroes at Bréda carried a complaint about Delribal's conduct to Monsieur de Bréda's nephews, the brothers Noé, who owned other plantations in the area of Plaine du Nord, but got no immediate relief. Delribal (as Bayon went on reporting to the absent owner throughout the fall of 1773) continued to pursue the poison plot. Bayon notes acidly that the one material improvement Delribal had accomplished at Bréda was the construction of a large torture chamber. At the sight of that, most of the adult male slaves on the plantation fled into the mountains, where they lived in *marronage* for nearly two months.

Delribal's own lengthy report to the owner fits neatly with Bayon's accusations: "I promised him* that if he was Guilty of having made the Animals die I would pardon him if he wanted to tell me the truth, But that I wanted to Know also, In Case he was not Guilty, who were the Negroes who made them Die? With what? And from Whom did they buy the Drugs? That if he declared to me everything that I asked for, I promised him further that I would ask you to give him Liberty, but if on the Contrary he did not want to confess I would make him Suffer, and that I would leave him for the Rest of his Days in the Dungeon."[13]

Under torture, Delribal's several victims did indeed declare to him everything that he asked for—and as he had done a good job of suggesting to them what he wanted to hear, the poison plot which he "discovered" came straight from his own morbid fantasies. "I will not Hide from you," he wrote to the owner, "that from the Acquaintance I have had during twenty-three years I have been in Saint Domingue Of the Malice of which the Negroes are Capable, to cause to perish from poison, Whites, negroes and Animals, as they have done in the past . . . I Am of the persuasion that In this Malady there is something supernatural."[14] Bayon, whose account agrees closely with Delribal's on the events (though not at all on their interpretation), confirmed in his own letters that Delribal believed that he himself was the ultimate intended victim of the poison plot—and that Delribal himself used witchcraft in

*The unlucky Louis referred to above.

his "investigation." "He had the simplicity to make a Magic Wand turn, which he said would let him know who were the poisoners on your plantation," Bayon wrote, soon after Monsieur de Bréda had decided to fire Delribal and restore Bayon. "It is a sad character of whom you have rid yourself."[15]

Sad indeed, but also typical. More masters resembled Delribal than Bayon—fearful and suspicious to the point of paranoia and at least as superstitious as the Africans they affected to despise for that weakness. Delribal's report of his own conduct reveals how the masters could imprison themselves in the endless vicious circles of the slave system. Bayon, for his part, was an exceptional case, as progressive as a slave master could possibly be. One need not call his attitude altruistic, but he was determined to create conditions in which the slaves of Bréda would multiply. Creole slaves, born in the colony, were considered infinitely more useful and manageable than those imported from Africa, but under masters and managers of Delribal's stripe, abortion and infanticide—notorious among the slaves of Saint Domingue—destroyed all hope of increasing them. In a system where Delribal represented the norm, Bayon's commonsensical approach was enough to make him respected and liked by slaves in his charge, perhaps even beloved by some of them.

"I hope," he wrote to the owner soon after his return to Bréda, "that henceforward there will be no such disorder. Your negroes seem to be very Happy that I command them, They Know how determined I am that no one will do them Injustice, that they will have provisions to live on in their place, that they will be Cared For When they are ill, but also that they will work for Their master."[16]

Substitute the word "liberty" for "master," and you have something almost identical to the policy that Toussaint Louverture would institute in 1801, as military governor of Saint Domingue.

The same day that Bayon de Libertat resumed his post at Bréda, most of the runaway slaves also returned to the plantation—some intermediary must have been able to find them and let them know that the regime was about to change. Against expectation, the slave Louis recovered from the self-inflicted wound on his throat, though Bayon reported that he now wheezed like an asthmatic and had a hard time making his speech understood. As the work gangs returned to their normal routines, the epidemic among the horses and cattle also subsided.

Apparently one of de Libertat's personal retainers, a man with a knowledge of veterinary medicine and a knack for diplomacy with discontented slaves, assisted considerably with restoring order at Bréda—assistance which may have been enough to justify his manumission. Toussaint was in his thirties at this time, still only approaching the prime of his powers, and it was a very unusual thing for a valuable male slave to be freed at that relatively young age. With the several skills he was known to possess, Toussaint à Bréda might have earned and saved the money to purchase his own freedom, or he might have had his liberty as a gift, in recognition of some extraordinary service such as playing an indispensable role in restoring the plantation from chaos to good order. In a letter to the French Directory in 1797, Toussaint himself credits Bayon de Libertat (not the comte de Noé) with having set him free: "Twenty years ago the heavy burden of slavery was lifted from me by one of those men who think more of their duties to fulfill toward oppressed humanity than the product of work of an unfortunate being. Here I speak of my former master, the virtuous Bayon."[17]

In the memoir he wrote in prison at the Fort de Joux, Toussaint touches on his life as a slave in a graceful but not especially informative arabesque: "I have been a slave; I dare to say it, but I never was subjected to reproaches on the part of my masters."[18] At the top of the arc of his career—as brigadier general, lieutenant governor, and finally governor general of Saint Domingue—he would often allude in this general way to the time he had spent in slavery. He never mentioned that he had been freed from his enslavement for seventeen years before he put himself at the head of the revolting blacks whom Sonthonax's proclamation of abolition had redefined as *nouveaux libres*.

The surviving list of Bréda's slaves is dated 1785, just six years before the insurrection on the Northern Plain put an end to the whole situation. In fact there is one Toussaint on the list, but his particulars bear no relation to those of Toussaint Louverture. The Toussaint who remained a slave in 1785 is listed as a sugar refiner (a skill that was never part of Louverture's portfolio), and is only thirty-one years of age—Louverture must have been at least ten years older by that date. However, Louverture's wife and her two sons are clearly identifiable on the list: Suzanne, a Creole, age thirty-four, and her four-year-old son Séraphin, who would later be known as Placide Louverture. Isaac, at the age of six months, is still recorded as a piece of property. His father, however, had been free for nearly ten years.

The first hard evidence of Toussaint's freedom was discovered in the 1970s: a document from the parish of Borgne attesting to the marriage of one "Jean Baptiste, negro of the Mesurade nation freed by Toussaint Bréda, a free negro."[19] Abbé Delaporte, *curé* of Borgne, added a marginal note to this description of Toussaint: "and recognized as free by Monsieurs the General and the Intendant in the year 1776."[20] This marriage certificate is enough to prove the date of Toussaint's freedom, the fact that he must have been formally and legally set free rather than informally granted *liberté de savane* (for otherwise the top officials of the colony would not have recognized him as a free man), and that he owned at least one slave: the one he had set free.

Toussaint Bréda also figures in three other notarial acts of the pre-revolutionary period. In a document dated 1779, he appears as the leaseholder of a plantation at Petit Cormier, in the parish of Grande Rivière (the same region where the rebel blacks were to camp in the fall of 1791). The lessor was Philippe Jasmin Désir, whom subsequent documents identify as Toussaint's son-in-law, married to one of his *filles naturelles,* Martine. The property consisted of sixteen *carreaux,* or about sixty-four acres, most of it planted in coffee and staples, and for the period of the lease Toussaint became responsible for thirteen slaves who lived and worked there. That one of these slaves had the quite uncommon name of Moyse is suggestive, for Toussaint treated the Moyse who was one of his key subalterns during the revolution as an adoptive nephew. A Jean-Jacques also appears on the list of slaves included in the lease, but since this name was more common in that day there is less reason to suppose that the man in question was Jean-Jacques Dessalines, future emperor of Haiti. It is known that Dessalines was the slave of a free black master and that he was born at Petit Cormier, but if he had been under Toussaint's authority during slavery time, this circumstance would probably have been noticed later on.

An act of 1781 dissolves the lease on the basis of a mutual agreement, well before its nine-year term, with no reason given. Chances are that Toussaint, who had by then been free for five years, had found means to purchase a property elsewhere. It seems unlikely that he abandoned the lease for lack of means to maintain it, since in the same year he appears as *fondé de pouvoir* (authorized representative) on behalf of his son-in-law Philippe Jasmin Désir in a minor dispute with the owner of a property Jasmin had leased in Borgne.

In his prison at the Fort de Joux, Toussaint declared that at the time the revolution erupted he was master of a considerable fortune; these three real estate transactions suggest how he (and other free blacks) achieved such prosperity. Sugar production required a heavy initial investment, not only in land, mill machinery, and refining equipment, but also in the large number of slaves required for such a labor-intensive operation—an investment out of range of the typical newly freed slave who would likely have spent all his resources on the purchase of his own freedom (though it seems likely that Toussaint himself was freed for meritorious service to Bayon de Libertat). Coffee plantations, however, were less labor-intensive and less expensive to operate, while the cultivation of staples which could be sold to the large slave gangs on the sugar plantations was cheaper still. Buying, selling, and renting plantations could also be extremely profitable in the 1770s and '80s, when most of the obvious arable land had already been developed. But if Toussaint Bréda had found an open road to riches, he did his best not to make himself noticeable as he traveled it. Though he almost certainly knew how to read and write at the time that these documents were executed, he declared himself unable to sign his name and allowed someone else to sign on his behalf.

The fact that Toussaint had a lot of business in Borgne suggests that he may have come with Bayon de Libertat from that parish, rather than having been born on Bréda Plantation at Haut du Cap. The location of the plantation sold by Bayon when he moved to Bréda has never been established; Gérard Barthélemy theorizes that Bayon may have come from Borgne. A substantial mountain separates Borgne from Haut du Cap and the Northern Plain, and it is not obvious why Toussaint would have involved himself in plantations there if he had no prior connection to the area. On the other hand, Borgne is an extremely fertile pocket in an out-of-the-way place, so it probably would have been easier for a free black to acquire land there than in the heavily cultivated region of the Northern Plain. And Toussaint's holdings were quite far-flung; Grande Rivière is also a good distance from Haut du Cap, and at the Fort de Joux Toussaint told his interrogator that he and Suzanne (who apparently had substantial means of her own, though still a slave in 1785) had purchased several properties in the canton of Ennery, a few miles northeast of Gonaïves and on the far side of the Cordon de l'Ouest from Toussaint's base at Bréda.

In 1791, then, Toussaint was not a rebel slave, but a free man who for whatever reason had joined their cause, and in 1793 he was not a *nouveau* but an *ancien libre.* Before 1791 he belonged to the class of *affranchis,* freedmen, within which slaves of 100 percent African blood who had won manumission by whatever means available had no legal distinction from *gens de couleur* who had been freed by their white lovers or fathers. Then too there was a class of black and colored free persons, legally distinct from the *affranchi* group, who had been born of free parents and thus were never slaves. Chemist and *houngan* Max Beauvoir reports having seen a marriage certificate for Toussaint and Suzanne which attests that Toussaint himself was born free, but this document is not found in the scholarly record, and the hard evidence that does exist supports the idea that he was freed in the 1770s.

He was thus a member of a very small group: free blacks who owned slaves as well as property, and enjoyed the same legal status (and lack of status) as free *gens de couleur,* but who were separated from the *gens de couleur* not only by a socially significant racial difference but also by differences in their social connections. Though often despised and abused by the *grands blancs,* the free *gens de couleur* had close kinship ties to the most wealthy and powerful white colonists in Saint Domingue, and more often than not those ties did prove useful to the educational and economic advancement of the free colored population. Allowing for exceptions like Toussaint's unusually close relationship with Bayon de Libertat, free blacks enjoyed no such advantage.

Baron de Wimpfen, a traveler in colonial Saint Domingue, puts it plainly: "the black class is the last.* That's the one of the free property-owning negroes, who are few in number."[21] For a mulatto born into slavery, son of a white father, manumission could be expected almost as an unwritten right. A black slave had no such expectation. A large number of those who were freed were too old to do plantation work anymore—they were *fatras,* in the unsentimental term used on the slave rolls. Others won freedom for particular merit, most commonly by service in the militia or the *maréchaussée.* Some, usually persons with a special skill like carpentry, blacksmithing, or the care and training of animals, worked on their free days to earn their recorded value and finally purchased their own freedom.

Since documents of the period don't reliably distinguish free mulattoes from free blacks, it is difficult to estimate just how many of the latter there really were. De Wimpfen says they were "few in number"; Haitian scholar Jean Fouchard suggests, on the contrary, that they may have been as numerous as the free mulattoes, especially if blacks with the status of *liberté de savane* are included. But if free blacks were to be educated, they paid for it themselves, having no white fathers to send them to the colleges for colonists' children in France. Nor did free blacks have family resources to help them enter the plantation economy on a large scale. Most operated as tradesmen and craftsmen: carpenters, masons, tailors, and the like. Some, it appears, were professional criminals. According to one account, many free blacks were less materially comfortable than slaves on the more humanely run plantations—such slaves might even look down on impoverished free blacks. Free blacks living in the countryside were constantly suspected of harboring maroons, and indeed it was sometimes difficult to distinguish a runaway from a legitimate free black.

Some free blacks made an argument that they ought to be seen as superior to the mulatto group: "The Negro comes from pure blood;

*Meaning they were at the bottom of the social order of free persons.

the Mulatto, on the contrary, comes from mixed blood; it's a mixture of the Black and the White, it is a bastard species . . . According to this truth, it is plain enough that the Negro is above the Mulatto, just as pure gold is above mixtures of gold."[22] But this scrap of rhetoric had no effect on the social reality of Saint Domingue, where even mulatto slaves felt superior to free blacks. Intermarriage between *gens de couleur* and free blacks was rare, and frowned upon by the former. Saint Domingue used an elaborate algebra to define sixty-four different variations of European-African mixture, and in this situation many mulattoes took an interest in lightening their children's skin through breeding.

Toussaint Bréda, then, was exceptional even within the small class of free blacks, for very few of them owned land and slaves on the scale that he did. And even if the free blacks really did amount to half of the *affranchis,* the group was simply too small to give him an adequate power base. He had perceived, earlier than most, that even the *gens de couleur* all together, though numerous and determined enough to put up a good fight, would be in the end too small and weak to win the ulti-mate battles. The wellspring of real power was within the huge majority of half a million African slaves, and therefore Toussaint Louverture did everything he possibly could to identify himself with them.

Between 1776, when he was freed, and 1791, when the rebellion began, Toussaint Bréda had a surprising number of common interests with members of the white planter class, despite the profound racial gap between him and them, and especially with the one white planter who had been his master and had willingly set him free. Some ten years older than Toussaint, Bayon de Libertat (like Napoleon Bonaparte) had roots in the Corsican petty nobility. One of his ancestors, known as Le Borgne (One-Eye), had won a certain celebrity in the service of King Henry IV of France. In France the family was based in Comminges, not far from an area called the Isle de Noé, so it is likely that de Libertat already had some connection to Louis Pantaléon, comte de Noé, as well as his uncle Pantaléon II de Bréda, when Bayon first came among flocks of impoverished noblemen and younger sons to seek his fortune in Saint Domingue. One Lespinaist, another manager who hoped to supplant de Libertat on one of the plantations he was in charge of, wrote bitterly that de Libertat owed all his fortune to the comte de Noé.

The count was a Creole, born in the colony, where his family had been established for nearly a century, and he was heir to several important plantations at Haut du Cap, Plaine du Nord, and Port Margot, in the mountains between Haut du Cap and Borgne. Bréda Plantation came to him through the marriage of his father, Louis, to Marie-Anne-Elisabeth de Bréda. Louis Pantaléon was born in 1728, two years after the marriage; when he was two his father was killed in a duel at Cap Français. The toddler count was thus left fatherless but very, very rich. In 1786, Louis Pantaléon de Noé was nearly sixty when he inherited Bréda Plantation from his childless uncle in France.

Bayon de Libertat was a smaller operator; in the middle of the eighteenth century he was just setting a foot on the bottom rung of the ladder which the Noé family had already ascended. While managing the vast holdings of the comte de Noé, de Libertat bought and sold smaller properties of his own, including undeveloped tracts and two one-eighth shares of existing plantations. The jealous Lespinaist estimated him to be worth *"150 mille livres de procurations."*[23]

Freed in 1776, Toussaint Bréda put a toe on the bottom of the ladder to prosperity and began to follow Bayon de Libertat, who by then had climbed about halfway to the top. Though he owned several properties by 1791, Toussaint went on living at Bréda Plantation, close to his former master. It is possible that Toussaint may have managed some of the Noé properties in de Libertat's stead, for Lespinaist's letter accuses Bayon of absenting himself to one of his own plantations and neglecting the lands he was supposed to be supervising.

Since free blacks were apt to be viewed with suspicion, especially if they lived in comparatively remote areas like Grande Rivière or Borgne, Toussaint's position was much more secure at Bréda, under the wing of his white protector. Working as a *commandeur* there would have given Toussaint a salary which he could invest in the properties he was acquiring. As a coachman he was apt to be charged with messages by his employers, and it is likely that he played some supervisory role at Noé properties other than Bréda, like Héricourt Plantation, near the town of Plaine du Nord, which he would later adopt as a headquarters.

Traveling on behalf of de Noé and de Libertat would allow him to learn about tracts of land in which he himself might be interested; for example, if he called at de Noé's coffee plantation at Port Margot, he didn't have much further to go to reach a small holding of his own at Borgne. Of course, Toussaint could never become a *blanc,* but up until 1791 his economic interests, at least, were closer to those of the *grands blancs* of Saint Domingue than to the great mute body of their slaves.

All evidence suggests that the relationship between Bayon de Libertat and Toussaint Bréda was one of friendship, as much as or more than that of master and slave. It's often noted that Toussaint accompanied and assisted Bayon in various escapades and slightly off-color adventures. Some of these were probably amorous; Madame de Libertat went on a long journey to France in 1775, to take the waters at Bagnères, and Toussaint's own youthful prowess with the ladies was proved by the number of his extramarital children. But in 1791, Madame de Libertat was in residence at Bréda, Bayon de Libertat was sixty-four years old, and both husband and wife had been sobered and saddened by the death of the younger of their two daughters at her school in France in 1784. "It is most Dolorous for a father and mother who love their children so," Bayon wrote to Monsieur de Bréda that year. "God has struck us in a sensitive spot."[24] He brought his sole surviving child back to Saint Domingue and swore he would not be parted from her except by death.

Toussaint, by his own reckoning, was over fifty in 1791. Both men had presumably outgrown the excesses of their youth, and settled down into a quieter, calmer level of companionship.

Colonel Cambefort, commander of the Regiment du Cap, was Bayon de Libertat's brother-in-law, and the regiment's second in command, Lieutenant Colonel Louis-Anne de Tousard, was Bayon's close friend and associate. Toussaint must have known both men well; aside from the family connection it is likely that all four were members of the same Masonic lodge; if Toussaint really was a Mason he could have had no more probable sponsor than Bayon de Libertat, who is known to have been a member of the lodge at Le Cap.

According to tenacious legend, a delegation of chafing royalists visited Bréda Plantation sometime in the summer of 1791, with the approval of Governor Blanchelande. The *petit blanc* faction, commonly called Pompons Rouges for the red cockades they wore in support of the French Revolution, now two years under way, had taken over the Colonial Assembly at Le Cap. The *grands blancs,* of a generally royalist disposition and wearing white cockades to show their loyalty to the king, were looking for a strategy to put the *petit blanc* canaille back in its place. Their notion, wild though it seems, was that a manufactured and secretly controlled uprising of the slaves on the Northern Plain could frighten the *petit blanc* faction back into submission to the Pompons Blancs, according to the old sociopolitical rules of the ancien régime.

It seems likely that the delegation to Bréda included either Cambefort or Tousard, if not both of them. Since both men were very familiar with Toussaint, it is not so incredible that one of them should have, in the words of Haitian historian Céligny Ardouin, "let slip a few words regarding that project for a rising of the slaves; too perspicacious not to recognize right away the opportunity for the future of his class in a general insurrection, Toussaint hazarded a few words in favor of the project; and added that the promise of three free days per week and the abolition of the punishment of the whip would suffice to raise the work gangs; but also, he demanded freedom for the slaves principally in charge of moving the others to action, as the price of their submission to the benevolent will of those who would deign to look after their well-being."[25]

Céligny Ardouin goes on to describe Toussaint as being the chief, though hidden, instigator and organizer of the meeting at Bois Caïman, to which he invited "his most intimate friends, Jean-François Papillon, Georges Biassou, Boukman Dutty and Jeannot Billet," all of whom were, like Toussaint, *commandeurs* on their respective planta-tions. Since Toussaint was already well known and well traveled all over the Northern Department, this mission would have been easy for him and would have attracted no unusual attention, though Blanchelande supposedly furnished him a special safe-conduct for these very special errands. "The conspirators met and distributed roles. Slyer than the others, Jean-François obtained the highest rank, Biassou the second; Boukman and Jeannot, being more audacious, charged themselves with directing the first movements. Toussaint reserved for himself the role of intermediary among the conspirators and secret movers of the insurrection: in any case he did not want to declare himself until he could be sure of the success of the enterprise."[26]

Though all the historians close to the events adopt it, the theory that the great slave uprising of 1791 had its origin in a white royalist plot has been dismissed and discredited by scholars of the late twentieth century, in part because it seems to belittle the achievement of Saint Domingue's revolutionary slaves in winning their own freedom and founding their own nation. However, if the *grands blancs* actually did light the fuse to the bomb that blew up their whole society, that is simply one of history's most magnificent ironies—it takes nothing at all away from the achievement of the black revolutionaries and their leaders, who almost immediately wrested control of the scheme away from the original plotters and took it over for themselves. Toussaint, especially, was always adept at redirecting the energy of others to serve his own ends.

Meanwhile, the strongest argument against the royalist conspiracy theory is its sheer preposterousness. The *grands blancs* had been in terror of a massive slave insurrection for at least a generation. What consequences could they possibly have expected if they started one themselves? What possible advantage could they have seen in the devastation of the plantations of the Northern Plain and the massacre of so many white inhabitants: men, women, and children, all members of their own class? How could they possibly have imagined that they could keep a general insurrection under control once it had begun?

If there are any answers, they lie in the state of extreme desperation among Saint Domingue's *grands blancs* at this time. Most of the upper strata of the colonial military and government consisted of French aristocracy. The world of the ancien régime was swiftly disintegrating in France, whence the nobles were racing into exile. Blanchelande and his cohort envisioned that the colony might become a refuge for the ancien régime—a notion compatible with the fledgling independence movement that existed among Saint Domingue's planter and mercantile classes, as well as with the idea of accepting an English protectorate there. But if any of these schemes were to come to fruition, the expansion of the French Revolution into the colony would absolutely have to be stopped.

From this point of view, the idea of instigating an essentially bogus slave insurrection could be made to resemble an acceptable risk. The conspiracy, if it did exist, was taking its cues from events in France of the previous two years, where what had become known as "the Paris mob" was launched at various royalist targets—the Bastille, Versailles, and so on—by a few manipulating hands well hidden behind the scenes. The royalist conspirators of Saint Domingue knew or supposed that these popular manifestations in Paris were not nearly so spontaneous as they were meant to appear.

So perhaps they really did believe that they could let the genie of mass slave revolt out of the bottle and then, when they chose to, put it back in. If so, they learned within twenty-four hours just how wrong they had been. Tousard, setting out at the head of his regiment to defend Limbé, was obliged to rush back to stop Jeannot from sacking Cap Français. Clouds of smoke from the burning cane fields on the plain had darkened the sky over the Jewel of the Antilles; before long the bedraggled survivors from the plantations began to drift in. If the black leaders of the slave revolt had ever been taking orders from royalist whites, on August 22, 1791, they definitively stopped doing so.

However, during the weeks and months that followed, vestiges of the royalist conspiracy did persist. Even in October 1791 the insurgent blacks seemed to cling to the idea that a deal was to be struck with their masters involving three free days a week and abolition of the whip. The otherwise mystifying royalist bent of so many of the rebel bands can also be explained in these terms.

Whether it really existed or not, the idea of a royalist conspiracy was adopted by Governor Blanchelande's political enemies—most notably by Léger Félicité Sonthonax, who ordered Blanchelande's deportation on these grounds. Later on, when it had become clear that the increasingly bitter conflict between Toussaint Louverture and Sonthonax would leave only one man standing, Sonthonax leveled the

same accusation at Toussaint: "By the impulsion of the same émigrés*
who surround him today, he organized in 1791 the revolt of the Blacks
and the massacre of the White proprietors."[27]

Former governor Blanchelande was shipped to France under suspicion of "having wanted to operate the counter-revolution"[28]—the
centerpiece of the desired operation was the slave insurrection of 1791.
The same writer, the Marquis de Rouvray, saw Blanchelande as an
"imbecile," the puppet of an "assembly of fools and intriguers."[29]
Blanchelande's accusers could always reiterate the evidence derived
from the eyewitnesses who survived the camps around Grande Rivière:
"that these rebels had nothing but white flags, white cockades; that
their device was Vive Louis XVI, Roi de France et de Navarre; that their
war cry was Men of the King; that they told themselves they were under
arms to reestablish the king on his throne, the nobility and the clergy in
their privileges."[30]

Blanchelande was convicted of treason, and sent to the guillotine
on April 11, 1793. A few years later, the French general Kerverseau
renewed the accusation against Toussaint Louverture: "Shaped by long
slavery to the merry-go-round of flattery and dissimulation, he knew
how to mask his feelings and disguise his steps and for that he was only
a more terrible tool in the hands of the disorganizers. It was he who
presided over the assembly where he had proclaimed as chiefs of
the insurrection Jean François, Biassou, and some others whose size,
strength and other physical advantages seemed to point toward command. For himself, weak and frail, known to his comrades by the name
Fatras-Baton, he found himself too honored by the position of secretary
to Biassou. It's from this obscure post, where he had placed himself,
that hidden behind the curtain he pulled all the strings of intrigue,
organized the revolt and prepared the explosion."[31]

A role as a deeply secret co-conspirator would help to explain how
Toussaint was able to remain quietly and calmly unmolested at Bréda
during the first several weeks of the insurrection, when all the sur-

---

*Aristocratic fugitives from the French Revolution were classed as émigrés and subject to various
sanctions if they returned to French territory.

rounding plantations had been burned to ash; the several pell-mell rebel assaults on Cap Français that occurred during these weeks had to pass directly in front of Bréda's gates. Soon after the first outbreak of hostilities, Bayon de Libertat went to join the militia in the besieged Jewel of the Antilles, but he left his wife at Bréda, in Toussaint's charge, apparently with perfect confidence that she would be safe there. Later on that fall, Toussaint seems to have had no serious difficulty bringing her to join de Libertat at Le Cap, and he had no more trouble sending Suzanne and their three sons through the war zone of the Northern Plain and the surrounding mountains to a safe haven across the Spanish frontier on the Central Plateau.

Within the supposed royalist conspiracy, as in so many other arenas of the colonial period, Toussaint is a potent but invisible presence. From his own words later in his career, and even more from his actions and inactions, we know that he never, ever liked to show his hand. Though perfectly capable of signing his name to legal documents, he would not reveal his ability to do so. Apparently he suppressed his own name from the rolls of the Masonic lodge of which he was a member. If he used his fourteen-year-old nephew Charles Belair as a proxy to sign that early letter to the colonial authorities, it is by no means unbelievable that he could have used Boukman, Jeannot, Jean-François, and Biassou as proxies in the early phase of the revolt. It's believable, too, that he knew from the start that the revolt could be transformed into a revolution.

What was his state of mind on that legendary afternoon when Cambefort, Tousard, and Bayon de Libertat "let slip" in his presence the gist of their plot for a rebellion? Toussaint was perfectly capable of reading the newspapers and probably was as well-informed as his *grand blanc* companions about the course of events in France. He would certainly have absorbed the revolutionary rhetoric of *liberté, égalité, fraternité* and recognized its implications for his race and his class. His link to the circle of the Providence Hospital in Le Cap and his frequent travels all over the Northern Department made him privy to whatever information passed by word of mouth.

The *petits blancs* had a bitter hostility to prosperous *affranchis,* which meant that Toussaint would have been likely to side against them—yet his loyalty to the other white faction would not have been complete. As a landowner and owner of slaves, Toussaint was to a certain extent in with the *grand blanc* proprietors, but because of his race he would never be of them. Even the leveling tendencies of Freemasonry and the Catholic Church were not enough to dissolve the racial barrier. French Revolutionary ideology, however, might very well break down the racial wall, if someone had the resources and determination to carry that ideology all the way to its logical and ultimate conclusion. Toussaint had already read the Abbé Raynal's prediction that a leader would materialize among the African slaves of the New World to lead them all to freedom. Mixed with French Revolutionary rhetoric, it made an interesting cocktail.

Toussaint had a large material investment in the colonial status quo which the royalist conspiracy was meant to restore and preserve. But the rest of his story shows that he also had an ability to see beyond that immediate practical interest; he was endowed with a greater foresight than Blanchelande, Cambefort, Tousard, Bayon de Libertat, and their kind. In a flash, he would have seen the whole future that they had failed to see. What a sweet irony it must have seemed to him, that the rulers of the colonial world should actually invite and encourage him to launch the series of actions that would, in ten years' time, replace French Saint Domingue with an independent black nation. And if he were careful, secretive, and discreet (as long practice had taught him always to be), Toussaint Bréda might emerge at the end as Toussaint Louverture, the nearly omnipotent master of his universe.

THREE

Turning the Tide

With the proclamation of Camp Turel, Toussaint came out from behind the curtain which had hidden his movements in 1791 and 1792, and placed himself squarely on the stage of the military and political theater of Saint Domingue. Still, his political motives remained somewhat obscure in the summer and fall of 1793. In the August 29 proclamation, he declared himself the partisan of liberty. That, however, did not necessarily mean that he intended to fall in with the French Revolution as it was being expressed in the colony by Commissioners Sonthonax and Polverel. Indeed, Toussaint was still at war with the Jacobin commissioners, still fighting, as the proclamation put it, for the king.

The declared royalism of the rebel slaves in the early 1790s has always looked peculiar. Macaya's equation of the kings of Congo, France, and Spain with the three wise men who followed the star seems, at first glance, a piece of perfect nonsense. However, a little better than half of the slaves who had risen in arms had been born in Africa and so had some direct experience of the African style of kingship. What they knew of European kings was conjectural—none had ever visited the Western Hemisphere. The kings of France and of Spain were almost as remote to these New World revolutionaries as the star that had shone on the birth of Christ so many centuries before. On the other hand, the

French king had put his signature on the Code Noir, which ordered a more lenient regime for Saint Domingue's slaves than the one which the colonists actually maintained. According to the legend of Bois Caïman, Louis XVI had in some sense been invoked there as the guarantor of the rights that the slaves were rising to claim: three days of liberty per week and abolition of the whip. From African wars and the sale of prisoners, Saint Domingue's slaves knew something about captured and imprisoned kings. By analogy, they could form an idea of Louis's increasingly fragile position as hostage of the Jacobins in France.

If his son Isaac's memoir is to be credited, Toussaint Louverture was the grandson of an African king, and something of that royal atmosphere was even preserved during his childhood, but Toussaint had been born on Hispaniola and never traveled off the island until the very end of his life. What he knew of Africa was legend. He knew as much about France as we do about the moon—yet we know quite a lot about the moon, even if we've never been there.

Just a couple of weeks before the proclamation of Camp Turel, Antoine Chanlatte, an *homme de couleur* who commanded for General Laveaux and the French at Plaisance, reported the failure of an attempt to win the rebels of that area to the side of the commissioners and the French Revolutionary government. The rebels in question were led by "Toussaint à Bréda," who had a headquarters at Marmelade, a key post in the all-important Cordon de l'Ouest. A movement of some rebel slaves to switch sides was scotched by Toussaint, who declared (in Chanlatte's paraphrase) "that they wanted a king, and that they would not lay down their arms until he was recognized."[1]

But Louis XVI had been dead since January, and Toussaint certainly knew it. Even if his communications with his *grand blanc* allies in the milieu of Bayon de Libertat had been completely severed by the slave rebellion (which is by no means certain), he had plenty of contact with the Spanish colonial military—of which he was now formally a part. The French Revolutionary government was now at war with the other nations of Europe, and also busy smashing down a Catholic-royalist revolt in the Vendée. Robespierre had become the single most powerful man in France, thanks to his chairmanship of the much-feared Committee of Public Safety, the body empowered to carry out the Terror on all enemies of revolutionary government, be they foreign or French. The guillotines began to run nonstop. Toussaint had some awareness of these developments, and in the summer of 1793 he was still maintaining his royalist bent.

On August 27, just two days before the proclamation of Camp Turel, Toussaint wrote a furious letter to Chanlatte, addressing the colored officer as "the scoundrel, perfidious deceiver."

"We know very well there is no more King, since you Republican traitors have had his throat cut on an unworthy scaffold," Toussaint fumed, "but you are not yet where you want to be, and who is to say that, at the moment when you speak, there is not another king? How poorly informed you are, for an agent of the commissioners. One easily sees that your doors are well guarded, and that you do not often receive news from France; you receive still less from New England."[2] Here Toussaint clearly meant to let Chanlatte know that his own sources of information were much better, both in Europe and in the newborn United States.

"It is not possible that you Fight for the rights of man, after all the cruelties which you daily Exercise; no, you are only fighting for your own interests and to satisfy your ambition, along with your treacherous Criminal projects, and I beg you to believe that I am not unaware of your heinous crimes . . . It is among us that the true rights of man and justice Reign!—we receive everyone with humanity, and brotherhood, even our most Cruel enemies, and we pardon them wholeheartedly, and with gentleness we coax them back from their errors."[3] The language of this conclusion is a rehearsal for the proclamation from Camp Turel two days later, and Toussaint even signed the letter to Chanlatte with the name "Louverture," though it was not a public communication. He would never answer to "Toussaint à Bréda" again.

It was extremely rare for Toussaint to express himself with such unbridled passion, and perhaps with a degree of disorientation. The royalist project had run on the shoals, both in France and in Saint Domingue. Louis XVI had died on the guillotine; so had Governor Blanchelande. Bayon de Libertat and most of the rest of Saint Domingue's royalist party had fled from the blazing Cap Français with Galbaud's fleet. Having landed at Baltimore, they were now doing their desperate best to regroup in the United States (while perhaps furnishing Toussaint Louverture with scraps of information from that country). A year or so earlier, Toussaint had lent his support to a settlement plan that would have put the majority of rebel slaves back to work on the plantations, in exchange for amnesty and manumissions for a handful of the leaders (meaningless to Toussaint himself, who was already free) and an amelioration of the basic conditions of slavery; the latter condition was consistent with the deal supposedly hatched in the original royalist plot for a "controlled" slave insurrection. By August 1793, any possibility of such a settlement had completely disintegrated. For the mass of *nouveaux libres* it was now liberty or death, and Toussaint Louverture would be the man to lead them to one or the other.

What, in the beginning, had he been fighting for? Prior to 1791 he had been a very successful participant in the economy of the colonial ancien régime. His economic interests made him a natural partner of the *grands blancs,* as did a number of his personal ties and his involvement in Freemasonry. But Toussaint was ever a proud man, though skilled in camouflaging his pride. He would have been as galled by the virulent racism of colonial society as Vincent Ogé and his kind, though far less likely to let his resentment show. By studying history he had trained his foresight; he may have expected from the very beginning that the first insurrection on the Northern Plain would inevitably lead to the abolition of slavery and an absolute reversal of the social hierarchies that had been based on slavery. Or he may have been radicalized by the course of events from 1791 to 1793, as many around him were.

From August 1793 onward, it was clear that he would be fighting to establish permanent liberty for all the former slaves of Saint Domingue. Who would be his allies in the struggle was a much more ambiguous question.

The survivors among the insurrection's first leaders, Jean-François and Biassou, had adorned themselves with extravagant titles ("grand admiral" or "generalissimo"), while Toussaint veiled himself with the description "general doctor." The Spanish colonial military installed Jean-François and Biassou as generals, while Toussaint became a comparatively humble *maréchal du camp*. At war with France in Europe, Spain hoped to reconquer French Saint Domingue with its newly engaged black auxiliaries: there were nowhere near enough white troops in Spanish Santo Domingo for any such undertaking. But Generals Jean-François and Biassou preferred to relax on what laurels they had been able to win earlier. Practically all the active campaigning was done by Toussaint, whose successes on the battlefield began to make a real impression.

Toussaint was angling for control of the Cordon de l'Ouest—the string of posts through the mountain range from Dondon in the interior to the western seaport of Gonaïves which divided Saint Domingue's Northern Department from the rest of the colony. He had a personal interest in the region, for he and his wife owned large plantations in the canton of Ennery, an area sheltered by the mountains just northeast of Gonaïves. These were important establishments from the military point of view as well, since Ennery offered the first line of retreat if Gonaïves, exposed on the coast, should prove untenable.

Toussaint also established a headquarters at Marmelade, a village centrally located between Ennery and Dondon. In the early summer of 1793, he took Marmelade from Colonel Vernet, a mulatto who commanded for the French republicans there. Vernet retreated to Pilboreau Plantation on the heights above Ennery, a major crossroads, where he had the ill luck to encounter Commissioner Polverel, who was hastening back to Le Cap from Port-au-Prince. Trouble with Galbaud was in the wind, so maybe Polverel was suffering from stress when he asked Vernet how many men he had brought back from his defeat; when Vernet told him two hundred, Polverel snapped, "Let's say two hundred cowards."[4] At that, Vernet took his two hundred men to join Toussaint, who eventually made him one of his most important commanders, and also adopted him as a nephew.

Toussaint's hard-fought engagements with Laveaux in the summer of 1793 were meant to protect the approaches from the Northern Plain to Dondon, at Morne Pelée and La Tannerie. Laveaux had won those battles, and his men occupied both La Tannerie and Dondon. Toward the end of June, a member of the French republican garrison at Dondon reported hearing two days' worth of lively cannon fire from the direction of Le Cap; he could also see the "inflamed air" from the burning of the colony's most beautiful city. He was witnessing from afar the outcome of *l'affaire Galbaud,* as Le Cap was sacked and burned by rebel slaves on June 22, 1793. At the same time, the Dondon garrison received an order from Galbaud to arrest Sonthonax and Polverel if they should pass through Dondon, but by then it was not the commissioners but Galbaud himself who was on the run, and the French soldiers at Dondon were in no position to do anything but try to get themselves out of what had suddenly become a frightening predicament.

They knew that the camp at La Tannerie had recently (and in their view treacherously) been surrendered to Toussaint. This development cut off their direct line of retreat to Le Cap, and also severed their lines of supply. Anticipating that the rebel slaves would soon make an attempt on Dondon, now that La Tannerie was in their hands, the French decided to try to escape by another route. Furnished with three and a half pounds of bread and a bottle of raw cane alcohol for each man, they set out in the direction of Marmelade, unaware that it too was occupied by Toussaint. Perhaps the ratio of alcohol to food in their supplies was poorly calculated, judging by how they fared along the way.

The way from Dondon to Marmelade goes over dizzying mountain peaks which in those days were covered with jungle. Toussaint, well aware of his enemy's movement, occupied Dondon as soon as the French had left it and laid an ambush for the French troops between Dondon and Camp Perly. Soon the French column encountered another group of rebel blacks ahead and was forced to a halt. The French commander, Monsieur de Brandicourt, ordered a cannon brought to the fore and was making ready to fire on the enemy when several voices cried out from the bush, urging him to come and parley with General Toussaint, to assure proper treatment for several sick men which the French soldiers, in the haste of their retreat, had left behind in Dondon.

With two companions, Brandicourt set out for the meeting, guided by "an officer of the brigands," and leaving the column in charge of a subordinate, Pacot. One of the men with Brandicourt grew mistrustful, and said that Toussaint ought to meet them halfway. But their guide pointed to a large gathering of blacks not far ahead, saying, "It's there that Toussaint is waiting for you."

"That's no more than a step away," Brandicourt said, shrugging off the warning. A misstep as it proved: when the three men reached the appointed spot they were seized, bound, and mocked by members of their own camp who had deserted to join Toussaint the previous night. Presently Toussaint himself appeared and asked that Brandicourt write an order for Pacot to surrender his surrounded troops. Brandicourt, seething with indignation, wrote that Pacot should follow "the most prudent course." At that, Toussaint grew annoyed and insisted that Brandicourt write a direct order for surrender. As one of his two fellow prisoners reported, Brandicourt, "believing that Pacot would take no step on an order dictated by violence, had the pusillanimity to do it."[5]

So runs the eyewitness account set down by the soldier captured with Brandicourt. Isaac Louverture's version (written many years later and at second hand) casts Toussaint in a more heroic light: rather than being taken by deceit, Brandicourt is captured fair and square by Toussaint's lieutenant and adopted nephew Charles Belair. Toussaint addresses Brandicourt in almost lyrical terms: "I admire your courage all too much . . . but I admire your humanity still more; as all retreat for your troops is cut off, you will give the order to avoid the effusion of blood."[6]

Regardless of their difference in flavor, the two accounts agree on the result. Pacot surrendered without a shot. When Toussaint marched the French column into his camp, his own six hundred men had to steel themselves to stand their ground, for the captured force was more than twice the size of theirs: some fifteen hundred strong.

This bloodless victory put Toussaint back in control of the eastern end of the Cordon de l'Ouest, restoring the line from Marmelade to Dondon and isolating the Northern Plain from the rest of the colony. It increased Toussaint's value in the eyes of his Spanish superior, Matías, Marquis d'Hermona, who well appreciated both the strategic value and the efficiency of the coup. And it vastly improved the morale of Toussaint's men. At the time he captured Brandicourt, Toussaint had six hundred well-equipped and well-trained troops in his personal force (along with about the same number of poorly armed and untrained men from the area of Dondon and Grande Rivière), but more were joining daily.

The maneuver also gained him a few more French officers. Those of royalist leanings, especially, could make themselves more comfortable in Toussaint's command than in the republican camp of Laveaux, and Toussaint found them very useful for shaping the growing number of his followers into an organized and disciplined army. In the end, Brandicourt himself went over to the Spanish side. Commissioners Sonthonax and Polverel interpreted his forced surrender as an act of premeditated treachery. There had been other events of that kind; Brandicourt's predecessor at Dondon, Monsieur de Nully, had willingly gone over to the Spanish not long before, and Captain de La Feuillée had done the same at Ouanaminthe.

The Cordon de l'Ouest protected the Spanish Central Plateau in the interior, including the towns of Saint Raphaël and Saint Michel. In the fall of 1791, Toussaint had sent his wife and sons into this area, where they would be safe from the anarchy spreading all over the Northern Plain. Probably it was during this period that he acquired the livestock ranchland he later told the interrogator Caffarelli that he owned. In the same 1793 campaign which captured Marmelade and Dondon, Toussaint also secured the region of Ennery and made a triumphal entry into Gonaïves, where the inhabitants treated him to "magnificent festivals," though a Spanish colonel remained at least nominally in command there.[7] In response to all these piercing advances, Commissioner Polverel is supposed to have exclaimed, "What! This man makes an Opening everywhere"[8]—one of the origins proposed for the name Louverture.

By 1793, the Saint Michel region was also hosting numerous French émigrés whom the Spanish authorities were encouraging to return there. It was one of these, a Monsieur Laplace, who wrote the letter complaining about Toussaint's "useless little posts" along the Cordon de l'Ouest and also accused him of plotting to "assassinate the whites." In fact, Toussaint preferred, during this period as throughout his whole career, to win whenever possible through diplomacy rather than force of arms. Although many of his positions in the Cordon de l'Ouest were challenged by Chanlatte, among others, Toussaint proved more capable than anyone else of providing real security to inhabitants of the region. His claim to "receive everyone with humanity" and to work with "gentleness" rather than violence is couched, interestingly, in terms like those of charismatic Christianity—and is also justified by his actions. In less than a year Toussaint expanded his personal command from a few hundred to several thousand increasingly well disciplined troops, and he continued to pick up stray French officers who helped him train his force of *nouveaux libres.* His men were better and better equipped, mainly thanks to Toussaint's successes in capturing arms and ammunition from the enemy. Both white and free colored landowners in the region found a genuinely humane reception if they were willing to offer genuine loyalty to him.

Still, Toussaint was not universally popular. Laplace, who styled himself "the deputy of the French émigrés residing at Saint Michel, all planters and land-owners of the parishes of Gonaïves, of Ennery, Plaisance, Marmelade and Dondon," complained to the Spanish governor that Toussaint "preaches disobedience" and "kidnaps and arms all the slaves from their plantations, telling these wretches that they will be free if they want to assassinate the whites." In his conclusion, Laplace declaims "we demand that the head of the guilty party fall."[9] This letter is dated April 4, 1794—a moment when as hindsight shows, Toussaint's loyalty to his Spanish commanders really had become rather questionable.

Though the Spanish commanders thought well of Toussaint's character and of his abilities in the field, his route to higher rank in their service was blocked by the presence of Biassou and Jean-François. Biassou, who had nominally been Toussaint's direct superior in 1791, and who still outranked him in the Spanish service, camped on La Rivière Plantation in the canton of Ennery and began to lay claim to positions Toussaint had taken in that area of the Cordon de l'Ouest— which Toussaint certainly meant to retain as part of his own strategic power base. Quarreling between the black leaders broke down into skirmishing.

Meanwhile, it was becoming reasonably clear from the actions of the Spanish, as opposed to lukewarm declarations they had made to the contrary, that they meant to reestablish slavery in French Saint Domingue, in concert with the French émigrés they had invited to return. Most of the latter (whom Laplace represented) were holed up in Fort Dauphin, the nearest port to the Spanish border on the north Atlantic coast. Their properties were peppered all over the interior, as Laplace described them, but for the moment the Spanish military would not support their return to their lands. About eight hundred of these French colonists eventually accumulated at Fort Dauphin, many of them returning from their flight to the United States with Galbaud's fleet. They were both useless and virtually helpless there, as the black leaders would not allow their former masters to be armed.

However, both Jean-François and Biassou had begun actively engaging in the slave trade themselves. They were rounding up women and children, as well as some insubordinate men—*mauvais sujets*—from their own ranks and selling them off to Spanish slave traders. A letter from Jean-François to a Spanish agent named Tabert craves permission to sell off some "very bad characters" in these terms: "not having the heart to destroy them, we have recourse to your good heart to ask you to transport them out of the country. We prefer to sell them for the profit of the king."[10] As Toussaint's own fighting force grew from hundreds into thousands, threatening the status of Jean-François and Biassou more and more, these two began kidnapping the families of men who joined Toussaint to sell them as slaves, and Toussaint's men themselves if they could catch them. No doubt this practice influenced Toussaint in proclaiming his own commitment to general liberty and in actually fighting for it more vigorously than before.

Toussaint's immediate Spanish superior, the Marquis d'Hermona, admired him to the point of declaring, "If God were to descend to earth, he could inhabit no purer heart than that of Toussaint Louverture."[11] D'Hermona was undoubtedly taken with the apparent fervor of Toussaint's Catholic devotions (though some more cynical observers claimed that Toussaint was actually plotting and scheming when he appeared to be praying). Jean-François and Biassou, as well as the French colonists represented by Laplace, were constantly trying to damage Toussaint's reputation with the Spanish governor, Don García y Moreno. When d'Hermona was replaced by Juan de Lleonhart,

Toussaint's fortunes among the Spanish took a turn for the worse. Moyse, his adoptive nephew and already one of his most important lieutenants, was arrested. His wife and three sons were briefly held as hostages—Toussaint could no longer be confident that they would be safe in the Spanish camp.

In late March 1794, an ambush organized by either Jean-François or Biassou or both of them took the life of Toussaint's younger brother, Pierre, who was shot from his horse at Camp Barade, at the head of the Ravine à Couleuvre a few miles southeast of Gonaïves. Toussaint, who was present, had a narrow escape. According to Isaac's memoir, Toussaint immediately pressed on from Barade to Saint Raphaël, arriving there with four hundred horsemen and in such a thunder that Don Lleonhart thought the town was being taken by the enemy. However, Toussaint did no more that day than register a bitter complaint about the attempts of the other black leaders against him. Returning along the Cordon de l'Ouest toward Marmelade, he raided Biassou's camp at La Maronnière Plantation, with such success that Biassou had to flee into the bush bare-legged, abandoning his horses, carriage, and a jeweled watch and snuffbox. Later Toussaint returned these personal effects to him with his (presumably sardonic) compliments.

Laplace, who apparently sometimes operated as Biassou's secretary as well as spokesman of the French émigrés, includes Toussaint's attack on Biassou into the complaint to Don García dated April 4. As of this date, Toussaint's situation vis-à-vis both his former black colleagues and the Spanish command would seem to have become intolerable, but he remained in Spanish service, at least technically, for another month.

By then the Spanish advance into French Saint Domingue had more or less stalled, thanks in part to dissension among the black auxiliaries. The Spanish did control Mirebalais in the interior and Fort Dauphin on the north coast. On the other side of Le Cap from Fort Dauphin, the Spanish held a pocket of territory around Borgne, where (coincidentally or not) Toussaint had been involved in various land transactions before the 1791 rising. The port of Gonaïves at the western extremity of the Cordon de l'Ouest was occupied by a small garrison of white Spanish troops, but Toussaint's lengthening shadow lay over that town. Given the chilled relations between Toussaint and the Spanish command, by April 1794 the whole length of the Cordon de l'Ouest had begun to look less like Spanish territory and more like Toussaint's personal fief.

Le Cap itself and its surrounding area were held for the French republic by the *hommes de couleur* whom Sonthonax had installed in the government and military, chief among them the mulatto General Villatte. But Toussaint almost certainly had a line of communication open to Borgne, via Limbé and Port Margot, and both Toussaint and Biassou were sometimes reported to have camped at Port Français (near today's cruise ship destination Labadie Beach), just over the mountain from the town of Le Cap, which was thus quite tightly encircled.

A narrow road running from Labadie through the pass over Morne du Cap to the area of the Providence Hospital and the uppermost military parade ground of Le Cap allowed the black rebels to threaten the town from that direction, as well as from the southern approach, where Biassou had carried out his successful raid on l'Hôpital des Pères in January 1792. If they entered from the pass over Morne du Cap, the rebels would have had access to the ravine which runs from the rear of the Providence Hospital all the way down the slope to the waterfront barracks and battery, through which they could have infiltrated the whole town. Toussaint, however, seemed not to want Le Cap to be overrun by rebels at this time, for he sometimes secretly warned Villatte of planned assaults.

A year before, in April 1793, the royalist colonists of Saint Domingue's Western Department had hoped for an English invasion to save them from the Jacobin commissioners Sonthonax and Polverel. On September 19, less than a month after Sonthonax's unilateral abolition of slavery, a British force landed at Jérémie on the southwest peninsula and was welcomed by French royalist colonists organized as the Confederation of the Grande Anse. Three days later, Major O'Farrel of the French army's Dillon Regiment surrendered Môle Saint-Nicolas, a key port at the end of the northwest peninsula, to a single British ship. The Dillon Regiment, mostly composed of Irishmen, had been alienated by Sonthonax's promotion of mulattoes in the colonial military and warmly welcomed a change of allegiance. This event left the French republican general Laveaux more or less trapped at Port de Paix, on the north coast between the English at Môle and the Spanish auxiliaries at Borgne.

In its first weeks, the English invasion was rather successful at rather low cost. Thanks to their warm reception by royalist colonists, the English soldiers were able to occupy a lot of ground without firing a shot. Indeed it soon developed that this particular batch of redcoats preferred not to fire any shots at all if that could be avoided, but instead to win territory with bribes whenever they could. But since the British were not directly dependent on black auxiliaries, there was nothing to stop them from arming French émigrés and colonists who took their part; these men formed militias who were willing and eager to fight. Thus, although the colored general André Rigaud held Les Cayes and the surrounding region on the southern peninsula for the French republicans, the British were able to bypass his positions and press as far north as Léogane, threatening Port-au-Prince, where Commissioner Polverel was in residence. To the north of Port-au-Prince, the British occupied Saint Marc and began building fortifications there and at Petite Rivière, a nearby town in the interior, in the foothills of the Cahos mountain range.

Allied with Spain in the European war with France, the British were theoretically supposed to cooperate with the Spanish in Saint Domingue, but in reality the two nations were in competition for possession of the sugar colony's vast revenues—provided either one of them could ever stabilize the situation there. Nonetheless a British delegation called at Spanish-controlled Gonaïves, where they were greeted by one "Tusan . . . a Negroe, who they called the Spanish general, commanding the place."[12] In the end, and despite some interesting proposals, the British and Spanish forces never managed to launch any combined operations against the French republicans; they left it at respecting each other's positions.

In the first eight months of their effort the British managed to gain a third of French Saint Domingue while losing no more than fifty men in battle. However, the tropical climate was equally fatal to all European troops, without any prejudice as to their nation. It was not yet known that malaria and yellow fever were mosquito-borne illnesses, though there was a general awareness that newly arrived troops were healthier in the mountains than cooped up in the miasmal towns of the coast. Occupying the mountains, however, involved combat risks that the British were reluctant to run. Illness soon began to make terrible inroads into their force, though for a while they could compensate by the use of the better-acclimated French colonial militias. The Spanish, in fact, had similar difficulties maintaining European troops in the field, though they could compensate with their acclimated black auxiliaries.

Despite these weaknesses of their adversaries, the French republicans were in a difficult spot. They too suffered from a shortage of European troops, and from the diseases to which new arrivals were prey. The strongest alliances Sonthonax had built were with the *gens de couleur* and the *anciens libres*—a significant faction but one vastly outnumbered by the huge mass of black *nouveaux libres,* who despite the abolition of slavery were conspicuously failing to flock to the republican banner. In April 1794, Sonthonax and Polverel were trapped under British siege at Port-au-Prince, while Laveaux was pinned down at Port de Paix. Communications between these towns and the other republican territories at Le Cap and Les Cayes were interrupted on sea by British naval power and on land by either British or Spanish occupation. Then there were sizable tracts of territory (at Gros Morne, Grande Rivière, Saltrou, and the Cul de Sac plain outside Port-au-Prince) which no one could say who controlled for certain—if anyone actually did control them.

When he looked at the checkerboard that French Saint Domingue had become, Toussaint could see plainly that all three colonial powers were in almost equally precarious situations. The weight he himself could bring to bear might be decisive—wherever he chose to throw it.

Did the British make him an offer? It would have been characteristic for them to have done so. At around that same time, the British made an overture to Laveaux, then in a truly difficult siege situation at Port de Paix, offering him a bribe of fifty thousand écus to yield his position and change sides. Perhaps the British thought that Laveaux, as a hereditary nobleman serving in the republican army, would welcome the invitation to abandon the Jacobins (as a fair number of officers had already done)—but Laveaux took enormous offense. "You have sought to dishonor me in the eyes of my brothers in arms," he wrote to the British colonel Whitelocke. "It is an outrage for which you owe me personal satisfaction; I demand it in the name of the honor which must exist among nations. In consequence, before there should be a general engagement, I offer you a single combat, up to the point that one of us falls. I leave you the choice of arms, be it on horseback or afoot."[13] Whitelocke apparently judged it impractical to accept the challenge.

Kerverseau claims that Toussaint turned down a similar offer from the British, for no reason of honor but because the price was too low—yet that may have been a simple slander. If the British did try to approach Toussaint, no document of the effort has survived. It is possible that they did not yet understand his importance, for at this stage of the game they seemed to have only a vague idea of the "Negroe, Tusan." On the other hand, Toussaint himself was extremely secretive and seldom left any trace of unconsummated negotiations behind him.

Sonthonax, of course, and then the more reluctant Polverel had meant for their abolition of slavery to win the *nouveau libre* rebel slaves to their side. As of April 1794, little had happened to justify this hope. A few bands of maroons here and there, notably the one led by Halaou in the region surrounding Léogane, formed queasy alliances with the commissioners. But most such bands were simply out for themselves, roaming mountainous areas which none of the three colonial powers could honestly claim to control, while the vast majority of *nouveaux libres* were opposing the republican French as Spanish auxiliaries. When General Laveaux tried to persuade Jean-François to embrace the republican cause in the fall of 1794, his reply was fully as contemptuous as the one Laveaux made to the British envoy—and was also keenly perceptive: "Although I might very well reply to all the chapters of your letter, I omit them because they are almost all detailed in a manifesto which I have circulated among my compatriots in which, without artifice, I let them know the fate which awaits them if they let themselves be seduced by your beautiful words . . . Equality, Liberty, &c &c &c . . . and I will only believe in all that when I see that Monsieur Laveaux and other French gentlemen of his quality give their daughters in marriage to negroes. Then I will be able to believe in the pretended equality."[14]

The question put so sharply in this letter was whether the French Revolution really meant to put its money where its mouth was with regard to freedom and equality for the blacks. Toussaint was certainly considering this same question closely by April 1794.

At the same time he had several pragmatic, not to say Machiavellian, reasons to switch sides. Hindsight shows that his chances for advancement in military rank were better with the French than with the Spanish. Toussaint (who didn't take up arms until he was over fifty) had discovered a surprising tactical ability and no doubt wanted to see it recognized and rewarded. Certainly he knew that in the Spanish military he had hit an impenetrable ceiling. But though in the end he would emerge as the highest-ranking French officer in Saint Domingue, in the beginning he accepted a lower rank in the French service than he'd had in the Spanish.

His brother Pierre had just been killed by his ostensible allies, and given his frosty relationship with the Spanish command, his wife and sons were no longer safe in their haven on the Central Plateau. Toussaint seems to have moved them briefly to the area of Trou du Nord on the Northern Plain, but this location was not very secure either. An alliance with the French republicans would include the mulatto commanders at Le Cap, whose power did reach into the Northern Plain.

From a distance, the British looked strong in the areas they occupied. They had several thousand redcoats on the ground, and the *grand blanc*–mulatto confederations of the west and the south were operating on behalf of the British invasion with some success. But Toussaint knew the value of intelligence, and he probably had intelligence of the weakening of the British force by disease. Also, the British positions were far distant from Toussaint's own areas of strength. The British were strongest on the southern peninsula, and at Môle Saint-Nicolas. They had occupied Saint Marc, the next important port down the coast from Gonaïves, and in April 1794 they looked likely to capture Port-au-Prince. All these areas, except for Saint Marc, were well away from Toussaint's current sphere of influence. Meanwhile, the Cordon de l'Ouest, which he personally controlled, formed a perimeter around the

French republicans in the north, and Toussaint considered the string of posts from Limbé through Port Margot to Borgne to be a logical extension of this line. To unite these positions with those currently in the hands of the French republicans would be a strategic thunderbolt. From the British post at Môle to Spanish-occupied Fort Dauphin, the whole north Atlantic coast would become, without interruption, French republican. Thanks to the Cordon de l'Ouest, the republicans could then secure the Northern Plain and practically all of the Northern Department except for a few points on the periphery. Suddenly they would become a serious threat to the British in the south and the west.

Then there was the question of general liberty. Toussaint claimed it had always been dear to his heart. Politically, it was now essential that he embrace it wholeheartedly, whatever he may have thought before. There was no other way to assure the loyalty of the great majority of *nouveaux libres,* who would henceforth be his power base.

Toussaint knew enough of European politics to doubt whether Sonthonax's proclamation of emancipation would prove durable. He knew that what really counted was the abolition of slavery by the National Convention in France. In fact, Sonthonax's proclamation had been ratified months before, in an ecstatic session of the legislature and in the presence of a delegation from Saint Domingue which included the white Louis Dufay, the mulatto Jean-Baptiste Mills, and a full-blooded African, Jean-Baptiste Belley, who like Toussaint had earned his own freedom from slavery under the ancien régime. On February 4, 1794, the convention passed, with no opposition, a law which "declares that slavery is abolished throughout the territory of the Republic; in consequence, all men, without distinction of color, will enjoy the rights of French citizens."[15] With that, the French Revolution had put its money where its mouth was. The decree did away not only with slavery but also with the whole structure of institutionalized racial discrimination that had plagued free blacks and free men of color until 1791.

However, the convention's decree was not officially proclaimed in Saint Domingue until June 8, 1794. The usual interpretation is that no news of this momentous event had reached the colony before this date, but such a long delay seems highly unlikely. The transatlantic voyage from France to the Caribbean took more or less six weeks, depending on wind and weather. Thus it is probable that rumors of the national decree would have begun to seep into Saint Domingue and the other French colonies no later than the end of March.

Officially, Toussaint Louverture is not supposed to have known of the decree until June. Yet in his letter to Chanlatte almost a year earlier, he boasted of the quality of the information he got directly from France. It is possible that he had his first inkling of the emancipation decree by the last days of March 1794, just as he was coming to blows with Jean-François, Biassou, and the Spanish military commanders.

On May 5, the emancipation decree was proclaimed in Guadeloupe—a negligible distance from Saint Domingue. On the same date, General Laveaux wrote Toussaint to acknowledge receiving an emissary who "announced to me that the national flag is flying in these two places [Terre Neuve and Port à Piment], and moreover he announced to me the return that you have just made, and that you have declared yourself Republican, and that for the triumph of Republican arms, you have raised the tricolor flag at Gonaïves."[16]

Toussaint had finally made his move, probably—as in the case of most successful politicians—for a mélange of pragmatic and idealistic motives. Whether he was influenced by the National Convention's abolition of slavery can never be known for certain. Chances are that at least a rumor of the decree had reached him. Sonthonax had gone so far as to announce it as early as February 27, but that was pure bluff and Toussaint probably would have recognized it as such. Laveaux's May 5 letter makes no mention of the convention's decree, referring instead to the advisability of "following the proclamation of the Civil Commissioners." Toussaint mentions having actually seen the convention's emancipation decree for the first time in a letter to Laveaux dated July 7.

Laveaux's May 5 letter describes Toussaint's move as a "return," and Toussaint's first reply, dated May 18, mentions that at some earlier point "the ways of reconciliation proposed by me were rejected." Some circumstantial evidence suggests that Toussaint and the republicans had tried for a rapprochement the year before, in the summer of 1793, before the catastrophic burning of Le Cap at the end of June. On June 4, the black leader Pierrot wrote to Governor Galbaud requesting written confirmation of a rumor he claimed to have heard that the French meant to declare the abolition of slavery. Since Toussaint was encamped with Pierrot at this time (a stone's throw from Le Cap, at Port Français), he was more than likely a silent partner in this probe. Toussaint was certainly aware of the trouble brewing between Galbaud and the Jacobin commissioners and must have been wondering which faction to back. Galbaud had roots in the *grand blanc* world to which Bayon de Libertat belonged; Toussaint was not necessarily convinced that even conservative royalists of this stripe would be absolutely attached to maintaining slavery.

After the conflict exploded and Galbaud's supporters had driven Sonthonax and Polverel out of Le Cap, the commissioners proposed freedom for any men among the black rebels who would fight for their cause against Galbaud. That offer was good enough for Macaya and Pierrot, but apparently not for Toussaint, who chose to withdraw, watch the battle from a safe distance, and then consider dealing with the victor. Toussaint always preferred to stand clear of any battle he didn't absolutely have to fight.

Once the Jacobin commissioners had emerged (however shakily) in the ascendancy, Toussaint reopened a line of communication with them, this time via Laveaux, who used Antoine Chanlatte as his emissary. Chanlatte was harassing several of Toussaint's posts along the Cordon de l'Ouest at this time, but also trying diplomacy in between skirmishes. His letter to Laveaux of August 10, 1793, reporting several scuffles and parleys in the area of Marmelade, Plaisance, and Ennery, ends with the startlingly offhand remark that Toussaint is in Le Cap and will soon be calling on Laveaux in person. Strange, since earlier in the same letter Chanlatte describes how "Toussaint à Bréda" had already rejected the republican overture. There was more than one man named Toussaint among the rebel slaves in the north of the colony, so perhaps it was a different Toussaint who meant to visit Laveaux.

Still, the idea that a clandestine meeting between General Laveaux and Toussaint Louverture might have taken place—just a couple of weeks before Sonthonax's announcement of abolition and Toussaint's proclamation from Camp Turel—is intriguing. If the encounter did happen, how did it go wrong? If it never happened, what was Toussaint doing in those two weeks, and whom was he talking to? At the time that Laveaux and Toussaint might have met, Sonthonax's proclamation of abolition was in the offing but had not yet come to shore. Toussaint's communications at the end of August suggest that he knew Sonthonax's proclamation was on the way—and that he meant to beat the French commissioner to that particular punch.

On August 25, Toussaint sent an open letter to a camp of free mulattoes fighting for the French republic from their base in Le Cap—Chanlatte and also Villatte were part of his intended audience. Not long before, Chanlatte had tried to win Toussaint over to the republican cause. In the August 25 letter Toussaint tried to persuade Chanlatte's troops to leave the republic and join him.

"The idea of this general liberty for whose cause you do battle against your friends, by whom was its basis first formed? Were we not ourselves its first authors?"[17] (This last sentence may be the only case where Toussaint identified himself, in writing, with the relatively small population of *affranchis* who had gained freedom under the old colonial system, rather than with the great mass of slaves in the process of freeing themselves.) He exhorted the mulatto troops to shake free of those who had hypnotized them with "a host of very vague promises"—Sonthonax and Polverel, that is, "two individuals charged with the title of Delegates of the Republic, which itself is not holding up."

Here, at the end of August 1793, Toussaint put plainly his belief that the French republic would not endure, that the monarchy would return, and that the rebel slaves must look to the restored French monarchy for ratification of the liberty they had claimed for themselves. In the next breath, however, he invoked the most famous passage of French Revolutionary rhetoric, albeit with a particular interpretation of his own: "Recall the sentiments to which your General Chanlatte bears witness, in favor of liberty and equality; liberty is a right given by Nature; equality is a consequence of that liberty, granted and maintained by this National Assembly."

Like so many of his generation, whether at first or second hand, Toussaint seems to have imbibed the idea of liberty as a natural right from Rousseau. Equality, in his view of things, may be more of a legal matter (and one which had for a long time preoccupied the free *gens de couleur*). If liberty is a right to be claimed, equality must then be socially constructed. Toussaint was for both, and by any means necessary: "It's for me to work toward them as the first to be swayed by a cause which I have always supported; I cannot give way; having begun, I will finish. Unite yourselves with me and you will enjoy your rights all the sooner."[18]

The colored troops were no more moved by this call than Toussaint had been a fortnight before by Chanlatte's appeal to join the republic. The reference to Chanlatte in Toussaint's August 25 letter is civil, at least, but perhaps Chanlatte sent a testy reply, for by August 27 Toussaint was denouncing Chanlatte in foot-high letters of flame as a "scoundrel, perfidious deceiver," and so on. No longer temporizing, he was again at all-out war with the forces of the French republic. "The ways of reconciliation" had failed.

Toussaint's letter of August 25 seems designed to preempt Sonthonax's abolition of slavery, proclaimed four days later. On August 29, when Sonthonax issued his edict in a page of dense prose (written in the phonetic Creole of the period, a language spoken by most of the slaves but read by practically no one), Toussaint was ready with his own proclamation from Camp Turel, which in a succinct five sentences boiled his August 25 letter down to its essentials: *I am Toussaint Louverture; perhaps my name has made itself known to you. I have undertaken vengeance. I want Liberty and Equality to reign in Saint Domingue. I am working to make that happen. Unite yourselves to us, brothers, and fight with us for the same cause.*

Toussaint was no longer addressing the *gens de couleur* as a separate group; he was speaking to anyone and everyone in the colony. Let all who heard choose between Toussaint Louverture and the French commissioners who were trying to hypnotize them. For the moment the rift seemed absolute. But Toussaint must have kept a back door open toward Laveaux during the following months, for in the spring of 1794 it seemed that these two had a relationship to resume.

The *when* of Toussaint's change of allegiance is as mysterious as the *why*. In a report written well after the fact, Laveaux states that Toussaint had stopped fighting the republican French by April 6, 1794. Elsewhere he says that the black leader "placed himself under the banner of the Republic on May 6th."[19] The apparent inconsistency is not so difficult to resolve. It is logical that Toussaint should have ceased hostilities against the French and opened a line of communication with Laveaux soon after the ambush on his party at Camp Barade in late March and his subsequent retaliation on Biassou's camp at Maronnière Plantation, and just as logical that he should have delayed any further attacks on the Spanish until he was completely ready to commit to Laveaux and the republic. White Spanish troops, after all, seldom ventured west of Saint Raphaël, and Biassou, after the whipping he had just taken, had reason to keep his distance from Toussaint, who probably spent most of April between Marmelade and Ennery, where neither the Spanish nor the other black leaders could learn much about what he was up to.

The determinedly hostile Kerverseau described Toussaint's shift to the republic this way:

> It was then that he put into practice all the tactics of slander and intrigue to corrupt the troops, create an independent force for himself, drive the former chiefs from the quarters they occupied and form from their debris a considerable arrondissement for himself.* It was then that he opened negotiations with the French and the English, and that he redoubled his devotional practices, assurances of loyalty and demonstrations of zeal to deceive the Spanish government, evading the orders that were contrary to his projects by stories of imaginary combats in which he had received dangerous wounds, and never ceasing to extract gold and arms for pretended expeditions which he never actually undertook, until finally, after a year of ruses and detours, unhappy with the English who did not put a high enough price on his betrayal, and aware that the president,† informed of his perfidy, was only waiting for the right moment to punish him, he commit-

*This summary of Toussaint's tactics in taking over the Cordon de l'Ouest has a certain ring of plausibility.
†The Spanish governor, presumably.

ted himself, made a surprise attack on San Raphael, whence
that same morning they had sent him, at his own request,
provisions and ammunition, then marched on Gonaïves
which he seized after slitting the throats of all the Whites who
had come before him to implore his protection—and declared
himself commander under the orders of the General Laveaux.
Such were the exploits with which he signaled his entry under
the flags of the Republic.[20]

Kerverseau never misses a chance to denigrate Toussaint, and this
narrative should be discounted accordingly, but the events of this day
(whatever its date) do reveal a man capable of absolute treachery,
absolute ruthlessness, and absolute hypocrisy—all qualities Toussaint
Louverture could claim, along with his more conventionally admirable
ones. His requisition of supplies from the very people he meant to
attack is classic.

Documents show that black auxiliaries attacked Gonaïves on April
29, but it is unclear whether this is the moment when Toussaint took
control of the port—other accounts give the date of his action as May 4
or May 6. The last date is implausible, as Laveaux's May 5 letter says
that Toussaint has already raised the republican flag at Gonaïves. A contemporary observer, Pélage-Marie Duboys, claims that Laveaux had
discussed Toussaint's capture of Gonaïves in advance (with an eye
toward using Toussaint's presence there to counterbalance the influence
of Villatte, the mulatto commander at Le Cap). By this account,
Toussaint permitted the Spanish garrison led by Villanova to depart
"with the honors of war," while the civilian population suffered
"the terrible fate of a place taken by force" once the garrison had
withdrawn.[21]

Toussaint wrote a couple of letters of his own from Gonaïves on
May 5. One was to the town's vicar ("I am most sincerely affected by
the harsh necessity that compelled you to leave the House of our
adorable creator. Having been unable to foresee such a disastrous event
fills my soul with despair"). The other, addressed to "Messieurs the
refugee inhabitants of Gonaïves," noted: "It is without a doubt painful

for me to have been unable to foresee the unhappy events that have just transpired and have obliged you to leave your properties. Such regret can be felt by me alone. Be assured, Sirs, that I did not at all participate and that everything was done without my knowledge and consequently against my wishes. God, who knows our most secret thoughts and who sees all, is witness to the purity of my principles. They are not founded on barbarous ferocity that takes pleasure in shedding human blood. Come back, Sirs, come back to your homes. I swear before our divine Creator that I will do everything to keep you safe."[22]

If there is any truth at all in Kerverseau's report of Toussaint's involvement, it is fair to say that Toussaint did sometimes take a certain pleasure in shedding crocodile tears. Those "magnificent festivals" he had lately enjoyed at Gonaïves had evidently slipped his mind. The capture of Gonaïves was a bloody affair: 500 fled to Saint Marc by boat, and 150 were reported slain. Kerverseau alleges a surprise attack on Saint Raphaël, and oral tradition describes a massacre at Marmelade that took place either May 4 or May 6. Toussaint's May 5 letter to the Gonaïves refugees ends with a cautionary postscript: "On second thought, I request that you do not return until after I have come back from Marmelade, for I am going up there today."[23] By one account of events at Marmelade, Toussaint attended mass with his Spanish superiors, taking the sacraments with his usual piety, then opened fire on them as soon as they had left the church.

Exactly what happened when can't be known for certain, but what had to happen to fulfill Toussaint's program is plain. He needed to secure the whole Cordon de l'Ouest from Gonaïves all the way to Dondon, meaning that he had to purge all Spaniards and Spanish sympathizers from every post along that line. There's no doubt that he did just that, and did it thoroughly. White Spanish troops found at Dondon, Gros Morne, and Petite Rivière were slain on the spot. Toussaint's reply to Laveaux on May 18 states calmly and confidently that "Gonaïves, Gros-Morne, the canton of Ennery, Marmelade, Plaisance, Dondon, l'Acul and all its dependencies including Limbé are under my orders, and I count four thousand men under arms in all these places."[24] Thanks to the drastic action he had just taken, Toussaint now had this "considerable arrondissement," and a considerable army occupying it, to offer to the French republic—on a platter.

Sonthonax and Polverel wrote to Toussaint to congratulate him on joining their cause. But Toussaint had switched sides too late to bail them out of their immediate predicament. On May 19, the British, encouraged by a reinforcement of nearly two thousand fresh troops, launched a full-scale assault on Port-au-Prince, supported by bombardment from ships on the bay, and forced the commissioners to abandon the town. Sonthonax and Polverel made their way to Jacmel on the southern coast, where on June 8, they hailed *L'Espérance,* the French ship which, with a weirdly bittersweet irony, brought not only the official news of the National Convention's abolition of slavery but also orders that he and Polverel return to France forthwith, to face charges of misconduct and misgovernance of the colony. As the Terror still ruled in France, such accusations strongly implied a swift trip to the guillotine.

The two commissioners wrote a batch of letters to their subordinates, including Generals Laveaux and Rigaud, then embarked on *L'Espérance* as deportees. No replacements for the commission had been sent from France. Before departing, Sonthonax gave the symbols of his authority—a medal and ceremonial sash—to Dieudonné, a black who had taken over Halaou's band after the latter was killed in a contretemps with a mulatto faction. Though his authority to do so was doubtful at this point, Sonthonax formally invested Dieudonné with all the powers he was surrendering as representative of France.

Upon the departure of the commissioners, General Laveaux became the senior French official in the colony. Perhaps Toussaint preferred it that way—he had early marked Sonthonax as a rival. His relationship with Laveaux waxed from the guarded respect of their first correspondence to a genuinely affectionate friendship and partnership. Between 1794 and 1798 Toussaint sent a ream of letters to Laveaux. He spoke standard French as well as Creole, but his spelling was purely phonetic, so he dictated his correspondence to several different secretaries, always reviewing the drafts with great care to make sure that his thoughts were exactly expressed. The letters to Laveaux amount to the largest body of Toussaint's writing that survives.

From the moment that he announced his shift to the republican side, Toussaint was exposed to attack on two fronts—or at least from two directions, as coherent fronts were hard to identify on Saint Domingue's difficult, mountainous terrain—from the English to the west at Saint Marc and from the Spanish and their remaining auxiliaries in the eastern mountains and the valley of Grande Rivière. By some accounts (unlikely as it sounds), Toussaint kept up some sort of diplomatic contact with the Spanish command for about a month after declaring his allegiance to Laveaux and the republic—the Spanish may have hoped he'd have another change of heart and mind—but that did not prevent hostilities from Jean-François and Biassou. On June 15 Toussaint reported to Laveaux an attack by Jean-François which actually succeeded in taking Dondon, an attack on La Tannerie by Biassou the next day, followed on June 11 by a British assault on his post at Pont d'Ester, the next town north of Saint Marc and at that moment the southern frontier of Toussaint's "considerable arrondissement."

"You see, Citizen General, how I am surrounded by enemies," he wrote, "on all sides, the right and the left."[25] In the same letter, Toussaint nevertheless proposes an attack on the Spanish force at Borgne, albeit in very coy terms: "I pray you, should it be an effect of your goodness to send out your army around Thursday or Friday, to appear before Borgne to threaten it as if you would attack it, I am sure that, by God's permission, we will have Borgne and Camp Bertin both together, by the maneuvers I will be there to combine."[26] This first joint operation between Toussaint and Laveaux, supported by a movement of Villatte's men from Le Cap, was a smashing success, and had the strategic importance of reestablishing republican control between Le Cap and Port de Paix, and further securing the Northern Plain.

On July 7, Toussaint reports his recapture of Dondon and decisive routing of Jean-François: "he owed his salvation only to the thickness of the brush into which he desperately hurled his body, abandoning all his effects . . . He saved nothing but his shirt and his britches."[27] Retreating to Fort Dauphin, Jean-François exercised his rage and disappointment by slaughtering the eight hundred unarmed refugee *grand blanc* planters who had been waiting there for a chance to fight for the Spanish royalists and the recovery of their lands. The Spanish garrison colluded in the atrocity, or perhaps felt it was too weak to prevent it; whatever their motive, the Spanish troops shut themselves into the fort during the massacre and refused entry to the helpless French victims, practically all of whom were slain, along with their families. This horrendous and almost inexplicable event, together with Toussaint's reoccupation of Dondon, crippled the Spanish project in French Saint Domingue, though Toussaint waited several weeks to deliver the coup de grâce.

In the same letter, Toussaint told Laveaux that he had just received word of Sonthonax and Polverel's departure and of the convention's abolition of slavery: "It is very consoling news to all friends of humanity," he wrote, "and I hope that in the future all will find themselves the better for it."[28] The definitive news of abolition inspired him to take much more vigorous action against the Spanish than he had done previously. The routing of Jean-François from Dondon meant that Toussaint was no longer hedging his bets: all pretense that he might still serve Spain was abandoned. Concerning the massacre at Fort Dauphin, Toussaint wrote to Laveaux on July 19 with an elegant simplicity: "General, you may count on my humane sentiments; I have always had a horror of those chiefs who love to spill blood; my religion forbids me to do it, and I follow its principles."[29] This line has a much stronger ring of sincerity than the rococo phrasing of the letters Toussaint sent to the survivors of his attack on Gonaïves.

Both Laveaux and Toussaint wanted very much to capture the town of Saint Marc, the strategic key to control of the Artibonite Plain, immediately south of Toussaint's forward post at Pont d'Ester. Since his days in the Spanish service, Toussaint had recognized the British commander there, Lieutenant Colonel Brisbane, as an extremely dangerous adversary. To dispose of him, he tried a combination of force and guile. Brisbane, who had observed Toussaint's activities with the same acute interest with which Toussaint watched his, believed that the black leader was mainly out for himself and perhaps could be purchased for the

British cause. Toussaint, hoping to lure Brisbane to Gonaïves where he could be captured, showed himself receptive to these overtures. The negotiations also gave him a chance to secretly court the mulattoes of Saint Marc and surrounding areas, who since the National Convention's abolition of slavery were cultivating a greater sympathy for the republic.

Brisbane would not put his head in the trap, but in the first week of September Toussaint did manage to lure him in the direction of Petite Rivière, with a feigned offer by the chiefs of that town to turn it over to the British. One purpose of this ruse was to facilitate the defection of Morin, Brisbane's colored aide-de-camp, who led three hundred men out of Saint Marc to join Toussaint's subordinate Christophe Mornet on September 3. The next day, with Brisbane still absent, Toussaint launched a lightning strike on Saint Marc, which then was not well fortified. He overran an exterior camp, whose officer, mysteriously, believed that Toussaint had come to negotiate a switch to the British side. Morin had conspired with colored men still inside Saint Marc to open the gates to Toussaint's army, which briefly took control of the town. But a British frigate sailed down from Môle to bombard Toussaint's men from the harbor, and Brisbane rushed back in the nick of time to recapture the place by land.

Toussaint eluded Brisbane's column and with forty dragoons rode full-tilt up the Artibonite River to capture Verrettes, a key post in the region whence Brisbane had just been hastily recalled. In this maneuver he was aided by Blanc Cassenave, mulatto commander of a unit in the Artibonite area called the Bare-Naked Congos, who had offered his allegiance to Toussaint at Gonaïves in 1793. With camps at Verrettes, and north of the Artibonite River at Marchand and Petite Rivière (where the British had begun building a fort on a hill called La Crête à Pierrot), Toussaint could control the passes into the Cahos mountains, an area as important to his strategy as the Cordon de l'Ouest. He could also threaten to isolate Saint Marc, where Brisbane was now hastily erecting more serious fortifications and launching an abortive sea attack on Gonaïves.

Laveaux believed Saint Marc was tottering and might easily fall. Before he sent Toussaint to attack the town again, he tried to soften the target by sending a proclamation to Saint Marc's citizens on September 12, 1794, urging upon the *gens de couleur* this point: "If you have had the courage to fight for those rights which alone distinguish man from the animals, then do have the generosity to recognize the beneficent decree which delivers your brothers from the irons that held them in slavery."[30] Although there was at this time a significant movement of *anciens libres* away from their alliances with the *grands blancs* and the British, Laveaux's missive had no apparent effect in Saint Marc. Toussaint proceeded to attack, deprived of any advantage of surprise, since Laveaux's proclamation had announced the planned assault—but he did succeed in capturing two forts on the heights above the town. Brisbane was shaken, but held out until he received reinforcements from Lapointe, a mulatto who commanded Arcahaye for the British, on September 18. Three days later, Toussaint gave up his attack on Saint Marc, after fifteen days of continuous fighting.

At the same time, Jean-François was gathering men for a fresh attempt on the eastern end of the Cordon de l'Ouest. On October 4 Toussaint reported his loss of several posts along the Artibonite River east of Saint Marc, which he attributed to "the perfidy of the colored men of that area."[31] "Saint Marc would now be ours," he went on, "if I had not had the misfortune to hurt my hand while mounting a cannon on a carriage. If I had been able to fight at the head of my troops according to my custom, Saint Marc would not have held out an hour, or I would have fallen, one or the other."[32] Instead Toussaint, nursing a painfully crushed hand, had to send his lieutenants Morin, Guy, and Blanc Cassenave into the fray in his place. The failure of the attack was assured by "the terrible treachery of the *hommes de couleur* who abandoned me to join our enemies."[33] In fact, three hundred mulattoes had been executed by the British in the wake of Toussaint's September 4 attack, and the survivors were doubtless discouraged from further collaboration with the French republic, at least for the time being. On top of that, Toussaint had run out of ammunition; such shortages would become one of his most chronic complaints to Laveaux. "The first time I attacked Saint Marc it was scarcely fortified at all," he concluded, somewhat bitterly. "At present it is very well bulwarked; its own ruins serve as its ramparts."[34]

Toussaint consoled himself for the failure at Saint Marc by whipping around 180 degrees to attack the Spanish and Jean-François. By October 21 Toussaint could send the much more cheerful report that he had driven the Spanish out of Saint Michel and Saint Raphael, capturing two officers and about fifty soldiers in the process. The towns were surrounded by horse and cattle ranches; Toussaint sent all the livestock into French Saint Domingue. "That operation accomplished," he wrote, "I razed the two towns, so that the enemy could not make any attempt on them and so he will keep his distance from us." In a very casual postscript he adds, "With the sabers of my cavalry I slew about ninety Spaniards—all those who in the end didn't want to surrender."[35]

This victory was a huge one, and hugely increased Toussaint's status with the French republicans. A white French general, Desfourneaux, had earlier failed in a campaign for the same objective. If there had been any lingering doubt, Toussaint's success decisively proved his value. As a Spanish officer, he had worn a crest of white feathers in his bicorne hat—an indication of royalist leanings. After this victory, Laveaux gave him a red plume, which Toussaint wore above the white ones ever after; his crest thus took on the colors of the revolution.

Now it was safe for Laveaux to leave Port de Paix and tour the Cordon de l'Ouest; he and Toussaint met face-to-face at Dondon. En route the French general was deeply impressed by what Toussaint had done to restore security and even tranquillity to the region: "Many whites had returned to their plantations . . . Many white women, whose properties had been invaded by the English, expressed to us how much attention and help they had received from this astonishing man . . . The parish of Petite Rivière offers the satisfying picture of more than fifteen thousand cultivators returned, full of gratitude, to the Republic: whites, blacks, mulattoes, soldiers, field hands, landowners—all blessing the virtuous chief whose cares maintain order and peace among them."[36] Following this encounter, Laveaux installed his headquarters at Le Cap; Toussaint returned to the campaign against the British.

Saint Marc remained a difficult thorn to pull from French republican flesh, and Brisbane was still a serious threat. Though his troops by now had more than a little training in the European style of warfare,

Toussaint was too wary to risk them against the redcoats in the open country of the Artibonite plain. He returned to a guerrilla program of ambush and temporary retreat. Brisbane's offensive, according to the British observer Brian Edwards, was "like a vessel traversing the ocean—the waves yielded indeed for the moment but united again as the vessel passed."[37] Toussaint's various European opponents would make the same complaint through the end of the decade. In February 1795, Brisbane himself was slain in one of these ambushes.

The fight for control of the posts on the south bank of the Artibonite gave Toussaint opportunity for some satisfying victories over *grand blanc* commanders in league with the British. He must have been practically cackling when, on August 31, 1795, he reported the humiliating defeat of one of these, Dessources, who "jumped down from his horse and, with the debris of his army, buried himself in the brush, shouting 'Sauve qui peut!' . . . I scattered bodies over the road for a distance of more than a mile; my victory was most complete, and if the famous Dessources has the luck to make it back to Saint Marc it will be without cannon, without baggage, and finally as they say with neither drum nor trumpet."[38]

As these tactics rendered the British at Saint Marc more or less ineffectual, Toussaint was content to forgo another wholesale assault on the town. During this same period he flushed the remainder of Jean-François's men out of the valley of Grande Rivière and established control of Mirebalais, an important town in a fertile valley near the Spanish border, at the opposite end of the Cahos mountain range from Saint Marc. Mirebalais was an area where French planters, both white and colored, had managed to remain on their lands and sustain a defense, and because of its remoteness the town's allegiance seemed to depend on the sentiments of these inhabitants more than anything else. Toussaint's attack which razed Saint Raphaël and Saint Michel had carried south toward Mirebalais, but local planters Despinville and Dubignuies encouraged the Spanish troops there to hold out; soon after the Spanish used Mirebalais as a platform for a counterattack on Toussaint's post at Verrettes, to the west along the Artibonite River. But then the locals decided to declare Mirebalais in favor of the French republic (at least temporarily). Toussaint undertook to secure these areas with a network of small camps like those with which he had created his first power base along the Cordon de l'Ouest; a letter of February 6 lists thirty-two of these.

Toussaint's successes in the interior had deeply damaged the Spanish-sponsored black auxiliaries there. By the Treaty of Basel, signed on July 22, 1795, Spain and France had ended their conflict, and Spain had agreed to cede its colony in the eastern half of Hispaniola to France. However, the French in Saint Domingue were spread too thin to occupy the new territory, and most of the Spanish colonists stayed on because they had nowhere to go. Flouting the treaty, Jean-François continued to harass Toussaint in the region along the border where the two black leaders had once queasily shared power. Not until November could Toussaint write to Laveaux, with enormous relief, "Thanks be to God: Jean-François is going to leave."[39] Rumors that Jean-François might shift his allegiance to the British invaders had caused the French republican camp some anxiety, but instead he retired to Spain with full military honors, while Biassou went to Spanish Florida with a few hundred of his men. What was left of his and Jean-François's followers then joined forces with Toussaint. Curiously, many members of Jean-François's family declined to accompany him into retirement, but stayed in Saint Domingue once Toussaint assured them of "liberty and tranquility." According to Toussaint's account of the episode to Laveaux, these relatives of Jean-François "had a horror of his principles, which generally tended to harm his brothers, and to perpetuate slavery."[40]

Between 1794 and 1796, Toussaint began to display unmistakably the same acumen (and sometimes the same ruthlessness) in politics as on the field of battle. His admirers as well as his detractors cannot help but notice that his potential competitors tended to come to harm during these years—not only enemy warriors like Brisbane but also several of his republican brothers in arms. Since the summer of 1793, the mulatto commander Blanc Cassenave had voluntarily reported to Toussaint; popular with his mostly black troops, Cassenave had been successful in engagements with the British outside Saint Marc and had been an important partner in Toussaint's assaults on the town. He had captured the half-built British fort at La Crête à Pierrot above Petite Rivière—

a point of importance to Toussaint's strategy in the region—and armed it with a couple of pieces of cannon. But relations between him and Toussaint broke down to the point that Toussaint had Cassenave arrested in January 1795. A long letter to Laveaux describes Blanc Cassenave as "an extremely abandoned, violent man," accuses him of plotting against both Toussaint and Laveaux, and of stealing eighty pounds of ever-scarce gunpowder.

Toussaint went on to accuse Blanc Cassenave of plotting to set up his own "arrondissement" in the Cahos mountains (where Toussaint had just recently extended his own reach), of keeping spoils captured from the enemy for himself instead of using them for the benefit of the troops, and of generally fomenting discord and rebellion, not only among the field workers of the area but also among the officer corps. (Cassenave briefly won over a couple of officers important to Toussaint: Guy and Christophe Mornet.) One of the differences between Cassenave and Louverture had to do with plantation work in the area: Toussaint had ordered that ground be prepared for planting; Cassenave persuaded the field hands that this labor was tantamount to the restoration of slavery.

Cassenave was imprisoned at Gonaïves. Before any trial could take place, Toussaint informed Laveaux, most silkily: "During his detention Blanc Cassenave was struck with a bilious choler which had all appearance of an unrestrainable rage; he was suffocated by it. *Requiescat in pace.* He is out of this world, we owe our thanksgiving to God on his behalf. As for myself, General, in having him arrested I did nothing but my duty; zealously I always seize the occasion to serve the fatherland. I will fight ceaselessly against enemies within and without. This death of Blanc Cassenave demolishes all procedures against him, as his crime had no accomplices."[41]

With a similarly honeyed tongue, Toussaint addressed himself to Dieudonné, leader of what had been Halaou's band of maroons and *nouveaux libres* outside Léogane, who was suspected by both Toussaint and General André Rigaud of contemplating a shift of loyalty to the English in that region. Although Sonthonax had invested Dieudonné with his commissioner's medal and, in theory, his commissioner's powers as well, apparently the impression this gesture had made was fading.

Rigaud, who commanded for the French republic in the southern peninsula, was trying diplomatic means to win the maroon leader to his side when Toussaint's missive reached Dieudonné's camp.

"Is it possible, my dear friend," wrote Toussaint on February 12, 1796, "that at the moment when France has triumphed over all the royalists and has recognized us as her children, by her beneficent decree of 9 Thermidor, that she accords us all our rights for which we are fighting, that you would let yourself be deceived by our former tyrants, who only use some of our unfortunate brothers to charge the rest of them with chains? For a time, the Spaniards hypnotized me in the same way, but I was not slow to recognize their rascality; I abandoned them and beat them well; I returned to my country which received me with open arms and was very willing to recompense my services. I urge you, my dear brother, to follow my example. If some particular reasons* should hinder you from trusting the brigadier generals Rigaud and Beauvais, Governor Laveaux, who is the good father of us all, and in whom our mother country has placed her confidence, should also deserve yours. I think that you will not deny your confidence to me, who am black like you, and who assure you that I desire nothing more in the world than to see you happy, you and all your brothers."[42]

The letter goes on in this vein for quite some time; meanwhile, as Toussaint advised Laveaux soon after, the net effect of "your dispatches and mine"[43] was that a mutiny led by Dieudonné's lieutenant Laplume took Dieudonné prisoner and turned him over to Rigaud. However, instead of bringing Dieudonné's band of three thousand to Rigaud as expected, Laplume put it under the orders of Toussaint. With this more or less bloodless coup, Toussaint was able to extend the range of his command much further south than he had ever done before.

Toussaint's reference to the "beneficent decree of 9 Thermidor" may have been a slip of his pen. In the context of his letter to Dieudonné the date of 16 Pluviôse, when the French National Convention had abolished slavery, would have made much more sense. There was no special decree promulgated on 9 Thermidor, the date when Robespierre and his faction fell from power and the Terror in France was brought to an

---

*These reasons may have included black mistrust for *anciens libres / gens de couleur.*

end. Within forty-eight hours Robespierre and his closest allies had followed the Terror's hundreds of victims to the guillotine, and a reconstituted National Convention reclaimed the executive functions previously carried out by the dread Committee of Public Safety. France's situation began to stabilize.

In August 1795, the Constitution of the Year III was ratified, reaffirming the rights and obligations of man and of citizen—a category in which the blacks of Saint Domingue were still legally included. In October, Napoleon Bonaparte was named commander in chief of all armies within France, thanks to his role in scotching a royalist insurrection in Paris, and a five-member directory elected by the legislature took over all executive powers. These developments overseas were likely to have been on Toussaint's mind in February 1796, though he had more than enough to think about at home in Saint Domingue.

Toussaint's letter to Dieudonné evokes the themes of black-mulatto racial tension most adroitly, as well as the stresses between the *anciens* and *nouveaux libres:* though technically a member of the former group, Toussaint was determined to position himself at the head of the latter. Indeed, conflict had been brewing between the mostly colored *anciens libres* and the mostly black *nouveaux libres* almost from the day Toussaint had decided to reposition himself beneath the French republican flag.

Sonthonax had empowered the mulattoes, but just before his recall to France he had begun to shift his weight toward the black *nouveaux libres.* Perhaps it was in the context of mulatto support of the *grands blancs* and the British that Sonthonax had remarked to Dieudonné, "You are the representative of France; do not forget that so long as you see colored men among your own, you will not be free."[44] Toussaint, though never a strong supporter of Sonthonax, probably agreed with this statement—privately. Up until 1796 he did not show it. In the south, victories by the colored commander Rigaud had been almost as important to the republic as what Toussaint had accomplished in the north and was beginning to accomplish in the Artibonite Valley. But so far, Toussaint's and Rigaud's spheres of influence had not come close to a collision.

With Villatte, the mulatto commander who'd been the supreme authority at Le Cap until Laveaux moved there from Port de Paix, friction came sooner. As early as September 1794 Toussaint began bickering with Villatte over control of posts in the area of Limbé. Toussaint insisted to Laveaux that these must remain under his authority—he felt that his natural cordon extended not only from Dondon through Ennery to Gonaïves but also from Ennery through Limbé, Gros Morne, and Port Margot to Borgne. An unspoken part of Toussaint's grievance against Blanc Cassenave was that the latter was more loyal to Villatte than to himself. Since both Toussaint and Villatte claimed authority around the edges of the Northern Plain, some contention between them was perhaps inevitable. Not long after the death of Blanc Cassenave, another mulatto commander, Joseph Flaville, rebelled against Toussaint's authority. Luckier than his predecessor, Flaville tucked himself under Villatte's wing at Cap Français long enough for Laveaux to broker a truce between him and Toussaint.

On July 23, 1795, the French National Convention had recognized the services of Toussaint Louverture by promoting him from colonel to brigadier general. Villatte, Rigaud, and Louis-Jacques Beauvais (a third colored officer who was based in the southern coastal town of Jacmel) received the same rank on the same day. Because of the distinction Sonthonax had conferred on him, Toussaint might have seen Dieudonné as just as serious a potential rival as the three mulatto generals. With the maneuver that disposed of Dieudonné, Toussaint also stole a march on Rigaud: Laplume was promoted to colonel by Laveaux on Toussaint's recommendation; thereafter Laplume and the force of three thousand he had wrested from Dieudonné reported to Toussaint.

Although Toussaint had done much to consolidate his personal power and to place it at the disposal of Laveaux and thus of France, the stability he was trying to bring to the colony was not as solid as it might have seemed. A lengthy report he made to Laveaux on February 19, 1796, reveals much about the problems of local dissension which Toussaint confronted, and also about his methods of solving them.

On February 13, while camped at his Artibonite outpost, Verrettes, Toussaint received two letters delivered by a white messenger, Gramont

L'Hôpital, informing him that the soldiers and field hands had revolted in the mountains above Port de Paix, the town so recently vacated by Laveaux. One of those letters had been dictated by the black commander of the region, Etienne Datty, who claimed that he had no idea of the cause of the rebellion. Toussaint wrote back to Datty at once, exhorting him to restore order. But soon after, "two citizens of the mountain of Port de Paix, more clear-eyed and more reasonable than the others,"[45] approached Toussaint at Verrettes and let him know that "many assassinations had been committed" in the region they had come from.

"Believing that all this might spread into neighboring parishes," Toussaint reported to General Laveaux, "I decided to leave myself to go to that area and try to remedy, if it should be possible, all the disorders." He put the fort he had just constructed at Verrettes into a "state of defense" and rode north to Grande Rivière, where he met a third deputation come to let him know that "the Disorder at Port de Paix was at its height," and that many had been killed. Toussaint had left Verrettes at eight in the evening; after circling through Grande Rivière, he rode southwest to Petite Rivière and halted at his headquarters on Benoit Plantation, where he arrived at eleven at night—in three hours he had covered an astonishing distance, given the difficulty of the terrain.

At six a.m. he rode on to Gonaïves, and stopped at his headquarters there to write letters and to ready a small detachment of dragoons for his expedition to Port de Paix. With this light reinforcement, he rode north from Gonaïves at four in afternoon, and reached the town of Gros Morne (about halfway to Port de Paix) at midnight. There he learned that an officer named Jean Pierre Dumesny had gone in search of Etienne Datty but had been unable to find him.

During Toussaint's halt at Gros Morne a large number of "citizens of all colors who had the Happiness to escape the assassinations which were being committed came to see me and gave me a recital which filled me with horror. As my Horses as well as my dragoons were tired I Gave the order to unsaddle, and to hold themselves ready, I had them given their rations . . . At three in the morning Jean Pierre Dumesny, having learned that I had arrived in the village of Gros Morne, came to join me and reported that he had not yet been able to find Etienne, that he had presented himself at the appointed rendezvous but had found no trace of him . . . At four o'clock in the morning I gave the order to the Dragoons to Saddle, and got on the road to Port de Paix by five."[46] On such maneuvers is founded Toussaint's reputation for rapid, unpredictable movement and for indefatigability.

A couple of miles outside of the town, Toussaint paused to send out a few advance messengers, Jean Pierre Dumesny among them, to try to coax Etienne Datty to meet him for an interview. Then he rode a little further, halting at Ravine Pourrie, where he "had the horses unbridled so they might graze on a little grass." It would have been full daylight by then; dawn comes quickly so near the equator. After an hour's wait, a couple of horsemen of Datty's troop appeared, then ten armed men on foot. Toussaint notes that while he reproached them vigorously for the riots and killings that had been going on, "they all seemed very satisfied to see me."[47] Having sent these people away with new messages urging Datty to present himself, Toussaint rode on, stopping at two in the afternoon at the river of Passe Seguier for long enough to compose a letter to the recalcitrant and thus far invisible Datty. This time Toussaint ordered Datty to meet him at the nearby Andro Plantation.

"I got back on the road; at three o'clock I arrived at Habitation Andro, where I found a black citizen named Baptiste who told me that he served as a herdsman for Citizen Andro, the owner, & also Two black women citizens and an old mulatress, of whom I asked, Why all these disorders?—they replied that they did not Know the cause. As soon as I arrived I wrote to Pageot, Commandant of the Northern Province, to inform him of my arrival, and I sent the said Baptiste, with Two of my dragoons, to carry this letter. At the same moment there came to see me a large number of men and women fieldworkers, who brought me provisions, some fowls and some eggs, and testified to the pleasure they had in seeing me, and that they Hoped that I would settle all these Disorders. I Gave them the order to go find me some forage,* which they did on the spot and seemed to do with pleasure. That seemed to me to be a Good omen and made me believe that settling these things would not be difficult."[48]

---

*For Toussaint's horses.

In all these maneuvers one begins to sense the delicate balance with which Toussaint walked the line between French military commander and African chieftain. He had arrived in the unstable region with just a few cavalrymen at his back; if Datty's rebellion were determined, his forces would hugely outnumber Toussaint's, though probably they would be far less well trained and disciplined. In his daylong meander through the area, Toussaint was spreading the news of his presence as broadly as he could, while being careful never to remain in one spot for more than an hour: he had no intention of making himself a stationary target until he had a better sense of the local mood. His letters to Datty were written in French military style, from commander to subordinate—but the verbal messages he sent, parallel to his written communications, must have been more like invitations to a sort of clan meeting. Toussaint drew his confidence from subtle harbingers in the locals' response to him that would likely have passed unnoticed by a European officer. When the field hands brought him offerings of food and willingly followed his directions to find hay for his horses, he was reassured that they accepted the style of patriarchal authority he was trying to assert. Secure in their support, he was encouraged to remain at Andro Plantation till Etienne Datty should come; without that support he might well have been as shy of Datty as Datty was of him.

"At seven o'clock in the evening, Etienne presented himself in conformity to the order which I had Sent him, with about five hundred men of whom a great Part were armed. I had my horse saddled and Gave the order to Etienne To have all the citizens who had come with him form a circle, as well as those who had just come in with the forage." With these directions, Toussaint managed to mingle Datty's men, whose intentions and loyalties were uncertain, with the field hands who had turned up earlier and had demonstrated their loyalty to Toussaint.

"I mounted my horse & entered into the Circle." To address the throng from horseback increased Toussaint's air of authority; he was also ready for a swift departure if anything should go wrong.

After having Preached to them the morals of reason and having reproached them for the assassinations which they had committed, I told them that if they wanted to save their liberty, they must submit to the laws of the Republic & be docile—that it was not by such [violent] conduct that they would enjoy their freedom, that if they had some claim or complaint this was no way to get it recognized, and that Jesus had said, 'Ask and you shall receive, knock at my door and it shall be opened to you,' but he did not tell you to commit crimes to demand what you Need.

I asked them if they knew me and if they were happy to see me; they replied, yes, they knew I was the father of all the blacks, that they also knew that I had never ceased laboring for their Happiness and for their freedom, but that they prayed me to Listen to them and Perhaps I would see that they were not so far in the wrong as I said that they were.[49]

At this point the encounter (as steered by Toussaint) had become a sort of court proceeding, African style, where grievances could be aired before the assembled community and resolved by the judgment of the patriarch. "I was silent," Toussaint wrote to Laveaux,

and listened to them. One Among them said, "My General, we all regard you as our father, you are the most precious to us after God, and in you we have the greatest confidence." I hushed him & told him that if they had considered me so, they would not have behaved as they did; that if they were afraid to address themselves to the Governor-General [Laveaux], whom we must all regard as our father and defender of our liberty, they should have addressed themselves to me & and that I would have worked to obtain satisfaction from the Governor-General of whatever claims of theirs I found to be just & that I would have Avoided their plunging into Crime.[50]

Here Toussaint is reinforcing a chain of command running down from Laveaux through himself to his subordinate officers and thence to individual soldiers and citizens. Though the hierarchy is orthodox, his style of asserting it is not. For the abstraction of European military organization, where all individuals can be replaced in their ranks, is substituted an alternative where the whole apparatus is held together by Toussaint's personal, paternal relationship with all the people under his authority—though he wields his authority in the name of Laveaux and the French republic.

"They replied that all loved the Governor-General, but that it was unfortunate that everyone was not like him." And then they got down to the real complaint:

> Since the beginning of the revolution Etienne has always been our Chief; it is he who has always commanded us; he has eaten all our misery with us to win our liberty—Why did they take the command away from Etienne to give it to someone else against our wishes & why do they treat him as nothing? To ask that question, my General, we took up arms; it is unfortunate for us that we have some bad men among us who have committed crimes, but few of us are implicated in all that. Alas! My General, they want to make us Slaves again; Equality is nowhere here—nothing Like it seems to be on your side. See how the Whites and the *hommes de couleur* who are with you are good, and are friends with the blacks till one would say they are all brothers born of the same mother— That, my General, is what we call Equality.[51]

This language, too, springs from the core rhetoric of the French Revolution, but here it has taken a peculiarly familial twist. Moreover, while these *nouveau libre* citizens of the Port de Paix region recognize Toussaint as "father of all the blacks," they also recognize two sides, it seems: theirs and his.

"They trouble us too much," the spokesman continued. "They don't pay us well for the harvests we make, and they force us to give our Chickens and pigs for nothing when we go to sell them in the town, and if we want to Complain they have us arrested By the police and they put us in prison without giving us anything to eat & we have to pay still more to get out again.—you can plainly see, my General, that to be dragged around like that is not to be free—but we are very sure that you are not at all like that, from the way that we see that everyone with you is happy and loves you."[52]

Once assured that the assembly had completely stated its case, Toussaint commenced his reply: "My friends—I ought not call you so, for the shame you have brought to me and all men of our color makes me see all too clearly that you are not my friends—all the reasons you give me strike me as Most Just, but although you do have a very strong case—"

But here, in the midst of reporting his own oration, Toussaint turned directly to Laveaux (whom he himself often addressed as "father") to explain, "I used that expression To make them understand that though they might have all the good reasons that One could possibly have, that they were still wrong and that they had rendered themselves guilty in the eyes of God, of the Law, and of men."[53] It was a ticklish matter for Toussaint to convince this audience, whose members were accustomed to resort to arms to settle injustices which looked obvious to them, that in the French republic, to which Toussaint insisted they belong, Law might trump Justice, at least from time to time.

> How is it possible, I said to them, that I who have just sent
> deputies to thank the national convention in the name of all
> the blacks for the Beneficent Decree which gives them all
> liberty, & and to assure the convention that they will do their
> best to deserve it, and will Prove to France and all the Nations
> by their obedience to the laws, their labor and their Docility,
> that they are worthy of it,—and that I answered for all and
> that Soon with the help of France we would prove to the
> entire universe that Saint Domingue would recover all its
> riches with the work of free hands—how shall I answer when
> the national convention demands that I account for what you
> have just done? Tell me—my shame makes me see that I have
> betrayed the national convention, that [what you have done]
> will prove to the national convention everything that the
> Enemies of our freedom have been trying to make it believe:
> that the blacks are in no way constituted to be free, that if

they become free they won't want to work anymore and won't do anything but commit robbery and murder.[54]

Here for the first time in public (and to the sort of audience he most needed to convince), Toussaint announced his ambition for the colony: he would manage Saint Domingue so as to prove to the whole European world that slavery was not necessary to the success of the plantation economy, that sugar and coffee production could be revived, and the Jewel of the Antilles restored to its former luster—with free labor. But for that project to succeed there was a surprisingly vast cultural rift to be bridged, and almost as soon as Toussaint had finished speaking, that rift began to widen once more.

The people whom he had addressed swore up and down to sin no more, to be good and obedient and peaceful, that they desired nothing more than to have Toussaint restore order among them. Toussaint exhorted them to prove these good intentions by returning to their plantations—and to work. Once they were gone he turned to Datty and pointed out that by no means all the inhabitants of the region had been present for this talking-to. Datty admitted that there were still three camps of rebels on the mountain above Port de Paix. Toussaint loaned Datty a secretary to draft a letter ordering those camps to report to Toussaint at Andro Plantation. That letter sent, Toussaint and Datty shared a supper. At ten thirty that night, Datty took his leave, promising to appear with the remaining rebels the next day. "I had the ration given to my dragoons," Toussaint wrote, "who had eaten nothing all day but a few bananas which the field hands had brought me, as I said before. I told them to pay good attention to their horses, and passed that night without anything new happening."[55]

By the next morning, however, it became clear that Etienne Datty had again slipped his leash. He sent emissaries but avoided appearing in person before Toussaint as he had promised, and the rest of the rebels remained where they were. Toussaint began sending letters once more.

Headquarters, Habitation Andro,
29 Pluviôse, year 4 of the French Republic, one and indivisible.

Toussaint Louverture, Brigadier General, Commander in Chief of the Cordon of the West, to Etienne Datty, Commander of the Africans

Immediately upon the reception of my letter, I order you to present yourself before me at Habitation Andro with all the citizens of the mountain and all those that I saw yesterday. My dear Etienne, I believe you to be too reasonable, not to Know what obedience is; I believe that you will present yourself right away, and spare me the pain of repeating this order.

Salut

(Signed)
Toussaint Louverture[56]

But Toussaint's belief was disappointed: Datty did not reappear, nor did he send a direct reply. Instead Toussaint received a letter from "the Citizens in arms at Lagon," explaining that since Datty had so often been entrapped in the past by "Beautiful Propositions" they themselves had restrained him from returning to Toussaint.

This cat-and-mouse game went on all day, with numerous exchanges of letters and circuits of messengers. By this time, Datty's insubordination was unmistakable, and the use of force seemed the inevitable next step. A white French officer might have taken it, but Toussaint had a different turn of mind. "Etienne's refusal made me spend the whole night considering what line I ought to Take. I reflected that if I used force, that might occasion Much more evil than there had so far been. At six in the morning, I decided; I left to go Find Etienne. I took with me Jean Pierre Dumesny, my Secretary,* and four of my dragoons."[57]

No wonder it took all night to calculate the risk of entering a rebellious encampment with this merely symbolic escort: in very similar circumstances, Toussaint had taken Brandicourt prisoner. But this gamble

*Guybre, a white Frenchman.

paid off: "I arrived at Camp Lagon at six-thirty; seeing me arrive, Etienne came before me; I scolded him and asked him Why he had Disobeyed, and what he could have been thinking of. He apologized and said that it was his troops who had kept him from coming. When I got down from my horse, all the Citizens, armed or not, came to tell me Good Day and to tell me how glad they were to see me."[58] The peaceful approach, however risky, allowed Toussaint to reoccupy his patriarchal role. The men of Datty's command were ready to recognize him as head of a household that included them all.

Toussaint then took Datty aside for another long session of remonstrance and coaxing, and finally "succeeded in making him hear reason." Then he inquired about Datty's secretary, one Maguenot (most likely a white Frenchman, one of several who served the black officers as scribes), and learned that he was lurking in another of the three rebel camps on the mountain. Maguenot was the probable author of the letter from "the Citizens in arms at Lagon" that Toussaint had received the day before. Between the lines of Toussaint's report to Laveaux, it appears that at this point Toussaint saw a possibility for laying the blame for Datty's insubordination on this Maguenot.

" 'You have a Secretary there who is a cunning, wicked man,' " Toussaint suggested to Datty. " 'He is deceiving you, I am sure of it,' and I asked him if he had seen a postscript he had put in the margin of the Letter that he wrote to me and sent by the citizen Gramont [i.e., the first news Toussaint had of the insurrection at Port de Paix, delivered to him at Verrettes], in these terms: The bearer of the Letter is the citizen Gramont, I am in No Way guilty, I am forced to live with wolves."[59] Etienne Datty declared that he had not seen this bit of marginalia, which suggests that perhaps he could not read: many of the black officer corps were illiterate and thus at the mercy of their secretaries. With the scales thus fallen from his eyes, Datty told Toussaint "no doubt he [Maguenot] could have put other bad things into the letters which I had him Write to the Governor General and the Commandant of the province, Without my knowing anything of it."[60]

It may well have been true that Maguenot helped stir up the trouble; it was certainly true that arresting him made it easier for Toussaint to reinstate Datty in his command without any punishment or reprimand—which, given the mood of Datty's men, was clearly the prudent thing to do. Maguenot was sent away under armed guard, while Toussaint and Datty dined together. After the repast, these two returned together to Andro Plantation.

"I arrived at Habitation Andro at four o'clock and found that everyone was there; I ordered Etienne to have them fall into line in front of the house. That being done I made them all Swear to put everything back into good order, to submit to the laws of the Republic, and I Gave them Etienne Datty To Command them." Whereupon Datty's men cried, "Vive la République! Vive la Liberté et l'Égalité! Vive le Général Laveaux! Vive le Général Toussaint!"[61] Then they all began to dance, while Toussaint retired to his room for a long-overdue rest; in the previous seventy-two hours he had taken scarcely more than a cat-nap. The next day he had to gallop back to Verrettes, for the English had taken advantage of his absence to attack his post there. In partnership with Laveaux, Toussaint had done a great deal to restore stability to much of the colony, but what he'd achieved was still constantly threatened, from both within and without.

Resolving the Datty affair had taken six rather hectic days, and Toussaint had needed to walk delicately over a long line of eggshells to avoid coming to blows with his own people—to the extent that Datty's people were his. Even the style of address of their letters underlines the gap between them: Toussaint is brigadier general in the French army, while Datty (in his own signatures as well as in Toussaint's salutations) is "Commander of the Africans." One is a French military officer who happens to be wearing a black skin; the other is a tribal leader. It is likely that all or most of Etienne's men really were "Africans" in the sense that, like the majority of the *nouveaux libres,* they had been born in Africa. The first instinct of these men was to trust the chiefs of their own group ahead of any Creole commander like Toussaint, though Toussaint, who knew how to operate both as a tribal leader and as a member of the French military hierarchy, was able to win Datty's men over, and without any serious show of force. His situation required him to shuttle constantly between these two roles, and he had a remarkable facility for doing just that, as his long report to Laveaux on the Datty affair is intended to demonstrate. A European officer in his place would have been far less likely to grasp, for example, that the willingness of the locals to find hay for his horses meant that they were likely to stand by him in the controversy, but it was through such subtle gestures that Toussaint maintained his connection to his popular base.

Toussaint was black, as he would often remind the *nouveaux libres,* but he was also (unlike the majority of them) a Creole, born in the colony and adapted to its ways from birth, and furthermore (unlike all the *nouveaux libres*) he had been a prosperous land- and slave-holding freedman well before the revolution whose principal leader he was now becoming. Much as he labored to disguise them, those differences did create a fissure between Toussaint and the roughly half million people he was trying to mold into a new black citizenry, competent to defend its own freedom on both the political and the military fronts.

The unrest in Port de Paix, settled in Toussaint's favor, is one example of this problem. In the Western Department, the uncertain loyalty of Dieudonné's force was another. This issue too was settled in Toussaint's favor by his letters and intermediaries, at roughly the same time that he himself was halfway across the colony managing the business of Datty. Toussaint wrote his crucial letter to Dieudonné on February 12, the day before he received the first news of the uprising at Port de Paix. Just ten days later, Toussaint was writing to Laveaux about similar trouble in La Souffrière "since Macaya went there with Charlôt after having escaped from the prisons of Gonaïves." Another tribal leader, Macaya had been a far more prominent figure than Toussaint when rebellion erupted in 1791, and with Pierrot had helped Sonthonax wrest control of Le Cap away from Galbaud in 1793. "I only had Macaya arrested because he was corrupting my troops and taking them to Jean-François," Toussaint wrote to Laveaux.[62] Perhaps it would be cynical to suppose that he also saw Macaya (like Blanc Cassenave, Dieudonné, and others) as a potential rival for advancement in the French military.

Certainly Toussaint and Macaya were of different breeds. After Macaya's escape from Gonaïves, Toussaint complained to Laveaux, "Every day he holds dances and assemblies with the Africans of his nation,* to whom he gives bad advice. As long as these two men remain at La Souffrière, people of ill intention will find them easily disposed to help them to do evil . . . It would be most suitable to have Macaya and his cohort Charlôt arrested, for they are staying too long in these neighborhoods . . . [Macaya] will now do all the harm he can so as to revenge himself on me. I pray you, my General, to pay careful attention to that, for if you don't cut the evil off at its root, it may grow very large."[63]

The episodes of Datty, Dieudonné, and Macaya show that unrest among the enormous African-born contingent of the *nouveaux libres* was very widespread. At the same time a completely different sort of outbreak was brewing among the *gens de couleur*. Toussaint's letter about Macaya is sprinkled with equally urgent complaints about Joseph Flaville, the mulatto commander who had vexed him not long before by making certain posts which Toussaint considered to be part of his own command report instead to Villatte at Le Cap. Indeed, Villatte's power and influence there were not only becoming more and more vexatious to Toussaint, but also more and more dangerous to Laveaux and to all French authority in the colony.

Toussaint's situation vis-à-vis these *anciens libres* was tricky. Like most in Villatte's colored contingent, he had been free well before 1791, and like them, he had prospered in the prerevolutionary plantation economy. His interest in political rights for freedmen was similar to that of the *gens de couleur*. Unlike them, however, he was black. It seems unlikely that the antipathy between Toussaint and men like Flaville and Villatte was altogether racially based, for Toussaint had mulattoes among his most trusted officers to the very end of his career (on terms like brothers born of the same mother, as Datty's men observed). However, it is likely enough that some colored officers were loath to accept a full-blood Negro as commander in chief, and certain that Villatte would have viewed the rapid growth of Toussaint's power in the Northern Department as a threat to his own position at Le Cap.

Events of the last two years had been extraordinarily empowering to the race of *gens de couleur* and the class of *anciens libres*. The *grands blancs*

*Macaya was a Congolese, an important tribal affiliation.

had been swept out of the north of the colony by the aftermath of *l'af-faire Galbaud*. Since the ratification of the National Convention had confirmed the abolition of slavery and of all racial discrimination among French citizens, the *gens de couleur* of the north had reason to believe that they had finally inherited the kingdom of their fathers.

So Laveaux's return to Cap Français was resented by many in the colored community there, which had restored and occupied many of the white-owned houses in the fire-ruined town, and had occupied the municipal offices. Toussaint foresaw trouble; on February 19 (in the midst of all the other turmoil) he wrote what for him was a frantic letter, advising Laveaux to stay clear of it: "Get yourself to Port de Paix if you can. Follow the advice of a son who loves his father, and don't leave there without letting me know . . . As soon as I have put my cordon in order I will write you everything I am thinking."[64] Either Toussaint never had a chance to write the follow-up letter, or Laveaux did not receive it, or he decided not to take it seriously.

Though never so fiery a Jacobin as Sonthonax, Laveaux did irk some sympathizers of the ancien régime in Le Cap by continuing Sonthonax's policies there: one inflamed observer accused him of setting up a "tribunal of blood."[65] Thus there was some hostility on the part of the remaining whites in the north, on which Laveaux's colored enemies could capitalize. It's also possible that the English invaders at Port-au-Prince, using the royalist Colonel Cambefort as their conduit, encouraged Villatte to depose Laveaux from his governorship. Still more probable was some degree of collusion with the mulatto commanders Rigaud and Beauvais, who between them controlled most of the Southern Department. The idea of mulatto rule of the whole colony was constantly sponsored by Pinchinat, an *homme de couleur* who despite his advanced age was a fierce personality: in 1791 he had calmly suggested, "Let us plunge our bloody arms into the Hearts of these monsters of Europe."[66] Pinchinat was a wily politician and skilled propagandist; Lapointe, commander at Arcahaie, declared that he feared the writings of Pinchinat more than an army. Certainly Pinchinat played some part in instigating what become known as *l'af-faire de 30 ventôse*.

On that date (March 20, 1796), the colored officials of Cap

Français imprisoned Laveaux and announced that he had been replaced in his governorship by Villatte. With his accountant, Perroud, Laveaux languished in jail for two days. Then, on March 22, Pierre Michel, a black officer acting on Toussaint's orders, entered Le Cap in sufficient force to rout Villatte and his followers, who fled into the countryside. Laveaux and Perroud were freed and restored to their offices, as a proclamation sent by Toussaint rebuked the population of the town for colluding with the coup attempt. On March 28, Toussaint himself appeared at the head of his army and received a hero's welcome.

In addition to disposing of another of Toussaint's rivals, this episode cemented the quite genuine friendship—and strategic partnership—between Toussaint and Laveaux. On April 1, Laveaux called an assembly on the Place d'Armes of Cap Français, where he proclaimed Toussaint to be not only "the savior of the constituted authorities," but also "a black Spartacus, the negro Raynal predicted would avenge the outrages done to his race."[67]

Toussaint had taken the coup attempt quite seriously as a threat to the stability of the whole colony, or more precisely as a threat to the administration he was building with Laveaux. He knew that the Villatte insurrection might well have gone colony-wide—Villatte had gone so far as to send notice to military officers all over the colony that he was now their commander in chief, and had also set about organizing a new colonial assembly. When Toussaint got the news at Gonaïves, he immediately sent two battalions, commanded by Charles Belair and Jean-Jacques Dessalines, to reinforce Pierre Michel at Le Cap, while he himself remained where he was, poised to strike in any direction, sending a stream of dispatches and messengers to other towns warning them not to rebel, as well as a report to the French consul in Philadelphia. When he marched north toward Cap Français he routed Villatte from a fort he'd occupied near Petite Anse; Villatte departed, snarling that he hoped "Laveaux would have his throat slit by the blacks he was caressing."[68] In fact, Villatte's party had managed to start a rumor that Laveaux and Perroud had imported two shiploads of chains for the restoration of slavery, and the two Frenchmen were threatened by a black mob until Toussaint opened the general warehouse to let the crowd see that no such chains were there.

In gratitude, and also to secure himself and his government against further suspicion from the *nouveaux libres,* Laveaux proclaimed Toussaint lieutenant governor that April 1 on the Place d'Armes, and announced that henceforward he would do nothing without Toussaint's approval. Toussaint, exhilarated, shouted to the crowd: "After God, Laveaux!"[69]—an exclamation he had recently heard addressed to himself by Datty's men around Port de Paix. On the same day, Dieudonné died in his southern prison, suffocated not by a "bilious choler" but by the weight of his chains.

FOUR

Closing the Circle

Trained as a lawyer and skilled as a diplomat, Léger Félicité Sonthonax was, above all, a survivor. The order for his and Polverel's arrest in Saint Domingue was signed by Robespierre, but by the time the two recalled commissioners arrived in France, Robespierre had fallen and the Terror was over. Sonthonax and Polverel were tried before a more moderate National Convention, by a committee predisposed in favor of abolition, though their accusers and prosecutors were a group of colonists who had lost their property. The various phases of the proceedings went on for over a year, from September 1794 to October 1795, and generated the first in-depth and reasonably objective report on events in French Saint Domingue since 1791, authored by Garran de Coulon, who presided over the commissioners' trial. Polverel died before it was over, but on October 25, 1795, Sonthonax won complete vindication, emerging from the cloud of his disgrace as a kind of hero. Three months later, he was appointed head of the Third Civil Commission to Saint Domingue, a body which also included Julien Raimond, an *homme de couleur* who had tirelessly lobbied for the rights of his class since the 1780s, and Philippe Roume de Saint Laurent, an experienced colonial hand who had been a member of the First Civil Commission. Marc Antoine Giraud and Pierre Leblanc brought the number of commissioners to five. Citizen Pascal, a white Frenchman who would marry one of Julien Raimond's daughters, was appointed as the commission's secretary general.

The ship bearing the Third Commission sailed into Cap Français on May 11, 1796; Sonthonax especially was received as a great emancipator. The French government had directed him to proclaim the abolition of slavery all over again, which he did with great enthusiasm; his popularity was also enhanced by his consort, Marie Eugénie Bléigeat, a *femme de couleur* attached to him since his first tour of the colony, who had borne him a son in Paris. During this honeymoon period of 1796, the head commissioner was so beloved by the *nouveaux libres* that they were supposed to have taught their children to pray especially for Sonthonax in their daily devotions.

But Sonthonax was the target of vicious rumors as well as blessings and bouquets. From the moment of his return, some began to spread the completely false tale that he had escaped execution in France on the condition that he would restore slavery in Saint Domingue. In July 1796, Toussaint Louverture wrote in a report to Laveaux: "The wicked are conspiring more than ever . . . I write to Commissioner Sonthonax by this same mail to let him know how the wicked ones are reducing his credit, so as to lead the gullible field hands, among others, astray. They are making them believe, among other absurdities, that he has returned from France to put them back into slavery. Several soldiers and field hands from the Artibonite have come to warn me about what is going on. I have dissuaded them from what the wicked have told them, and sent them back home reassured."[1]

For his part, Sonthonax noted (despite the euphoria surrounding his return) that "the regime established in Saint Domingue at our arrival was perfectly similar to the eighth-century feudal regime."[2] Considerable arrondissements had been carved out by various black and mulatto military leaders, who could as reasonably be compared to twenty-first-century warlords as to medieval barons, and the tension between *nouveaux* and *anciens libres* was palpable. One of Sonthonax's first acts was to deport Villatte and his chief supporters to France—an endorsement of the steps recently taken by both Laveaux and Toussaint Louverture. To underline that endorsement, Sonthonax also promoted

Toussaint to general of division, advancing him a rank ahead of any other non-French officer in the colony.

By the time the Third Commission reached Saint Domingue, Toussaint Louverture was plainly the most powerful commander in the colony (though André Rigaud, in the south, was a close second) and also the most useful to France. With the exception of Môle Saint-Nicolas, where the English still held the forts and the harbor, he had secured all of the Northern Department for the French republic. His campaigns in the interior during the summer and fall of 1795 had won the regions of Mirebalais and of Grande Rivière for France. Fort Liberté, once the stronghold of the Spanish black auxiliaries under Jean-François, was now garrisoned by Toussaint's troops, commanded by Pierre Michel. Following the Treaty of Basel and the departure of Jean-François and Biassou from Saint Domingue, most of the men those two had commanded in the name of Spain had fallen into Toussaint's ranks.

For Toussaint, as for Sonthonax, the two matters of chief concern in the summer of 1796 were the potential for another mulatto rebellion in the style of *l'affaire Villatte,* and the English invasion, which still had a lease on life. In the Cordon de l'Ouest, Toussaint had made his posts impregnable, but he was still disputing the south bank of the Artibonite River with the redcoats, and in September 1795, the English had recaptured Mirebalais from Toussaint's brother Paul, thus opening an important supply line to the livestock herds on the grassy Central Plateau. Throughout 1796, Toussaint harassed the English at Mirebalais guerrilla style, making use of an alliance with a local maroon community known as the Dokos, but he could not commit the forces to dislodge them altogether.

Toussaint's military management of the north was developing a certain authoritarian quality which some among the *nouveaux libres* were inclined to resent. Toussaint had thought it best to undermine and eliminate many of the more traditional African chieftains who, like Biassou, doubled as *houngans,* or Vodou priests. The complaint he wrote to Laveaux about Macaya in February 1796 was one example of this program; his overthrow of Dieudonné was another.

Vodou was, and remains to this day, fundamentally unresponsive to command and control from the top. Each of the myriad temples scattered over the colony was a sort of cell that could network with others by many different horizontal routes. Toussaint, who like many of his people found it comfortable to combine a private practice of Vodou with a public and equally sincere profession of Catholicism, understood the revolutionary potential of the Vodou networks and used them to his own advantage when he could. He also understood that Vodou would always be resistant to any centralized authority, including the authority he was trying to build.

A related issue was Toussaint's determination to restore the plantation economy, which his enemies could turn into an accusation that he meant to restore slavery. This claim had been a feature of Blanc Cassenave's abortive rebellion in 1795. In June of that year, "a citizen named Thomas" spread a rumor among plantation hands at Marmelade that Toussaint was "making them work," so as to "return them to the slavery of the whites." "I went there myself to preach to them and make them hear reason," Toussaint reported to Laveaux; "they armed themselves against me and as thanks for my efforts I received a bullet in the leg, which still gives me quite vivid pain."[3]

In April 1796, not long before the arrival of the Third Commission, Toussaint had to subdue a similar revolt in the parish of Saint Louis du Nord. His proclamation to the inhabitants there strikes the tone of a disappointed but affectionate father: "Oh you Africans, my brothers, you who have cost me so much weariness, sweat, work and suffering! You, whose liberty is sealed by the purest half of your own blood, how long will I have the grief of seeing my stray children flee the advice of a father who idolizes them! . . . Have you forgotten that it is I who first raised the standard of insurrection against tyranny, against the despotism that held us in chains? . . . You have liberty, what more do you want? What will the French people say . . . when they learn that after the gift they have just given you, you have taken your ingratitude to the point of drenching your hands in the blood of their children . . . Do you not know what France has sacrificed for general liberty?"[4]

As fervently as Toussaint claimed brotherhood with the mass of the *nouveaux libres,* he also addressed them as "Africans"—not as Creoles like himself. The two cultures had real and large differences between them, and the "Africans" were perennially resistant to the work ethic Toussaint was trying so urgently to get them to adopt. Any ruler who wanted productivity for the colony faced the same obstacle, which was described with a certain loftiness by a French commentator in Port-au-Prince: "Work, which produces wealth and nourishes commerce, is the child of our artificial needs; needs which the Negro ignores, just as the philosopher disdains them."[5] Toussaint's task was to dissuade the *nouveaux libres* from this disdainful attitude (philosophical or not) and to convince them that work was essential to the defense of their freedom. At the same time the African-Creole cultural gap must be bridged by a universal black solidarity.

Generally well informed about events in France, Toussaint probably knew in advance that Sonthonax was returning to Saint Domingue. The language of his address to the people of Saint Louis du Nord, even as it affirms the liberating role of France, also (like the proclamation of Camp Turel) stakes Toussaint's own claim to be the chief emancipator of the *nouveaux libres.* Later in the same address, his reassurances become more frank:

> Pay close attention, my brothers: there are more blacks in the
> colony than there are colored men and whites together, and if
> some disturbance occurs it will be us blacks that the Republic
> holds responsible, because we are the strongest and it is up to
> us to maintain order and tranquility by our good example. I
> am, as chief, responsible for all events, and what account can I
> make to France, who has heaped us with so many good deeds
> and has granted me its trust, if you refuse to hear the voice of
> reason.[6]

Toussaint liked to illustrate such speeches by displaying a jar of black corn with a thin layer of white grains on top. With a couple of shakes the white particles would vanish completely into the black mass. Meanwhile, Toussaint's "voice of reason" was saying two things at once:

at the same time that it preached obedience to France it also reassured the audience that the black majority would eventually prevail, no matter what, because "we are the strongest."

To a considerable extent, Sonthonax and Toussaint Louverture shared a similar agenda at the point that the Third Commission arrived in Saint Domingue. Sonthonax's abolitionism was completely sincere, and he was enthusiastic about his assignment to level the society of the ancien régime, uprooting the old divisions of race and of class, even to the point of empowering the black majority (since Sonthonax felt he had been burned, during his first tour in the colony, by the mulatto race and the class of *anciens libres*). Toussaint could meet Sonthonax on the ground of this egalitarian social project, and of their common commitment to general liberty for all. And Sonthonax could meet Toussaint on the ground of ultimate loyalty to the French republic. There is no evidence that Toussaint was nurturing any scheme for independence during this period. All his public proclamations insisted that the *nouveaux libres* owed a debt and obligation to France as the sponsor of general emancipation and supporter of the Rights of Man, and his actions reinforced his words. On the practical plane, Toussaint and Sonthonax had roughly the same program: to reestablish the plantation system with freedmen's labor.

Sonthonax was wise enough to court Toussaint's personal goodwill—the strong friendship that already existed between Toussaint and Laveaux was helpful in this regard. In July 1796, Sonthonax wrote to Toussaint: "As a private individual, you have all my friendship; as a general, all my confidence."[7] During the same summer Sonthonax helped arrange for Toussaint's oldest sons, Placide and Isaac, to travel to France for their education—a project apparently favored, if not initiated, by Toussaint, who wrote to Laveaux on June 16: "Receive, I beg you, my sincere thanks for the goodness you have wished to have for my children; count in advance upon my gratitude; I assure you it is without limit. The Commissioner Sonthonax has written me the most obliging letter in that regard; he will give them passage to France on board the *Wattigny.* How many obligations I have to him and to you!"[8]

Placide and Isaac Louverture sailed for France on the same ship that had brought the Third Commission to Cap Français, and afterward Sonthonax bestirred himself to ensure that their passage into the French educational system was smooth (the costs were assumed by the French government). Under the ancien régime it had been traditional for the more prosperous (and mostly mulatto) freedmen to send their children for education in France, and this move would help Toussaint's sons to advance as French citizens under the new world order. But Toussaint was too canny not to have realized that his sons would also be hostages; perhaps the formality of his thanks was slightly strained.

Sonthonax and Toussaint were also in basic agreement about the two most serious threats to the French republic as it existed in Saint Domingue: the English, who in their collaboration with the royalist *grands blancs* frankly intended to restore slavery along with all other aspects of the ancien régime; and the potential for a colony-wide mulatto revolt, of which Villatte's rebellion might have been only a harbinger. The mulatto class (traditionally a property- and slave-owning class) was less than wholly enthusiastic about Sonthonax's project for eradicating all class and racial distinctions and for the empowerment of the largely black *nouveau libre* majority.

In the north, open resistance to this program had been scotched by Sonthonax's deportation of Villatte and his cohorts. The most powerful colored general in the south, Rigaud, was fighting on the republican side and threatening the British positions in the Western and Southern departments. Rigaud had emerged as the most important military leader for the *gens de couleur;* in diplomacy and propaganda he was abetted by Pinchinat, who had been implicated in the Villatte rebellion. With another colored brigadier general, Beauvais, Rigaud had established a considerable arrondissement from Jacmel to Les Cayes on the south coast, which he occupied in a state of quasi independence, since communication with the French authorities in the north was difficult. The military regime which he headed was accused of maintaining slavery in all but name (an accusation which would also be leveled against Toussaint Louverture from time to time).

From the moment of their recall to France, Sonthonax and Polverel had lobbied for a substantial force of European troops to be sent to the colony, but without success. In 1796, Sonthonax arrived in Saint

Domingue armed mainly with his powers of diplomacy; he had to obtain military support from the commanders already in place—chiefly Toussaint Louverture and André Rigaud. Sonthonax did, however, receive a shipment of twenty thousand muskets, which he distributed with great gusto among the *nouveaux libres,* saying to each recipient: "Here is the liberty which Sonthonax gives you; whoever would take this gun from you means to make you a slave again."[9] The prodigious rhetorical effect of this gesture made Sonthonax again a rival for the immense popularity of Toussaint Louverture. And when he urged the field hands to work, Sonthonax told them in the same breath, "Don't forget that nobody has the right to force you to dispose of your time against your will."[10] Meanwhile, most of the guns Sonthonax passed out wound up in the hands of Toussaint's men, while some, unwisely given to uncommitted supporters of the recently departed Jean-François, were immediately used against the French republican forces.

Sonthonax needed the cooperation of both Rigaud and Toussaint, and he needed them to cooperate with each other. The latter goal was difficult to achieve, though both generals were persistent in attacking their common enemy, the English. Sonthonax sent a delegation to the south, seeking to confirm French governmental authority there. At first, the field hands turned to the delegates (Kerverseau, Rey, and Leborgne), protesting the slavery-like labor conditions they suffered and showing the irons and isolation boxes with which they were punished. However, Rey and Leborgne seemed to have been poorly chosen for a sensitive mission; these two were notorious for their debauchery even before they arrived in Les Cayes—where Leborgne went so far as to seduce Rigaud's fiancée, then boast of the conquest all over town. Justly infuriated by this sort of outrage, Rigaud and his partisans managed to rouse a popular rebellion on the rumor that it was really the commissioners who intended to restore slavery. After considerable violence, the delegates fled to Spanish Santo Domingo, followed by some fifteen hundred French families from the region. Rigaud and his group managed to turn a nice profit by selling them passports. Mulatto domination of the military, the civil service, and the plantation economy continued unchecked in the south. A proclamation from the commissioners defending the conduct of their delegates and rebuking the mulatto leaders was paraded through the streets of Les Cayes—pinned to the tail of a jackass.

The breakdown of relations with Rigaud made Sonthonax and the Third Commission ever more dependent on the military power of Toussaint. Both Sonthonax and Laveaux urged the black general to make a move against the English at the oft-disputed town of Mirebalais, which was in fact a key point in Toussaint's whole strategy along the south bank of the Artibonite River. Mirebalais was the principal town of a fertile valley which produced many commercial crops and which also offered access to horses and cattle on the formerly Spanish ranches of the Central Plateau. Toussaint needed to secure a route from Mirebalais to a west coast port, and after his failure to capture Saint Marc he had shifted his sights to Arcahaie, a smaller coastal town to the south. Arcahaie was the stronghold of Lapointe, a cultivated mulatto commander with an army of three thousand men whose first loyalty was to their leader, but which he had put at the disposal of the English invaders. Lapointe was not easily driven out of his base, though several intermediate points along the Artibonite (Petite Rivière to the north and Verrettes to the south) were already in Toussaint's hands.

The British had a new officer at Saint Marc, General Simcoe, the most redoubtable fighter they'd had on the scene since Brisbane. Toussaint adapted his strategy to suit this new opponent. In April 1797, he recaptured Mirebalais, which had been occupied for the English by the vicomte de Bruges. Recovering this position allowed him access to the plain of Cul de Sac, across which he could threaten the outskirts of Port-au-Prince, which was still in English hands. He advanced as far as Croix des Bouquets, where British resistance finally forced him to retreat. General Simcoe was then inspired to challenge Toussaint along the length of the Artibonite and to reclaim Mirebalais for the English. Dessources, the *grand blanc* ally of the English who'd been humiliatingly whipped by Toussaint not long before, came out from Saint Marc with two thousand men to occupy Verrettes—in a simultaneous maneuver the British general Churchill recaptured Mirebalais. Toussaint moved out from Gonaïves with a force of ten thousand and again annihilated Dessources and his legion as they attempted a retreat from Verrettes to Saint Marc. One of Dessources's artillery officers shot himself to avoid capture; Dessources himself staggered into Saint Marc "almost naked and covered with mud."[11]

Colonel Cambefort, the royalist commander of French forces at Le Cap before 1791 and an associate of Toussaint's through his brother-in-law Bayon de Libertat, had collaborated with the British from the beginning of the occupation of the west. With no great success, the British had tried to use him to win influence in the region of Le Cap during the months when Villatte's rebellion was coming to a boil. Once Toussaint routed Villatte's party, Cambefort was put in command of Saint Marc, until Simcoe replaced him there in May 1797. Fresh from his victories in the interior, Toussaint launched a new assault on Saint Marc; soon after Cambefort departed for Port-au-Prince.

This attack left Mirebalais undefended, but Toussaint knew that if Saint Marc fell, Mirebalais would be easily retaken. In his first rush he captured several camps north of the town, then organized an attack on Fort Charvill, on the peak called Point à Diamant. A battery firing on Saint Marc proper prevented any sortie from the town, while Toussaint's men charged the walls of Fort Charvill with ladders. The attack failed when the ladders turned out to be too short. The following day, the English got reinforcements from Port-au-Prince and recaptured the posts Toussaint had taken. Toussaint was obliged to retreat in some haste, abandoning a couple of cannon and a wallet containing a note from Sonthonax urging him to use those guns against Saint Marc.

Though Saint Marc remained in English hands, Toussaint's threat there had obliged Simcoe to recall his forces from Mirebalais, which Toussaint easily reoccupied. His access to the grasslands and livestock of the Central Plateau was now assured. The English would not seriously challenge him again in the interior, and they had permanently lost the line along the south bank of the Artibonite River.

For Toussaint's successes in this campaign, Sonthonax promoted him to commander in chief of all the French army in Saint Domingue. And on May 23, 1797, Toussaint reported this achievement to Laveaux, and expressed his hope for still more complete victory: "Inspired by love of the public good and the happiness of my fellow citizens, my dearest wishes will be at their zenith, and my gratitude perfected, if I am happy enough to be able, after having expelled all enemies from the colony, to say to France: The standard of liberty flies over all the surface of Saint Domingue."[12] This letter reached Laveaux in France, where he had sailed in October 1796 to take up an elected office as representative of Saint Domingue in the French National Convention.

The repair and the reform of the plantation economy was hindered by the damaged state and the dubious status of the plantations themselves. Most had been abandoned by their *grand blanc* owners and managers during the first phase of extreme destructive violence beginning in 1791, but under varying circumstances. Some had fled their lands and the colony, purely and simply as refugees. Others had been deported as counterrevolutionaries during Sonthonax's first tour in Saint Domingue. A great many had sailed from Cap Français with the fleet that carried away the defeated Governor Galbaud. The deportees and those who sailed with Galbaud were apt to be classified as émigrés, counterrevolutionary enemies of the French republic; as such, their lands could be confiscated by the state. Yet no official list of émigrés existed for Saint Domingue, so these plantations were sequestered, rather than confiscated outright, and could not legally be sold to any-one who might redevelop them. Leasing these plantations to temporary managers struck both Sonthonax and Toussaint Louverture as a stop-gap solution; many were taken over by members of Toussaint's officer corps, who used various degrees of military force to put *nouveaux libres* back to work in the cane fields, and some by Toussaint himself.

Sonthonax was adamant in refusing to allow anyone to return to Saint Domingue who might be considered an émigré. Friction between Toussaint and the commissioner developed around this point, for Toussaint courted the return of many *grand blanc* landowners. In gen-eral, this group possessed a lot of managerial and technical knowledge which Toussaint felt was essential to the restoration of Saint Do-mingue's prosperity (and its value to the French nation), particularly in the skill-intensive area of refinement of white sugar. In particular, the group included men like Bayon de Libertat, who had fled Cap Français with Galbaud's fleet in 1793. During Bayon's years of exile in the United

States, Toussaint faithfully sent him the proceeds from his plantations in Saint Domingue, and in 1797 he authorized Bayon's return to the colony.

Thanks to his unusually close connection to Bayon de Libertat's circle, and to his own status as an *ancien libre* and sizable landowner before the revolution, Toussaint had a certain standing (by class though not by race) in the group of returning proprietors. This connection, and Toussaint's policy of advancing the claims of white landowners to recover their property and redevelop plantations with free labor, suggested, not only to Sonthonax and the white Jacobins but also to many among the *nouveau libre* black majority, that Toussaint's loyalty was dangerously divided. The numerous small rebellions against his authority in the past few years had mostly been provoked by his effort to restore a system of plantation labor; putting white former slave masters back in authority was, in the eyes of many, more suspicious still.

Toussaint, like Sonthonax, was apparently working to build a new society, which would replace the hierarchies inherent in a slave-based system with a new triracial egalitarianism founded on regard for the Rights of Man. Freedom for the former slaves of Saint Domingue was absolutely fundamental to his plan, and Toussaint never wavered in insisting on that point—on which his support from the *nouveaux libres* depended. But among the colony's other races and classes, implementation of this program proved tricky.

Following Villatte's deportation and Sonthonax's disastrous mission to Rigaud, the mulatto-dominated Southern Department had to all intents and purposes seceded from the colony—at least it no longer recognized the commission's authority—while the *gens de couleur* elsewhere were quietly alienated from both Sonthonax and Toussaint. The military situation, though improved since Sonthonax's previous sojourn, was still difficult. The Treaty of Basel had formally ceded Spanish Santo Domingo to France, but there was no military force sufficient to occupy this large tract (which was twice the size of the French colony), and until Toussaint permanently conquered Mirebalais it was actually the English who enjoyed the supply line into the Spanish Central Plateau. Though the English could not expand their territory, the French were having no better success in dislodging them from the key towns they occupied on the coast.

Ill at ease with the military predicament, Sonthonax began trying to persuade Toussaint to decommission many of his troops and send them back to work on the plantations, while at the same time requesting more European troops from France. Naturally, Toussaint's suspicions were aroused. Moreover, the effectiveness of Sonthonax's rhetorical gestures, along with the sincerity of his commitment to permanent general liberty, made him a serious rival for Toussaint's popularity among the *nouveau libre* black majority. Field hands had begun to address Sonthonax as "Father," and among them his name had the force of a magical talisman.

In this rather uneasy situation (in September 1796), elections were held to choose colonial representatives to the French National Assembly. In a curiously double-edged letter, Toussaint urged Laveaux to stand as a candidate:

> My general, my father, my good friend,
>
> As I foresee, with chagrin, that in this unfortunate country, for which and for whose inhabitants you have sacrificed your life, your wife, your children, something disagreeable will happen to you, and as I would not wish to bear the pain of being witness to that, I would desire that you should be named deputy, so that you will be able to have the satisfaction of seeing your true country again and all that you hold most dear, your wife, your children—and so you can be sheltered and not be the pawn of the factions which are gestating in Saint Domingue—and I will be assured, along with all my brothers, of having the most zealous defender of the cause we are all fighting for. Yes, general, my father, my benefactor, France possesses many men but where is the one who would be forever the true friend of the blacks, like you? There will never be one.[13]

This tortuously mixed message undoubtedly springs from an equally complex mixture of motives. Who is really threatening Laveaux in those ominous opening phrases, the "factions which are gestating in Saint Domingue" or Toussaint Louverture himself? Either way, the warning to leave or face dire consequences would have been difficult to miss.

It's also difficult to understand just why Toussaint wanted Laveaux off the Saint Dominguan scene, for Laveaux was his strongest, most loyal ally in the French administration, one whom he could sincerely call a benefactor. But Laveaux had been a long time in the colony, and did indeed miss his family in France. And Toussaint, whose information from overseas tended to be quite current, was aware of a counter-revolutionary movement brewing in France, and thus he saw a need for a faithful friend in Paris—a "zealous defender" not only of general liberty but also, especially, of Toussaint Louverture. Laveaux departed to take up his office in France in October 1796, but Toussaint continued to write to him regularly for the next two years, filing the same minutely detailed reports on military and political events that he had done when Laveaux was his immediate superior in the colony.

Sonthonax was also elected deputy to the French National Assembly in the September 1796 election—whether under pressure from Toussaint or not is less clear. As his conflicts with Sonthonax worsened, Toussaint had a stronger motive to get the commissioner out of the colony, but while some accounts claim that Toussaint threatened to destroy Cap Français (again!) if Laveaux and Sonthonax were not elected, others say that Sonthonax campaigned for his own election, to the point of ordering Toussaint out of town and sending a friend "through the streets armed with a sword, distributing the list of those who were supposed to be named to the legislature."[14] General Pierre Michel arrived in force on election day, promising to "turn all to fire and blood if Sonthonax and his candidates were not named"[15]—but Pierre Michel usually acted on the orders of Toussaint.

Though elected at the same time as Laveaux, Sonthonax seemed far less eager to leave Saint Domingue. Given his earlier experience of recall, it seems likely that he wanted to use the election to secure a line of retreat for himself in France in case he should be forced out of the colony a second time. On the other hand, some observers suspected that Sonthonax did not ever intend to leave the colony. Instead, he and his partisans who had also won election to the National Assembly in September 1796 would form the core of a new colonial assembly which would make Saint Domingue independent of France. In November 1796, Sonthonax began to write letters to the home government requesting his recall, yet he stayed on for nearly a year longer, and sometimes seemed determined to stay indefinitely.

Between the election of September 1796 and August 1797, the "factions gestating" began to split the colony between Sonthonax and Toussaint Louverture. At the same time, fissures opened among the five members of the Third Commission. Giraud, almost from the moment of his arrival, had been fearful of "the savage ferocity of the Blacks" and "the refined perfidy of the colored people and the *ancien libre* Negroes."[16] Giraud believed that Raimond was plotting to slaughter all the whites in the colony, and Sonthonax and Leblanc exploited his fear to isolate Raimond and make him powerless on the commission. (Roume, the fifth commissioner, had been sent to represent the French in Spanish Santo Domingo.) With Pascal, who was now his son-in-law as well as the commission's secretary general, Raimond turned to profiteering from the leasing of plantations confiscated from their émigré owners—an activity which reinforced their relationship with the sector of Toussaint's black officer corps which was enriching itself under this system. Then Giraud disintegrated into nervous illness and returned to France, and Sonthonax and Leblanc had to bring Raimond back into the commission's decision making.

For his own part, Leblanc began to compete with Sonthonax, courting popularity with the prominent blacks in the region of Le Cap. Toussaint was shocked to be included in these overtures, or he pretended to be, and wrote to the commission as though Leblanc had offered him a bargain with the devil. Thus far, Toussaint had remained on good terms with Sonthonax, with whom he had frequent private conferences during this period. Then Raimond quietly approached Toussaint to warn him that Sonthonax was scheming for independence with the other recently elected delegates to the National Assembly.

Wary, Toussaint told Raimond that the accusation might stem "from the bitterness you cherish against your colleague, for I know that you don't have a good understanding between you."[17] Nevertheless, he agreed to sound Sonthonax out on the matter without revealing that Raimond was his source. Sonthonax denied any such ambition and promised to send the delegates to France without further delay—though in fact he sent only a few of them.

Since Sonthonax's return, a quarrel had been simmering between him and Toussaint over the matter of émigrés in general. The particular case of Bayon de Libertat brought it to a head. On July 4, 1797, Sonthonax sent Toussaint a remarkably hotheaded letter protesting Bayon's return to Saint Domingue, with a copy of "the law which condemns to death the émigrés who return to the territory of the Republic after having been banished, and condemns those who have aided or favored their return to four years in irons. It is in the proclamations of the Commission as well as in the deposition of Bayon that you will read your duty with regard to this man, the brother-in-law of Tousard and the intimate friend of Baron de Cambefort, commander of Saint Marc. I am too much your friend to recommend you a weakness . . . The Commission, always compassionate, does not ask or require the blood of the guilty man, but only that he purge Saint Domingue of his unworthy presence."[18]

This ultimatum was rash in all sorts of ways—aside from the insult and threat of injury to Toussaint's friend and former master, it was ill considered for Sonthonax to threaten Toussaint himself with four years in irons. On July 18, Toussaint took the matter over the commissioner's head, writing to the Directory in Bayon's defense. Barely five weeks later, Sonthonax himself was compelled to leave Saint Domingue.

In August 1797, Toussaint called on Sonthonax in the commissioner's house at Cap Français. Toussaint was accompanied by Raimond and Pascal, but Sonthonax preferred to see Toussaint alone. Their conversation was interrupted, but on August 20 Sonthonax visited Toussaint to continue it—again with no witnesses. The next day, Toussaint summarized both halves of the interview to Raimond and Pascal, who set it down as a dialogue ten pages long. This *pièce de théâtre* may very well be a work of fiction but it served as Toussaint's justification for pressing Sonthonax to leave the colony:

TOUSSAINT: Recall, when you proposed independence to me, you personally told me that to assure liberty it would be necessary to cut the throats of all the great planters, and you made the same propositions to other blacks, who reported them to me.

SONTHONAX: That was a long time ago, but that project was never carried out.

TOUSSAINT: I'll answer you as creoles do—If you have a hog that eats chickens, you may put out its one eye, you may put out its other eye, but it still will eat chickens whenever it can.

SONTHONAX: What's that supposed to mean?

TOUSSAINT: It means that the wicked are incorrigible. The other time, when you came here, you told the *hommes de couleur* to slit the throats of all the whites, and the *nouveau libre* blacks to slit the throats of all the *anciens libres*. That's what caused the civil war and caused so much French territory to be turned over to the English and the Spanish. And then you left, and you left us nothing but trouble.

SONTHONAX: How can you have such a bad opinion of me?

TOUSSAINT: It's a true fact and all the world knows it.[19]

How much truth was there in any of this? At least enough to blacken Sonthonax's reputation. Sonthonax's exhortation to Dieudonné to fear and mistrust the mulattoes had been a public statement—in Toussaint's construction of the dialogue, the rest seemed to follow quite logically. The idea of an independent Saint Domingue had arisen before 1791, and Sonthonax certainly suspected a pro-independence motive in Toussaint's resistance to his own authority. This dialogue neatly turned that accusation on the accuser. Still, it is not impossible that Sonthonax did have his own dream of leading Saint Domingue to independence.

His role (as reproduced from Toussaint's formidable memory) is not a noble one. Before the play is over, Toussaint has reduced Sonthonax to pleading:

TOUSSAINT: Commissioner, this conversation will never be finished, but to conclude it, I tell you that you must prepare yourself to leave for France.

SONTHONAX: No, General, let us forget the past.

TOUSSAINT: Comissioner, you are too well known; the salvation of the colony requires that you leave for France; it is absolutely necessary that you go; her security depends on it.

SONTHONAX: Let's forget all that, let it all be over; I promise that I will give you all I own—everything that you want.

TOUSSAINT: I want nothing, I need neither gold nor silver nor anything at all. You must go; the salvation of the colony requires it.[20]

And so the stage was set. On August 20, the commissioner received a letter similar to the one earlier sent to Laveaux, though this one was signed by Generals Moyse, Henry Christophe, and Clervaux and several junior officers, as well as Toussaint: "Named deputy of the colony to the Legislative Corps, commanding circumstances made it your duty to remain for some time still in our midst; then your influence was necessary, troubles had disturbed us, it was necessary to settle them. Today, when order, peace and zeal for work, the reestablishment of agriculture, our success against our external enemies and their impotence permits you to present yourself to your function—go tell France what you have seen, the prodigies to which you have been witness. Be always the defender of the cause which we have embraced, of which we will be the eternal soldiers."[21]

Sonthonax sent at once a letter of acquiescence, then stalled for time, and investigated to see if he might find any military support for his staying on among the garrisons of Cap Français. Toussaint, meanwhile, gathered his own forces at Petite Anse, a few miles outside the town. At four in the morning on the fourth day of Sonthonax's delay, he fired a cannon, then sent the French general Agé with a message to Julien Raimond: "If your colleague has not left before sunrise, I will enter Le Cap with my dragoons and embark him by force."[22] On August 24, Sonthonax boarded the ship *L'Indien* and began his voyage to France.

"He was still in the intoxication of triumph," wrote General Kerverseau of Toussaint, "when I arrived at Le Cap. I saw the hero of the day, he was radiant; joy sparkling in his glances, his beaming features announced confidence. His conversation was animated; no more suspicions, no more reserve . . . He spoke of nothing but his love for France and his respect for the government; he presented himself as the avenger and the support of the rights of the metropole, and all the friends of order and peace made their best effort to persuade themselves of his sincerity."[23]

The sincerity of Toussaint's loyalty became a matter of debate in France as soon as Sonthonax arrived there—as Toussaint had certainly anticipated it would. On September 4, 1796, he sent a version of his dialogue with Sonthonax (so incriminating to the latter) as a report to the minister of marine in France, who supervised overseas colonies; the gist of this communication was to accuse the commissioner of scheming to make Saint Domingue independent for his own personal profit and to bring about that independence through a series of racial massacres in the style of the worst excesses of the French Terror. The accusation had at least some credibility, for Sonthonax had publicly inveighed against the white slave-owning colonists, denouncing them as "a horde of ferocious tyrants" and "bloody men," rejoicing that such "slave traders and cannibals are no more."[24] Toussaint reiterated his complaints against Sonthonax in a long letter to Laveaux (whose presence in the French legislature he hoped might counterbalance that of the evicted commissioner) and was seconded by letters sent by Julien Raimond to the minister of marine.

Sonthonax retaliated by accusing Toussaint of pro-independence and counterrevolutionary intentions, starting with the first secret beginnings of the black leader's political and military career in 1791 or before. Toussaint's close association with Catholic priests (the Abbé Delahaye and a couple of others had become part of his entourage since his rise to power) could be made to appear culpable in this context, as could his connections to the *grand blanc* circle of Haut du Cap, which included not only Bayon de Libertat but also the well-known royalist conspirators Colonel Cambefort and Colonel Tousard. In conclusion, Sonthonax denounced Toussaint as a royalist reactionary to the core: "At the instigation of those same émigrés that surround him today, he organized in 1791 the revolt of the Blacks and the massacre of the landowning Whites. In 1793 he commanded the army of brigands at the orders of the catholic king."[25] Thus Sonthonax lent his support to the old rumor of a royalist counterrevolutionary conspiracy behind the original slave revolt in the north. However, it is almost impossible to verify any real fact in this exchange of slanders between Sonthonax and Toussaint.

In France, the spring 1797 elections had brought a royalist majority to power. In the new National Assembly the dispossessed land and slave owners of Saint Domingue found a vigorous advocate in Vincent Marie Vienot de Vaublanc. His speeches were bitterly critical of Sonthonax, "who has sacrificed everything to the Africans, in the hope of dominating them through each other," but instead finds himself "reduced to trembling before them and to seeing his orders despised by men who owe only to him the authority with which they abuse him."[26] In Vaublanc's view, Sonthonax had become the prime example of the humiliation of whites brought about by his own misguided policies, notably the abolition of slavery. Vaublanc's rhetoric called more or less openly for the restoration of the ancien régime in Saint Domingue.

Toussaint Louverture was well aware of these developments and of the menace they represented to liberty for all. One theory suggests that he forced Sonthonax out of the colony as a sacrifice to Vaublanc's faction, which had indeed called for Sonthonax's removal. But Vaublanc's rhetoric was also aimed directly at Toussaint and his officers. "And what a military government! To whose hands is it confided? To vulgar and ignorant negroes, incapable of distinguishing the most unrestrained license from the austere liberty which yields to the law."[27] In September 1797, Laveaux made a speech defending Toussaint against such vitriol, describing him as "a man gifted with every military talent" and "a Republican full of sentiments of humanity"[28] and protesting that his loyalty to France was absolute.

In November, Toussaint himself wrote to the French Directory, reminding the government that he trusted in France enough to send his children there. At the same time he made it painfully clear that preserving liberty for the former slaves of Saint Domingue would be more important to him even than the welfare of his children should circumstance force him to make that choice. The conclusion of this letter, much as it tries to insist on his belief in French support for general liberty, is riddled with doubt and crowned with defiance: "could men who have once enjoyed the benefits of liberty look on calmly while it is ravished from them! They bore their chains when they knew no condition of life better than that of slavery. But today when they have left it, if they had a thousand lives, they would sacrifice them all rather than to be subjected again to slavery. But no, the hand that has broken our chains will not subject us to them again. France will not renounce her principles . . . But if, to restore slavery in Saint Domingue, you were to do so, then I declare to you, that would be to attempt the impossible; we knew how to face danger to win our liberty, and we will know how to face death to keep it."[29]

France decided to try a diplomatic course. On March 27, General Joseph d'Hédouville arrived in Saint Domingue as the agent of the French government. On March 27, 1798, he landed in Ciudad Santo Domingo, on the Spanish side of the island which had been ceded to France by the Treaty of Basel but into which Toussaint's power did not yet reach. En route overland to French Saint Domingue, Hédouville consulted with Commissioner Roume and with General Kerverseau. The latter was Toussaint's sharpest critic in the French military, but Hédouville had also been briefed by Colonel Charles Humbert Marie Vincent, who was Toussaint's greatest military friend and supporter after Laveaux.

When Toussaint wrote to Laveaux following Sonthonax's forced departure, he blamed much of the trouble on the difficulty of governing by committee, for the Third Commission really had squandered much of its energy on internal strife. Far better, Toussaint reasoned, that France should be represented in Saint Domingue by one sole leader. "I want him to be European, this chief, because I want us not to lose sight of the country from which emanates the power that rules a colony two thousand leagues away from its metropole."[30] Of course, Laveaux himself had met this description better than anyone. The new agent was a different sort of officer.

Hédouville's recent service in the region of Poitou, which had been a hotbed of counterrevolutionary and royalist uprisings since 1793, had earned him the sobriquet "Pacificator of the Vendée." Sonthonax, upon his second return to France, had drawn a comparison to Saint Domingue by denouncing Toussaint as "one of the chiefs of the Vendée of Saint Domingue."[31] Villaret-Joyeuse, a partisan of Vaublanc who would later command the fleet that brought Napoleon's invading army to the colony, made that comparison more precise: "Why don't you try in Saint Domingue what you have done with so much success in the Vendée? Saint Domingue is also a Vendée to be reconquered; it is devastated by the double scourge of civil war and foreign war; it's only by force of arms and by energy mixed with gentleness that you will succeed in bringing it into submission."[32]

Hédouville, whose successes in the Vendée had relied on diplomacy as much as battle, arrived in Saint Domingue better supplied with gentleness than with force: the home government had allowed him scarcely any fresh European troops. Kerverseau, having sized up his situation, advised him to display confidence, though he had very little material strength: "I must tell you then, that despite your character as Agent of the Directory, Toussaint will be more powerful than you. An order signed by him will have more force than all your proclamations, than those of the Directory, than all the decrees of this Legislative Corps. But all his power will be yours, once he is certain of your principles."[33]

Hédouville installed himself in Cap Français on April 20, 1798. Toussaint, wary of the newcomer, was not there to meet him; in a series of letters, he excused himself by citing his campaigns against the English invaders on the west coast and the distance over difficult terrain. In view of his notoriously rapid movement all over the colony, the latter explanation was not very convincing. In fact, Toussaint was busy conducting his own negotiations for a British withdrawal with General Thomas Maitland, who had arrived to take over the British operations in Saint Domingue just three weeks before Hédouville's landing.

The adventure in Saint Domingue had not turned out as the British hoped. They had not been able to make the area of the colony they occupied anywhere near as profitable as it had formerly been for France. They earned something better than £500,000 from exports during the occupation, which, on the other hand, cost them more than £7 million in money, as well as about 20,000 casualties. At Maitland's arrival, the British had only 2,500 European soldiers under arms, plus a few thousand black and colored troops of doubtful reliability, while Toussaint was reputed to have 20,000 men to bring against them.

Having driven the British from Mirebalais and the interior, Toussaint was now able to put pressure on the cordon of forts which protected Arcahaie. In March 1798, he broke through it. Though the formidable Lapointe was still holding out for the British in Arcahaie itself, Toussaint's advance allowed him to seriously threaten the British positions to the north, at Saint Marc, and to the south at Port-au-Prince. The British situation in the Western Department looked less and less tenable.

Maitland had studied the rivalry between Rigaud and Toussaint and concluded that the two generals were unlikely ever to cooperate. He believed that Laplume, who since the overthrow of Dieudonné had commanded a large force for the French republic just to the south of British-held Port-au-Prince, was a quasi-independent third factor; for Laplume's loyalty to Toussaint was never certain. The British general knew that possession of Port-au-Prince would greatly empower whichever leader it was yielded to. If Toussaint got the prize, the British would still have both Laplume and Rigaud in a buffer zone between Port-au-Prince and the British post at the port of Jérémie toward the western tip of the Grande Anse. Furthermore, by dealing with Toussaint, Maitland might drive a wedge between him and Hédouville, whose arrival made an easy exit for the British less likely.

On April 23, Maitland offered to withdraw all British forces from the west of Saint Domingue, on condition that the French colonists who had collaborated with the British be granted amnesty. Over the next few days, Toussaint negotiated that the forts and their cannon would be turned over to him intact—a major and rather surprising concession. The accord was signed on April 30, and not until the following day did Toussaint write to Hédouville at Le Cap to notify him of the fait accompli. Teeth presumably clenched, Hédouville approved his action, noting marginally that French law and the French Constitution permitted no one to come to terms with proscribed émigrés. But Hédouville could not influence events in the Western Department from where he sat, and troops commanded by Christophe Mornet and Toussaint's brother Paul were already advancing toward Port-au-Prince across the Cul de Sac plain.

A great many Frenchmen chose to depart on British ships; those who remained were understandably apprehensive. Laplume was also present in force outside Port-au-Prince, and when he struck a peace agreement with the mulattoes of Croix des Bouquets, Bernard Borgella, the *grand blanc* mayor, sent a delegation to thank him. Then Christophe Mornet arrived in Port-au-Prince to assure Borgella that the transition would be orderly. A Frenchman in the town described Mornet's men:

> His tattered troops, covered in a few rags molded to their trunks, true sans-culottes, starving and in want of everything, naturally should have breathed nothing but pillage; so far from anything like that, not only did they not commit the lightest insult, but we even saw them, upon entering a city evacuated by the enemy, go without rations for two days without a murmur. Where are the European soldiers who, in such a case, could maintain so exact a discipline?[34]

When Toussaint entered Port-au-Prince soon afterward, the amnestied French colonists came out to receive him with tremendous fanfare—doubtless born of their relief at the extraordinary self-control of the black troops already occupying the town. Toussaint appeared with extreme modesty, wearing a plain field uniform without epaulettes, his customary head-cloth tied beneath his tricorner hat. He declined the most extravagant gestures of the welcoming whites, declaring, "Only God should walk beneath a dais; only to the sole master of the universe should one offer incense."[35] He had, however, promised to respect their property, and he backed up the promise by sending the stray cultivators of the region back to work on the plantations. On May 26, he announced to all citizens of Port-au-Prince: "The times of fanaticism are no more; the rule of law has succeeded that of anarchy."[36] When the British fleet sailed on May 28, Toussaint arranged a Te Deum in the Port-au-Prince cathedral to celebrate.

The evacuation of the west left the British with only two posts in the colony. Though the naval bases at Jérémie (threatened by Rigaud at nearby Tiburon) and at Môle Saint-Nicolas (which Maitland judged could not withstand a siege backed by the artillery which Toussaint could bring to bear from land) were valuable to the defense of Jamaica, Maitland judged that they were not worth their cost. On July 27, he reported to Governor Balcarres of Jamaica that he was on the verge of deciding to evacuate Saint Domingue altogether.

Throughout the summer of 1798, Maitland received emissaries from both Hédouville and Toussaint, still with the goal of promoting dissension between them—as Hédouville warned Toussaint in a July 5 letter. Aside from the particular differences developing between the agent and the general in chief, the traditionally contentious division of power between Saint Domingue's civil and military authorities was there for Maitland to exploit. On July 30, he decided to close the deal with Toussaint, having concluded (as Kerverseau had done) that as commander in chief of the army the black general held the real reins of power.

The accord for the evacuation of Jérémie, signed by General Huin for Toussaint and Colonel Harcourt for Maitland on August 13, was immediately put into practice; the English were gone from the south by August 23. This agreement, as well as the one for the evacuation of Môle concluded on August 30, contained favorable terms for émigré colonists which were irritating to Hédouville—not to mention that

Maitland had promised earlier that he would surrender Môle to no one but Hédouville himself. But to complete the undermining of the agent's authority, Toussaint and Maitland signed a secret agreement at Point Bourgeoise on August 31: a nonaggression pact and trade deal which lifted the British blockade from Toussaint's Saint Domingue, and gave him a free hand within its borders so long as he honored a promise not to export the black revolution to the British Caribbean colonies. (Toussaint kept his end of the bargain a year later by betraying a conspiracy to raise a slave revolt in Jamaica.) The arrangement concluded, Maitland and Toussaint repaired to the last British base at Môle, where the white general treated the black one to a festive dinner, and afterward gave Toussaint the elaborate silver service used at the meal, with the compliments of the king of England.

Toussaint and Maitland shared amiable feelings toward members of the *grand blanc* group in exile, and Toussaint let Maitland know that he would welcome the return of such refugees not only from the United States but also from Jamaica—meaning that the French collaborators who had fled the Western Department with the English would be allowed to come back almost right away. Hédouville, for his part, was expelling *grands blancs* pardoned by Toussaint as émigrés, though not so fast as Toussaint was admitting them.

Toussaint's policy gave him a burst of popularity among the whites of the Western Department. The ladies of Port-au-Prince, who had caught on to his taste for elaborate religious ceremonies, took up a collection for a thanksgiving mass. Toussaint, far less reserved than when he had first taken possession of the town, mounted the pulpit to declaim: "I am going to imitate Jesus Christ, whom we adore in this temple—he forgave in the name of his Father; I will forgive in the name of the Republic."[37]

Rumors of the secret treaty with Maitland soon leaked, further damaging Toussaint's shaky relationship with Hédouville. He had called on the agent at Le Cap for the first time soon after he'd taken possession of Port-au-Prince and the west from the English, but had not stayed long, preferring to retire to the security of his own base at Gonaïves. In July, he visited Hédouville again, this time in the company of General André

Rigaud. The latter was technically still under order of arrest since his rebellion against Sonthonax and the Third Commission in 1796, and as wary of the new agent as Toussaint was, it seemed. A volatile character, Rigaud was irked that the British had yielded the towns of the Western Department to Toussaint rather than to him, but when the two generals met in Port-au-Prince, they manage to smooth over that difference. United by a common mistrust of Hédouville, they traveled from Port-au-Prince to Le Cap together.

But once he met Hédouville in person, Rigaud dropped his reserve, so that the agent found him a warmer and more congenial figure than the suspicious, aloof Toussaint. This development reactivated Toussaint's mistrust of Rigaud, and Hédouville, who felt that he would have better luck managing these two generals if they were at odds with each other, encouraged the breach between them by favoring Rigaud. Before he left the south, however, Rigaud had been worried that Hédouville might have him deported to France to face charges related to his 1796 rebellion against the Third Commission, so he had arranged for an insurrection to break out at Anse à Veau during his absence—one that only his return to the south could subdue. As there was no time to call it off, the insurrection began on schedule and Rigaud, now trapped by his own artifice, had to rush home to settle it, leaving Toussaint to sort out his problems with Hédouville alone.

So far as labor policy went, Toussaint's and Hédouville's ideas were not so very dissimilar. Both wanted to restore the plantation economy by sending *nouveaux libres* back to work in the cane and coffee fields. Both were inclined to bind the freedmen contractually to plantations for periods as long as three years, and often to the same plantations where they had previously been slaves. When Toussaint undertook such measures himself he thought of them as necessary for the restoration of prosperity, but when they were undertaken by Hédouville, Toussaint could easily be persuaded that the agent was a tool of Vaublanc and the faction in France that was maneuvering for the restoration of slavery in fact, if not in name. One of his letters to the agent makes much of the idea that he, Toussaint, had been set free by the principles of the postrevolutionary French Constitution—and no mention of the fact that he had been free for more than a dozen years before. Toussaint preferred to identify himself with the *nouveaux libres* as much as he could—but the stringent labor rules were hugely unpopular with that group, no matter who was pushing them.

Hédouville had brought no significant military force with him, but he did have a team of civil servants with which he intended to replace most of the men Toussaint had appointed to various civilian posts in the government. Like Idlinger, who was in charge of the government's accounting in Le Cap, many of Toussaint's appointees were white Frenchmen, and many were considered to be corrupt, but Hédouville's efforts to replace them with his own people quickly became another sore point. In an effort to interrupt Toussaint's negotiations with the British, Hédouville ordered that enemy envoys should be admitted only at Le Cap, but Toussaint paid no attention to that. When Hédouville rebuked him for his leniency toward the émigrés, Toussaint wrote tartly to the Directory, "Ah, since one reproaches the blacks for throwing out their former tyrants, isn't it part of their duty to prove that they know how to forgive—to welcome the same men that persecuted them?"[38]

One of the French naval captains told Toussaint "how flattered he would be, after having brought General Hédouville, to return with General Toussaint Louverture, whose services would find in France all the sweetness and honor which they so richly deserve." The shades of sarcasm and menace in this remark did not escape Toussaint, who responded darkly, "Your ship is not big enough for a man like me."[39] Officers of Hédouville's largely symbolic honor guard persisted in teasing him with the prospect of a perhaps involuntary journey to France, until Toussaint finally pointed to a nearby shrub and said that he would make the trip "when that is big enough to make a ship to carry me."[40] Toussaint wore a red head-cloth under his general's bicorne; this *mouchwa têt* had a Vodouisant significance—it represented a bond between Toussaint and the warrior spirit, Ogoun Ferraille. Hédouville's supercilious young staff officers boasted that four of them would be enough to arrest "the ragheaded old man." Ogoun did not take the insult lightly; not very long after, a couple of these witty young blades were slain in an ambush south of Port-au-Prince.

If Hédouville was playing Rigaud against Toussaint, Toussaint was not much troubled by his game. "Let Monsieur Rigaud go take his instructions from the Agent of the Directory," he said, in a moment of unusual frankness, to one of the French colonists he had amnestied in the region of Port-au-Prince. "I could very well have him arrested, but God forbid—I need Monsieur Rigaud . . . the caste of Mulattoes is superior to mine . . . ; if I were to remove Monsieur Rigaud, they would perhaps find a leader worth more than he . . . I know Monsieur Rigaud . . . ; he loses control of his horse when he gallops . . . ; when he strikes, he shows his arm . . . Me, I know how to gallop too, but I know how to stop on a dime, and when I strike, you feel me but you don't see me."[41]

Hédouville's efforts to contain and limit Toussaint's power, via Rigaud or any other counterweight, were rapidly coming to nothing. After the British withdrawal he wanted to reduce the size of the black army, but could do nothing toward this end. He mistrusted Toussaint's cadre of black officers, many of whom were illiterate and thus in Hédouville's view too easily led, or misled, by their white secretaries— who were apt to belong to the suspicious *grand blanc*/émigré class. And despite all Hédouville's remonstrations and proclamations to the contrary, Toussaint persisted in favoring this latter group, which was not only protected by his agreements with Maitland but also had an important role in his own project for rebuilding the economy of the colony. Most of the civilian bureaucracy was reporting to Toussaint's officer cadre, and the military had infiltrated most branches of administration. Hédouville's struggle to reassert civilian control created still more friction.

When Hédouville urged him to cut the number of his troops, Toussaint told him, "Ah well, if you are able, you can do it yourself." The reaction of Toussaint's adoptive nephew Moyse, who then commanded at Fort Liberté, was still more pointed: "That agent wants to diminish the troops, and I want to increase my regiment. If there are no soldiers, there won't be any more general."[42] Moyse was also more and more openly hostile to labor policies which would attach former slaves to their former plantations, regardless of their source.

In the fall of 1798, rumors began to spread that a massacre of the whites was in the offing. The French Revolutionary calendar's New Year came in late September, and the *nouveaux libres* circulated more widely and generally than usual during this period, holding dances and assemblies which fed the fear among the whites that an insurrection was being planned. Toussaint sought to scotch the rumor, telling his officers: "Show how absurd is the intention they have imputed to the blacks, and don't allow any assembly to take place."[43]

In this tense atmosphere, quarreling broke out between soldiers of the Fifth Regiment, commanded by Moyse at Fort Liberté, and planters in the area. Hédouville was alarmed enough by that situation to order Moyse replaced by Manigat, a black magistrate in the town backed by some of the few white troops at the agent's disposal. Moyse was away on a tour of inspection of the countryside when Manigat took over, and when he returned, Manigat declared him a rebel. After an exchange of gunfire between Manigat's supporters and his own, Moyse left town with many men of the Fifth Regiment and began raising the field workers of the Northern Plain in an insurrection against Hédouville. By some accounts, Toussaint met Moyse at Héricourt Plantation and helped coordinate the rising.

Hédouville sent for help from Toussaint at Gonaïves, but Toussaint would not receive the messengers, though one was his close friend Colonel Vincent and the other his sometime confessor, the Catholic priest Anthéaume. Instead, Toussaint had them briefly imprisoned in the Gonaïves fort. When Hédouville learned what had happened to them, he resigned himself to leave Saint Domingue. In an address to the citizens of Le Cap, Hédouville blamed the trouble on an émigré plot to make the colony independent of France. By then the population of the Artibonite Valley had joined the insurrection, and Dessalines was marching north from Saint Marc at the head of the Fourth Regiment, with an order in Toussaint's own handwriting and phonetic spelling (which meant that it must have been composed in great haste): "I spoke to you yesterday about Fort Liberté—well, it is now in the power of the white troops by the order of Hédouville . . . Hurry up and get twelve hundred men ready to march against Le Cap and arrest him before he embarks."[44]

By the time Toussaint and Dessalines reached Le Cap, riding the wave of the huge popular insurrection, Hédouville was already on ship-board, with his honor guard and a handful of local sympathizers, including the mulatto commissioner Julien Raimond and Belley, the retired black delegate to the French National Convention. He sent ashore a few of Moyse's officers whom he had with him in exchange for an assurance that the harbor forts would not fire on his vessel as it departed. Toussaint promptly wrote to the Directory, denying any ambition for independence and blaming the trouble on Hédouville. Though the church of Le Cap had not yet been fully reconstructed since the fire of 1793, Toussaint had a Te Deum sung on the site to celebrate the departure of all enemies from the colony; the French agent was apparently lumped into this category, along with the British troops and navy.

Hédouville sailed for France on October 22, 1798. He had lasted for less than one year in Saint Domingue. As a parting shot, he transferred all his authority as representative of the French government to General André Rigaud. It remained to be seen whether this gesture would be as ineffectual as Sonthonax's similar appointment of Dieudonné a few years previously.

Ignoring Hédouville's promotion of Rigaud, Toussaint invited Roume (who, since his experience began in the early 1790s, was probably the most seasoned French diplomat still in Saint Domingue) to return from the Spanish side of the island and replace Hédouville. Roume had been authorized by the home government to take over as agent if Hédouville died, and Toussaint now invoked this clause, despite a slight difference of circumstances. Leery of this proposition at first, Roume eventually accepted it, arriving at Port-au-Prince in January 1799. Perhaps he could serve as the sole European chief that Toussaint had been longing for. On his way into French Saint Domingue from the Spanish side of the island, Roume ran into several intimidating demonstrations by large mobs of blacks, whipped up by Toussaint to remind the Frenchman just how real power was balanced. A delegation met Roume at Croix des Bouquets just outside Port-au-Prince and warned him that his authority would be recognized only if he acted in concert with

Toussaint—perhaps a deliberate echo of the similar promise Laveaux had made to the citizens of Le Cap when he appointed Toussaint lieutenant governor in 1796.

Despite the color of French authority that Roume's presence could provide, recent developments, especially the imperfectly kept secret treaty with Maitland, gave rise to suspicion that Toussaint meant to make the colony independent, if he had not, for most practical purposes, already done so. There were leaks of the Toussaint-Maitland accord in the correspondence of English merchants and even American newspapers like the *Baltimore Telegraph*, where English agents were wont to plant propaganda stories from time to time. The *Telegraph* also reported that Toussaint expelled Hédouville because the agent was planning to invade the United States. In December 1798, a London newspaper put it in the plainest English: "With this treaty, the independence of this important island has, in fact, been recognized and guaranteed against any efforts the French might make to recover it."[45] Yet this sally might have been more a taunt of the French than a description of the actual situation in Saint Domingue.

Toussaint, meanwhile, continued to make substantial gestures of loyalty to France. With a series of local proclamations, letters to Laveaux, and reports to French official entities like the Ministry of Marine, he built a case for Hédouville's misconduct, analogous (in his representation) to that of Sonthonax. The foundation of these arguments was the old, prerevolutionary competition which the home government had intentionally fostered between the military governor of the colony and the civil intendant (Thomas Maitland had known how to play on this built-in fissure). Thus the civil chief, Sonthonax, with right and the law on his side, had in 1793 emerged bloody but more or less victorious over the military governor, Galbaud. Toussaint, as military governor with right on his side, had righteously deported the civil chief Sonthonax in 1797. The abrupt departure of Hédouville was explained in a similar manner. In his letter to the Directory, Toussaint accused the agent's entourage of counterrevolutionary dress and demeanor coupled with "the most liberticide propositions, the same that Vaublanc proclaimed."[46] A work policy announced by the agent, which required field hands to engage themselves to their plantations for three years, smacked altogether too much of slavery, Toussaint claimed (though his own labor policy was not much different).

In sum, Hédouville had come to introduce strife where Toussaint had carefully constructed peace. "According to his reputation as Pacificator of the Vendée," Toussaint wrote to Laveaux, "that is to say, as a benefactor of humanity, I should have thought that General Hédouville would have at least preserved the good harmony which he found among us; well, either General Hédouville was carrying a different spirit during his mission to pacify the Vendée,* or his character changed enormously as soon as he set foot in the colony. For he showed himself every day to be suspicious, brusque, and carried away against everyone."[47] Increasingly inclined to offer the honor of his victories to divine powers of one kind or another, Toussaint gave credit for the preservation of public order against the threat represented by Hédouville to the colony's "Tutelary Genie." "Whatever may be the injustices of the agents of the government," he assured Laveaux, "I shall be no less constant in my principles and no less obedient to the authorities of the Motherland, because I am a long way from dumping the blame for the misconduct of her agents on her. I only want to express my wish that the Directory, instructed by experience, shall henceforward send no more men to govern the most beautiful colony of the Antilles who, so far from advancing it toward prosperity, do nothing but slow it down—partisans who follow only their passions and for whom the destruction of the country is nothing, so long as they reach their goal."[48]

With Hédouville gone (and so long as no other vicious partisans like him should arrive), Toussaint's peace would be just as fastidiously restored—all with the object of retaining the colony, and restoring its vast economic potential, for France. The credibility of this presentation was undercut by a couple of circumstances: Toussaint had made independent agreements with England, otherwise an enemy of France. Also, at the end of the 1790s, he began extremely discreet explorations (abet-

---

*In Vodou, drastic changes in behavior and/or personality are explained by an individual's being possessed by different spirits at different times; metaphorically, the individual is seen as a horse that carries different spirit-riders.

ted by his new British allies) of the possibility of rescuing his older sons, Placide and Isaac, from the Collège de la Marche, where he had sent them as proof of his own loyalty and commitment to a future under the French republic. Soon after Hédouville's departure, Maitland reappeared in Jamaica and sent Colonel Harcourt to confer with Toussaint, a move that made some think that Maitland had influenced Toussaint to expel Hédouville. There were rumors that Saint Domingue would be turned over to the English and their émigré allies, but (though émigré refugees were returning in force from the United States) Toussaint did his best to quiet the whispering, and proclaimed his loyalty to the French republic as loudly at home as he did in his letters to Laveaux and the Directory.

On November 15, 1798, Toussaint issued a proclamation requiring all the able-bodied blacks in the colony who were not attached to the army to return to work for wages on the plantations (generally the same plantations where they had formerly been slaves). The *grand blanc* planters were elated, and Toussaint had to struggle to stop them from exulting too loudly and telling the *nouveaux libres,* "You say that you are free, but here is a letter from the General in Chief that forces you to come back to work for me!"[49]

Such remarks did nothing to sustain the idea that Toussaint still stood for general liberty first, last, and always. What troubled him now was the cost of freedom. As he saw it, the former slaves had no choice but to work productively, for the defense of the freedom they had won. Toussaint did his best to defuse the renewed hostility between former masters and former slaves by having the work policy enforced by the black military officers, rather than by the white planters. The edict was designed to help restore the export economy based on production of sugar and coffee, in cooperation with mulatto planters and returning *grands blancs* who had the requisite technical skills, and were now expected to manage their properties with freedmen's labor—the workers were free, but constrained by Toussaint's edict, backed by military force. Toussaint was eager to establish trade relations with countries other than France, for diplomatic reasons and also to get revenue for the purchase of arms, in case diplomacy should fail.

The end of the Terror in France had brought about a conservative swing in the home government, one which had a stabilizing effect. By the end of 1795 the rebelliousness within French borders had all been subdued, and Napoleon was beginning his series of victories which drove the Austrians out of Italy. France's increased confidence in foreign affairs led to friction with the United States, then under the presidency of George Washington. The many French privateers operating out of Saint Domingue's ports often failed to distinguish between British and American targets, and in 1796 Washington was told (mistakenly but damagingly) that Sonthonax had authorized the taking of American prizes. France, on her side, was irked by recent accommodations the United States had made with Britain. In 1797, the Directory did license French privateers to capture American merchantmen—despite the fact that much French trade was carried on American boats—in order to discourage U.S. trade with Britain. When John Adams succeeded Washington as president, he made a new effort to rectify this situation, but his emissaries in Paris were rebuffed and even insulted.

The United States had sent Jacob Mayer as consul to Cap Français, mainly to see to the repatriation of American sailors stranded ashore in Saint Domingue after the capture of their ships. In the spring of 1798 Congress passed a law suspending all trade with France and areas under French authority for a period of nine months—the act was viewed as a prelude to a declaration of war. However, Jacob Mayer was advised by Secretary of State Timothy Pickering that the suspension was "limited to places under the acknowledged power of France. Consequently, if the inhabitants of Saint Domingue have ceased to acknowledge that power, there will not . . . be any bar to the prompt and extensive renewal of trade between the United States and the ports of that island."[50]

At the same time that Maitland was negotiating special British trade arrangements with Toussaint, Jacob Mayer was commissioned to let the black general know that the United States would also support such a step toward Saint Domingue's independence from France—and perhaps even an outright declaration. But these intimations came

Toussaint's way just as Hédouville arrived in the colony, and under these circumstances, Toussaint was too canny and cautious to take the bait immediately or openly.

As soon as Hédouville departed, though, Toussaint sent one of his French administrators, Joseph Bunel, on a mission to the United States, accompanied by Jacob Mayer. (Of Bunel, Colonel Vincent wrote, "I believe him to be the most dangerous advisor to Toussaint, whose confidence he has more than anyone; this man does infinite harm to France.")[51] These emissaries carried a letter from Toussaint to President Adams: "You can be assured, Mr. President," Toussaint wrote, "that Americans will find protection and security in the ports of the Republic and St. Domingue, that the flag of the United States will be respected there, as that of a friendly power and ally of France."[52] The mission had provisions such as yams—which were more easily produced in quantity than sugar or molasses—to offer in trade, and could also offer to put a stop to the taking of American prizes in Saint Domingue's waters if trade should be renewed.

Bunel immediately fell foul of the French consul in Philadelphia, Philippe André Letombe, who wrote to Paris that Bunel had not even bothered to visit him, but instead was collaborating with Maitland and, aside from arranging exceptional trade agreements, was courting firm U.S. support for an independence bid in Saint Domingue. But in the currently awkward state of French-American relations, Bunel had better access to the Adams administration than Letombe, and the encouragement Toussaint was giving for the return to Saint Domingue of *grand blanc* refugees who were now scattered all over the U.S. Eastern Seaboard no doubt helped improve Bunel's position.

The possibility of independence for Saint Domingue aroused violently mixed feelings in the American Congress, with the case against it most strongly stated by Albert Gallatin of Pennsylvania:

> Suppose that island, with its present population, under present
> circumstances, should become an independent state. What is
> this population? It is known to consist, almost entirely, of
> slaves just emancipated, of men who received their first educa-
> tion under the lash of the whip, and who have been initiated to

liberty only by that series of rapine, pillage, and massacre that have laid waste to that island in blood. Of men, who, if left to themselves, if altogether independent, are by no means likely to apply themselves to peaceable cultivation of the country, but will try to continue to live, as heretofore, by plunder and depredations. No man wishes more than I do to see an abolition of slavery, when it can be properly effected, but no man would be more unwilling than I to constitute a whole nation of freed slaves, who had arrived to the age of thirty years, and thus to throw so many wild tigers on society.[53]

To the anxiety that an independent Saint Domingue would spread slave rebellion across the Caribbean and into the southern United States was added the fear that such a state would become a base for pirates—like the pirates who threatened American shipping along the Barbary Coast (often with the covert encouragement of the British), but much, much closer to home. That French Saint Domingue had to all intents and purposes been founded by pirates had by no means been forgotten.

However, the declared subject of the congressional debate was not Saint Domingue's independence but the possibility of renewing trade relations, which had been lucrative and important for American merchantmen for many years. The embargo against trade with France was to be renewed—but exceptions could be made "either with respect to the French Republic, so to any island, port, or place, belonging to the said Republic, with which a commercial intercourse may safely be renewed."[54] It was so well understood that Saint Domingue was the island in question that the rider was commonly called "Toussaint's Clause." But free trade with Toussaint's Saint Domingue had its own set of risks, at least for the slaveholding south of the United States. Thomas Jefferson, marginalized in the Adams administration, fretted about that: "We may expect therefore black crews & supercargoes & missionaries thence into the southern states . . . If this combustion can be introduced among us under any veil whatsoever, we have to fear it."[55]

Despite all such reservations, the bill was passed, and soon afterward the USS *Constellation* captured the French *L'Insurgente* in Caribbean waters. A naval war between the two countries was clearly under way, for all it had not been officially declared. In that context, Toussaint's negotiations with the United States had to be interpreted by the French Directory as treating with the enemy, though the Directory said nothing about it for the moment (for fear that Toussaint would declare the colony independent). Bunel returned to Le Cap to report the success of his mission, accompanied by Jacob Mayer and a new American envoy, Edward Stevens—and a cargo of supplies to launch the new trade agreement. Idlinger, the French accountant called by cynics "Toussaint's creature,"[56] was there to receive them, and Maitland's emissary, Colonel Harcourt, sailed into Le Cap at the same time. Not long after, Maitland arrived in person to take part in the conference with Toussaint which confirmed all the terms of the deal.

American ships were to be admitted only at Le Cap and Port-au-Prince; however, American consuls in those two towns could issue these ships passports to visit other ports on the Saint Domingue coast, as could the chief of the American consulate, Edward Stevens. British vessels were to be admitted at all ports without exception, though under false colors, normally the Spanish flag. The British would have their own representative installed in the colony, in a role analogous to that of Edward Stevens. Toussaint agreed to shut down all privateers and corsairs and prevent their operating out of Saint Domingue's ports, and he also agreed to keep his own citizens off the sea, which allayed the fears of southerners like Jefferson. The trade would be carried by American or British ships, Saint Domingue would not develop a merchant fleet, and crews of black "wild tigers" would not sail into Charleston or any other U.S. port. But Toussaint could operate transport vessels up and down his own coasts, under protection of the U.S. and British ships, which would also provide him with some local transportation services. Perhaps most significantly of all, Toussaint was to be furnished with whatever munitions of war he requested. Shipments of flour and gunpowder began right away.

The rather complicated terms of this arrangement had been negotiated in stages. First Toussaint worked out the fundamentals in private meetings with Stevens at Le Cap (while Maitland's messenger,

Harcourt, was kept waiting in the wings). Then Toussaint induced Roume to sign off on the deal with Stevens to permit U.S. shipping in Saint Domingue's ports—not without difficulty, since Roume was more than a little reluctant to grant such privileges to ships of a nation currently in the midst of a naval war with France.

The conference with Maitland took place later, at Arcahaie; Stevens was present for it, but Roume was not. In addition to the very tricky terms for admitting British ships to Saint Domingue's ports under false flags, Toussaint renewed his pledge not to interfere with Jamaica or other neighboring islands, and to halt the depredations of French privateers. Another secret rider on the deal committed Toussaint to refuse entry to any French warships armed outside the colony—a condition which would exclude practically any French naval vessel. This term was intended to further allay the concern shared by the British and the Americans that the French might use Saint Domingue as a base for expanding the French Revolution, and especially a black slave revolution, into their own slave states in North America (as indeed the French, or Toussaint and his army independently of the French, might well have done). When President Adams announced the trade deal in the United States, these secret terms, and especially the British participation, were carefully kept quiet.

A risky game—but Toussaint was playing it with consummate skill. While constantly, adamantly proclaiming his and the colony's loyalty to France, he had managed to place Saint Domingue under the protection of an enemy naval power. Enemy ships now had more privilege in the French colony's ports than the ships of France herself! But Toussaint would not let British and American naval protection tempt him to a declaration of independence, in part because only France had abolished slavery, while Britain and the United States showed no sign of doing so any time soon. Trade with the United States was essential for Saint Domingue's survival and British acquiescence was essential to that trade. At the same time, remaining French was Saint Domingue's best guarantee of general liberty for its people.

Whatever other intentions he might have had, the preservation of general liberty was always Toussaint's first and ultimate purpose. So long as France remained firmly committed to the abolition of slavery,

Toussaint's attachment to France was quite real. And he knew that, for the moment at least, the risk that he might go so far as to declare Saint Domingue independent outright would discourage the Directory from punishing him for behaving, in some respects, as if Saint Domingue were already independent in fact. In this way, Toussaint had achieved a delicate balance for his fledgling state among the superpowers of his time—powers he seemed expert in playing against one another.

There were still internal problems to confront. As Maitland had anticipated, the evacuation of the British had helped to make Toussaint more powerful than any other leader in Saint Domingue. His armament had become very imposing; not only did the British leave him their forts with cannon intact, they also left sixty thousand muskets in good working order. Though the colored commanders Rigaud and Beauvais still shared the Southern Department between them, no one could challenge Toussaint's dominance in the north and the west. Despite Hédouville's strenuous effort to set them against each other, Rigaud and Toussaint sustained a spirit of cooperation for several months after the agent's flight. On February 3, 1799, Beauvais, Rigaud, and Laplume traveled to Port-au-Prince to meet Toussaint and Roume for a celebration of the anniversary of the National Convention's abolition of slavery. But a few days later, the entente between Toussaint and Rigaud began to crack when Roume took a couple of military districts out of Rigaud's command and turned them over to Toussaint.

Suspicious that Rigaud was plotting a mulatto takeover in Port-au-Prince, Toussaint delivered a harangue in the capital's largest church, warning Rigaud and all the *gens de couleur* that he could do away with them all if he only chose to raise his left hand against them; it was just their good fortune that for the moment he chose to use the tools of law instead. This threat had a double resonance: in Vodou, malicious black magic is understood to be the work of the left hand, while the right is in charge of healing, benevolent action.

Toussaint's largely secret negotiations with the British and Americans were still going on. Suspicious of the secrecy, Rigaud accused Toussaint of conspiring with Maitland to restore slavery. Toussaint then revealed one of the secrets he had kept with the British general: he let Rigaud know that Maitland had wanted either Beauvais or Laplume to assume command of Jérémie (near Rigaud's hometown, Les Cayes, on the Grand Anse) when the British evacuated, but that he, Toussaint, had insisted that Rigaud take control of the port. At that point, Toussaint would likely have chosen Rigaud as his successor as general in chief (an early indication that Toussaint had already begun to think that this choice would be his to make), but now, thanks to Rigaud's abuse of his trust, he was beginning to prefer Beauvais. Rigaud, Toussaint charged, had shredded Toussaint's order for thanksgiving masses following the departure of the British, offending "the supreme being, to whom I always give credit for the success of my operations." The next accusation was distinctly more serious: "I know," said Toussaint to Rigaud, "that in the design to get rid of me you have posted men sworn to you along the road to Arcahaie"[57]—that is to say, assassins.

The ink was barely dry on the last secret convention Toussaint had signed with Maitland when Rigaud, exasperated to the point of no return, published the letter in which Hédouville had transferred his authority as agent to him. It was June 15, 1799, and Rigaud was already marching in force toward Petit and Grand Goâve, the two posts which Roume had transferred to Toussaint's command not long before. He captured those two towns so swiftly that Laplume was barely able to escape by throwing himself into a boat. At Arcahaie, having eluded whatever assassins Rigaud might have sent to waylay him there, Toussaint met Richter, one of the American consuls, to hurry up his arms shipments. Barrels of gunpowder with British stamps were offloaded at Port-au-Prince. Clearly, the United States and Britain were backing Toussaint in the conflict, while some observers thought that Rigaud had been incited by Anglophile French colonists and remnants of the old Colonial Assembly who had always hated the *gens de couleur* and hoped the whole race would be wiped out in a civil war with the blacks.

Toussaint began taking a similar line. The address he made to an assembly of field hands on the Cul de Sac plain is his longest speech in Creole ever recorded:

Am I not a black as much as the rest of you? Was I not a slave like the rest of you?—well what do they want to say? Don't listen to them, my friends. We are all brothers. Who fought for you from the beginning of the whole business until now . . . wasn't it me? You didn't know me well back then, because I was at Le Cap. Wasn't it the blacks of Le Cap who fought first for freedom? The mulattoes have fought on their own account in this area, and if they tell you they were fighting for you they are deceiving you. Wasn't it them that gave up the blacks around here to be sent to the Mosquito Coast?* Ah, look at Rigaud today—who's looking for trouble, and what does he expect to get out of it? He says I want to sell the blacks to the English. He's crazy, oh!—wasn't it me who chased all the English out of here! Don't listen to people who come around to stir you up against me. Seize them and bring them to me. It's Rigaud and his people, or rather it's the mulattoes who want to make the rest of you go back to slavery. It's they who owned slaves and are angry to see them free. Isn't it I who was a slave myself exactly like the rest of you? The whites had slaves, but they know what is called a revolution, they love the law . . . they are friends of the blacks, so watch out!—if you do harm to them, you'll make me very angry.[58]

The view here expressed of the whites' benevolence and commitment to general liberty was perhaps a little exaggerated. Christophe Mornet, Toussaint's commander in the Cul de Sac region, was enforcing the labor policy with such enthusiasm that one gratified white observer commented that "little remained to be done for the gangs to be working just like in the old days."[59] But in this same speech

*Toussaint is reminding his audience of the black regiment bizarrely known as the "Swiss," who were recruited in the same region and promised freedom for fighting for the mulatto-*grand blanc* Confederation of Croix des Bouquets. When the fighting was finished, the Swiss were betrayed, shipped first to the Mosquito Coast, then stranded in Jamaica, then returned to Saint Domingue by the British. Most of them were slain on board ship in a Saint Domingue harbor. Toussaint had always been outraged by this episode and knew how to share his outrage with his listeners.

Toussaint apologized for that severity, shifting the blame to Christophe Mornet, and offered all his listeners passports to leave their plantations and go where they liked. As the conflict with Rigaud flowered into all-out civil war, Toussaint found it expedient to rally his black base by suspending his stringent labor policy. He promoted several days of festival that brought swarms of blacks into Port-au-Prince from the outlying area, and on the gallery of the government house he joined in Ibo warrior dances, to help whip up enthusiasm for battles which were sure to come.

On July 3, Roume, under pressure from Toussaint, declared Rigaud a rebel and traitor to France, though the agent still hoped to mediate a peaceful settlement. Five days later, Toussaint sent his main force, which now amounted to between twenty and thirty thousand men, to confront Rigaud at Petit and Grand Goâve. Though Rigaud's main strength was in the south, particularly in his home region of Les Cayes, his faction had footholds all over the colony, particularly in the coastal towns. Beauvais, commanding at Jacmel on the south coast, hoped at first to remain neutral, but when *gens de couleur* in the surrounding countryside were attacked by Mamzel and the Doko maroons (probably on Toussaint's orders), he was forced to join the struggle on the side of Rigaud and his race. Meanwhile, Toussaint was riding rapidly all over the Western and Northern departments to suppress rebellions in the Artibonite Plain and at Môle Saint-Nicolas. On July 25, he broke a siege of Port de Paix, where Rigaud's partisans had attacked Toussaint's General Maurepas.

Not so very long before, Cap Français had been a mulatto stronghold. In the summer of 1799, Toussaint executed Pierre Michel (the officer who'd been first to rescue Laveaux from mulattoes then led by Villatte) for an attempt to turn over this important town to Rigaud's supporters; fifty other conspirators were put to death at Le Cap on August 4. Rigaud's partisans wanted to assassinate Toussaint, if they could not defeat him on the battlefield; during the summer of 1799 Toussaint had three narrow escapes from ambushes which seemed to target him personally: at Pont d'Ester in the Artibonite Valley, near Jean Rabel on the northwest peninsula, and at Sources Puantes on the road to Port-au-Prince. He broke up another ambush on Desdunes Plantation in the Artibonite, and ordered six ringleaders to be blown to bits by point-blank cannon fire on the parade ground at Gonaïves.

In the midst of all the fighting, Toussaint waged a propaganda war. During the early stages of the conflict with Rigaud, Agent Roume had done his best to defuse it, writing an open letter to Rigaud which urged him not to be trapped in Hédouville's scheme to set him and Toussaint against each other. Roume saw the racial dimension of the conflict and was alarmed by it. An elegant passage turned on the point that Roume himself was married to a *femme de couleur:* "Toussaint Louverture knows only two kinds of men, good ones and bad ones; it is I who assures you of that; I, the husband of a mulatress; I, the father of a quarteron; I, the son-in-law of a negress—believe me, my mulatto brothers-in-law, believe me, who has long known the sentiment of the General in Chief, believe that I have come to the degree of admiration which he inspires in me by recognizing him the impartial friend of the Blacks, the Reds, and the Whites."[60] This familial view of Saint Domingue's racial situation was one that Toussaint could certainly share. In peacetime he could rise to the level of impartiality which Roume described here, and even during the civil war he liked to point out the numerous loyal mulattoes who remained in his army, many of them in high-ranking, trusted positions.

But now, Toussaint claimed that Rigaud had built his party by assuring all the *gens de couleur* that "the Mulattoes are the only natives of Saint Domingue, that in consequence the country belongs to them by right, that it is theirs, as France is for the Whites, and Africa for the Negroes."[61] In his efforts to incite the blacks against the whites, Toussaint argued, Rigaud proved himself "faithful to the principles of Machiavelli."[62] The author of *The Prince* was much on Toussaint's mind these days; he had also accused Hédouville of fleeing his post "to escape the disastrous effects of his Machiavellianism."[63] Now he returned to the Villatte rebellion to demonstrate the Machiavellian cast of Rigaud's faction, alleging that in 1796 the mulattoes were already plotting to seize all three departments of the colony—Villatte in the north, Beauvais in the west, and Rigaud in the south—in a plot master-minded by Pinchinat. Should there be any doubt that the mulattoes hated all the blacks and wanted to destroy them, there was always the example of the Swiss.

The product of this kind of thinking was a war of racial extermination. Toussaint's rising second in command, General Jean-Jacques Dessalines, emerged as the chief executioner. In regions where Toussaint had run into ambushes and assassination attempts, the reprisals were crushing. Dessalines was always more consistently hostile to mulattoes than Toussaint. "The Blacks," he said, "are friends of repose; whenever they get stirred up it's because someone else put them in motion, and you will always find colored men behind the curtain."[64] Dessalines respected courage wherever he found it, and colored men who stood up to him were often invited to serve in his command—as many of them did. To those unable to bear arms, Dessalines would say, "What are the rest of you good for?—to give bad advice. Enough!"[65] His men understood the remark to be a death sentence.

Toussaint was determined to settle all internal conflicts quickly and absolutely, because there were plenty of external threats still on his horizon as the eighteenth century drew to a close. The Directory had given him no definite reaction to his expulsion of Hédouville; in an increasingly shaky state itself, it had decided simply to watch and wait. In France, both Hédouville and Sonthonax were outraged against him, while the Vaublanc faction was still pressing for the restoration of slavery. Despite some tactful efforts (abetted by his new British allies) to extract them, his two eldest sons were still hostages in France.

Though Toussaint had not been censured for his conduct toward Hédouville, his deals with the English and the Americans might also have provoked the French government, especially the prohibition of French military vessels in Saint Domingue. Though he had made no open bid for independence, it was becoming more and more apparent that Toussaint did not especially want to see French military vessels in port anywhere on the island—which meant that he needed to bring the Spanish region of Hispaniola under his control. But while the civil war continued he could spare no troops for that operation. Therefore, Rigaud's rebellion had to be utterly crushed. Thus far, Toussaint's ruthless repression of the mulatto revolt resembled the Terror in France, whose original purpose, as declared by Robespierre, was to create seamless internal solidarity for the confrontation of foreign enemies.

By November 1799, the civil war between the mulattoes and the blacks had settled on the siege of Jacmel, which Toussaint delegated to Dessalines, who had routed Rigaud from the positions he had taken further to the north. During the same month the Directory collapsed in France, and Napoleon Bonaparte assumed executive rule of the nation. Though this arrangement described Napoleon as "first consul" in a consulate of three, it was patently clear that France's new system of government was a military dictatorship, controlled by a single dictator. Such a hard swing to the right was apt to be favorable to proponents of slavery, as Toussaint could not help but suspect. In December, the Consulate issued a constitution stating that the colonies would henceforth be governed by "special laws"—alarming news for Toussaint and all the *nouveaux libres* of Saint Domingue, as such exceptions to the laws that governed the French homeland had previously been used to permit and justify slavery.

Agent Roume, though rapidly falling out of sympathy with Toussaint, wrote to First Consul Napoleon Bonaparte to complain of the effects which such decisions at home were having in the colony, in the souls of men whom Roume characterized as "simple but good."[66] The notion of "special laws" for the colonies led the blacks of Saint Domingue to suspect they were going to be governed by "a new *code noir* based on the old one."[67] Worse, a flurry of letters had begun to circulate, all claiming that an army with a mission to restore slavery would appear on the Spanish side of the island and attack French Saint Domingue across the frontier. The effect of such rumors on Toussaint is not hard to imagine.

On April 27, 1800, Toussaint extracted an order from Roume to take possession of Spanish Santo Domingo. Well aware that the home government did not want this region to fall into the control of its black general in chief, Roume had been refusing since January to sign the order. His once congenial relationship with Toussaint had gone sour. Aware of Maitland's semisecret visits, Roume disapproved of Toussaint's dealings with the British; and the civil war distressed him so much that he concocted a covert plan to halt it by bringing in a Spanish fleet from Cuba to draft both Toussaint's and Rigaud's armies for an all-out assault on Jamaica. Toussaint knew nothing of that fantastic scheme; it was the issue of Spanish Santo Domingo that brought him to a crisis with Roume.

He had Roume locked up for a time in Fort Picolet, on the cliffs above the harbor of Le Cap, but when the agent still held out, Toussaint applied pressure from different angles. A committee of prominent whites led by Mayor Borgella of Port-au-Prince issued a proclamation that Toussaint was "the only man who can seize the reins of government with a certain hand"[68] and giving him authority (which it had no legitimate power to give) to overrule Roume's decisions. At the same time, a false rumor that Toussaint had been appointed "proconsul" by the new French government was being circulated by the American consul Stevens and by General d'Hébécourt, one of the French officers in Toussaint's inner circle. Toussaint, headquartered in Port-au-Prince to direct the campaign against Rigaud in the south, made a quick run up the coast to Gonaïves, whereupon huge demonstrations broke out all over the Northern Department, with *nouveaux libres* calling for Roume's deportation. General Moyse was, ostensibly, unable to contain these riots—the same sort of riots he himself had incited against Hédouville. Six thousand men assembled in Le Cap and voted Roume out of his position as agent.

Roume had recently annoyed the British by expelling one of their agents, Douglas, from Le Cap, and Toussaint's British allies were quietly pressuring him to get rid of Roume altogether, but Toussaint did not really want to go so far. He preferred to keep the colony's interests balanced between the interests of the superpowers of his day, and if no representative of the French government remained in Saint Domingue he would be in open rebellion against France, thus wholly dependent on whatever protection he could expect from the United States and from the British navy. At about the same time, his old friend Laveaux, who had been turned away by local authorities from a mission to Guadeloupe, was expected to land in Spanish Santo Domingo. Here was one agent of France whom Toussaint might have welcomed without ambivalence. But Laveaux's ship was captured by the British before he could land, and taken to Jamaica as a prize. Roume would be the agent, or no one would. When Roume finally signed the order to take over the Spanish territory, Toussaint invited him to resume his office.

Toussaint's troops were still so tied up in the civil war that he could send only General Agé, a white French officer but up to now a Toussaint loyalist, to carry out the mission. Agé traveled alone, or the next thing to it. When he reached Santo Domingo City, Governor Don García refused to acknowledge his authority, though Agé threatened the arrival of Toussaint's army. Don García gave him six soldiers for an escort back to the French border. When Agé returned discomfited, Roume rescinded the order, announcing (honestly enough) that it had been extracted by force. Toussaint was furious, but for the time being he was too consumed by the civil war to do anything about it.

For months, Toussaint's tremendous black army had been halted outside the defenses of Jacmel. Beauvais, never wholly enthusiastic about war with the overwhelming black army, had finally decided to leave his post and the colony—only to be shipwrecked and drowned. In January 1800, the redoubtable mulatto officer Alexandre Pétion—who had previously served in Toussaint's command but now decided to switch sides—slipped through the lines around Jacmel and took over the defense. During the next few months, the tightening siege gradually reduced the inhabitants to a state of starvation.

With such a huge numerical advantage, Toussaint's army could easily have surrounded Jacmel on land, but to seal off the town by sea was trickier. Though the British were supposed to allow Toussaint to operate in Saint Domingue's coastal waters, the four ships he sent to blockade Jacmel were captured and hauled off to Jamaica. This event, which coincided with Roume's expulsion of the English agent Douglas, put a strain on Toussaint's arrangement with Maitland. Still worse, the French Jew Isaac Sasportas had just traveled from Saint Domingue to Jamaica to raise a slave rebellion there, and got himself arrested. If Toussaint had ever had anything to do with that conspiracy, he disavowed it now—by some accounts it was he who betrayed Sasportas in the first place. Agent Roume, however, would have been happy to disrupt Toussaint's coziness with the English, and may well have had a hand in Sasportas's doomed expedition. For whoever might have been concerned, the Jamaican authorities made a point of hanging Sasportas on a gallows high enough to be visible from the shores of Saint Domingue. Toussaint sent General Huin, who had handled much of the original Toussaint-Maitland dealings, to Jamaica to iron out these difficulties. In the end the British stood back and allowed the Americans to support Toussaint at Jacmel.

When the USS *General Greene* joined the blockade, Jacmel's situation became truly desperate, and when the *General Greene* finally bombarded the harbor forts, the defenders held out for less than an hour. Pétion managed to evacuate the women from the town, then led the male survivors on a sortie to rejoin Rigaud on the Grande Anse. Broken elsewhere in the colony, the Rigaud rebellion was now confined to the southwest peninsula. Dessalines soon followed up the Jacmel victory by taking the town of Miragoane, and from there he pursued Rigaud's remaining forces into the plain of Fond des Nègres. Toussaint, meanwhile, made a triumphal visit to Jacmel, where he addressed the survivors in evangelical terms: "Consider the misfortunes which threaten you; I am good and humane; come and I will receive you all . . . If Rigaud presented himself in good faith, I would receive him still."[69]

New delegates from the French Consulate arrived in Hispaniola in June 1800: the experienced Julien Raimond, General Jean-Baptiste Michel, who had been part of the Hédouville mission, and Toussaint's friend and partisan Colonel Vincent. The armed force meant to accompany them proved unavailable at the last minute, so these three took the precaution of landing on the Spanish side of the island (as Hédouville had done). Vincent traveled separately from the other two, accompanied by false rumors that he had orders from the home government for Toussaint's arrest. He was supposed to have been halted by an insurrection in Arcahaie, but the riot was forestalled when a local commander who either had been left out of the loop or pretended to be arrested the officer in charge of stirring up the rising before he could trigger it. Vincent continued north along the coast, passing unmolested through Toussaint's stronghold at Gonaïves, but at Limbé he was seized by an angry mob of *nouveaux libres,* beaten, and stripped of the papers he carried. The crowd took his epaulettes from him too, and dragged him several miles over the mountains on foot. During one halt he was blind-folded and led to believe he was about to be shot. "I will never forget," Vincent wrote later, "another black man named Jean Jacques, comman-der of the northern plain; he had never seen me before, but seeing me mistreated by these Revolting Negroes who seemed very much decided to take my life, he covered me with his own body, in the desert to which I had been taken."[70]

Michel, who took a different route to Cap Français, suffered simi-lar treatment. In both cases the apparent object was to confiscate the envoys' papers and make sure they had no secret mission. Meanwhile (as Dessalines's army smashed into the Grande Anse in pursuit of Rigaud), Toussaint was making a triumphal progress north from Jacmel. When the people of the towns along his way came out to honor him as Saint Domingue's sole ruler, he seemed much less shy of accept-ing such accolades than when he had first taken over Port-au-Prince from the British.

In fact, though the new emissaries brought news that Napoleon had confirmed Toussaint in his position as general in chief (which, given the Hédouville controversy, should have greatly relieved the black leader), and a reassuring proclamation from Bonaparte to all the *nou-veaux libres* ("Brave blacks, remember that only the French people rec-ognize your liberty and the equality of your rights"),[71] they were also under orders to forbid Toussaint to occupy Spanish Santo Domingo. Furthermore, the new emissaries were supposed to bring the civil war to an end, but Toussaint, who was not immediately to be found in either Port-au-Prince or Le Cap, was intent on taking care of that mat-ter himself. When he finally met Vincent and Michel, on June 25, he did not seem overjoyed by the confirmation of his rank, and he declined to have the sentence ("Brave blacks, *etc.*") embroidered in gold on the battalion flags as Napoleon had ordered.

On July 7, Dessalines handed Rigaud a crushing defeat on the plain of Aquin. In light of this event, it meant little for Toussaint to permit Vincent to carry the "olive branch of peace" into Rigaud's last redoubt in Les Cayes. Indeed, when Rigaud learned that Napoléon and the Consulate had confirmed Toussaint in his military functions, he tried to stab himself with his own dagger.

On August 5, Toussaint himself entered Les Cayes, and Rigaud took flight, first to Guadeloupe and then to France. Toussaint announced an amnesty for his erstwhile mulatto opponents but left General Dessalines to administer it in the south. Dessalines exercised very little restraint in his reprisals. The French general Pamphile de Lacroix described the result as a "human hecatomb," with some ten thousand colored persons of all ages and both sexes left dead, often by mass drownings, "if one can believe the public voice,"[72] though biographer (and staunch Toussaint defender) Victor Schoelcher objects that if all the alleged slayings had really occurred, the known mulatto population would have been exterminated three times over. But it is clear the amnesty was something of a sham. Toussaint had once mocked Rigaud because "he groans to see the fury of the people he has excited,"[73] but now, when he saw what Dessalines had done, he groaned on quite a similar note: "I said to trim the tree, not uproot it."[74]

The instigation of "spontaneous" riots by the sector of the citizenry sometimes called the "Paris mob" had become a tried-and-true strategy for French revolutionaries during the late 1780s. According to some theories, the royalist conspirators in Saint Domingue were following that model when, with the help of trusted *commandeurs* like the Toussaint who had not yet become Louverture, they planned the first slave insurrection on the Northern Plain in 1791. The *gens de couleur* understood this method: Villatte's brief overthrow of Laveaux was marked by a riot in the town, and Rigaud planned one in the Southern Department to give himself an emergency exit from his first meeting with Hédouville. Toussaint, always a savvy observer of such events, almost certainly adapted the strategy for his own use—using popular uprisings to restore Laveaux to his governorship, to drive out both Sonthonax and Hédouville, and to intimidate Roume, Michel, and even his good friend Vincent. He was more careful than most not to let his own hand show in the instigation—instead he entered those anarchic scenes (even those of his own devising) to rescue the victims and restore order. "I won't tolerate the fury," he said. "When I appear, everything has to calm down."[75]

Vincent, who had opportunity to observe this "great art of the chief" from several angles, described it with a grudging admiration:

"with an incredible address he uses every possible means to stir up, from afar, misfortunes which only his presence can make stop, because, I think, for the most part it is he alone who has engineered them."[76] For better or worse, the same strategy has been used in Haitian politics from Toussaint's time to ours.

In October 1800, Toussaint gave thanks for the victory over Rigaud and his faction before the altar of the principal Port-au-Prince church. Among other things this orison shows how well he had mastered the priestly language of his time—and how smoothly he could blend it with his own political messages:

> What prayers of thanksgiving, O my God, could be equal to the favor which your divine bounty has just spread out over us? Not content to love us, to die for us, to pour out your blood on the cross to buy us out of slavery, you have come once again to overwhelm us with your blessings, and to save us another time. They have been useful to me, your celestial bounties, in giving me a little judgment to direct my operations against the enemies of the public peace who still wanted to spoil your creation: thus my gratitude is without limit, and my life would not be enough to thank you for it . . .
>
> Make me to know, O my God, the way that I must follow to serve you according to your wishes. It's for that that I lift up my soul toward you. Deliver me, Lord, from the hands of my enemies and teach me to do nothing but your supreme will, for you are my God. Give us constantly your holy blessings, and guide us in the path of virtue and of your holy religion; make us always to know a God in three persons, the father, the son, and the holy spirit, so let it be.[77]

Toussaint would stop at practically nothing to secure himself—and the principle of general liberty for all the former slaves—from present or potential enemies, within and without. As important as eliminating any possibility for further rebellion on the part of the mulatto caste was the extension of his authority over the entire island. The last two delegations from the French government had penetrated Toussaint's realm via Spanish Santo Domingo, and with next to no military force at their disposal. Observing the rise of Napoleon Bonaparte had caused Toussaint to begin considering the possibility of a serious armed incursion by the same route.

Vincent, Michel, and Raimond had arrived with an order forbidding Toussaint to take possession of the Spanish side of the island. In this first week of November, Minister of Marine Forfait reiterated this order. In a separate letter to Roume he requested that the latter remain in his role as agent of France in Saint Domingue and give Toussaint the benefit of his counsel—pending Napoleon's planned reorganization of the colony's administration which (Forfait assured Toussaint) "will convince you of the special esteem he has for you and for your brave Blacks."[78]

Given the earlier promise, or menace, of "special laws" being once more applied to French colonies, Toussaint was not much comforted by Forfait's dispatches, except in that they confirmed the authority of Roume. Not long before, a French fleet carrying reinforcements to an army in Egypt had published a false destination: Saint Domingue. Toussaint had been spooked by this carefully deployed rumor and moved to believe that the next expedition supposedly bound his way might actually arrive where it was advertised.

Roume had always been a reluctant partner in Toussaint's project to take over Spanish Santo Domingo. Toward the end of November 1800, Toussaint accused him of sabotaging that plan. On this and other less specific charges (like Sonthonax and Hédouville before him, Roume was said to have "sowed discord among us and fomented trouble"), Toussaint had Roume arrested. Instead of deporting him to France, he had Moyse escort him to Dondon, to remain with his family, guarded by twenty men, in a mountaintop shack sometimes described as a chicken house, "where he will stay until the French government recalls him to make an account of himself."[79] Nine months later, Toussaint sent Roume to the United States, where he lingered a while in Philadelphia before finally returning to France.

Roume had come to Saint Domingue with the First Commission in the early 1790s, which gave him much longer experience than most of his

French counterparts there; moreover, the family relationships he described in his admonitory letter to Rigaud gave him special insight into the culture of the colony's blacks and *gens de couleur*. To Kerverseau, Roume praised Toussaint as fervently as he did to Rigaud, writing in January 1799, "Whatever high opinion I had of his heart and his spirit, I was still a long way from the reality. He is a philosopher, a legislator, a general and a good citizen. The merit of Toussaint Louverture is so transcendent that I have a lot of trouble understanding why so many intelligent people don't see it, and only try to mock and slander him. If, after the justice I have just rendered to this astonishing man, I was not afraid of seeming too vain, I would add that since we have been together, two things are one: either he tells me just what I was about to tell him, or it's I who advances just what he wanted to propose to me. The same zeal for the Republic, the same love for Saint Domingue, the same urgency for the reestablishment of order and agriculture, and for the constitutional organization of the country."[80] A few months later, the symbiosis between Roume and Toussaint had very much decayed, and even at this writing Roume may have suspected that the letter to Kerverseau might end up in Toussaint's hands, for Toussaint certainly did try to intercept Roume's correspondence later on, when the trust between them was broken.

Once Roume was out of Toussaint's keeping, he wrote from Philadelphia, perhaps with a freer hand, frankly accusing him of a "project to make Saint Domingue rebellious against France and to usurp for himself the supreme power in the island." Everything he had won up to now, "so far from slaking the insatiable Toussaint, has only increased his avarice, his pride, and his passion for conquest."[81] The latter passion, Roume suggested, might move Toussaint to launch his armies on Jamaica or Cuba or both. In a subsequent letter, Roume (who himself could never begin to control Toussaint) portrays him as the pawn of his white advisers: "In spite of the fanatical ambition and profound rascality of Toussaint, I affirm one more time that he is less guilty than those vile white flatterers, Agé, Idlinger, Collet and the others. The most terrible of his passions, the desire to rule, had made this old negro, barely escaped from the chains of slavery, mad and enraged."[82] In a letter to the Spanish ambassador to the United States, Roume mentioned his feeling that Toussaint might soon be betrayed and overthrown by certain officers in the black army, and explored the notion of having him kidnapped for trial and imprisonment somewhere outside Saint Domingue.

The extreme contradictions in Roume's view of his subject over the years make one wonder if the Frenchman had himself been deranged by his experience with Toussaint—sometimes his picture of Toussaint's "Machiavellianism" seems downright paranoid—or if all his opposite statements were somehow necessary to cover the contradictory quality of Toussaint's actual character. Even in his most hostile letters, Roume remained fascinated. Toussaint is "an extraordinary being," he wrote, and "he alone holds the thread through the labyrinth"[83] of Saint Domingue's peculiarly complex story.

With Roume under wraps in his Dondon chicken house, Toussaint was not immediately concerned with what the French agent might think of him. He notified Governor Don García that he meant to carry out Roume's order of April 27 by sending Moyse with a sufficient force to take control of the eastern portion of the island for France, ignoring not only the more recent orders of Forfait to the contrary, but also the fact that Roume himself had rescinded the April 27 order on June 16. Accounts of the progress of the black army across the formerly Spanish territory differ. Though Toussaint had promised that private property would be respected (a usual feature of his rhetoric which was usually supported by his actions), one Spanish observer claimed: "The flight of the Spaniards who abandoned their lands was found justified by the abominations committed by this army and especially by the General Maurepas, that execrable tiger, who, with impunity, behaved himself just like his bandits who went to the last excesses against people of both sexes and their property."[84] Moyse and Toussaint himself were accused of appropriating rich Spanish plantations for themselves and of looting livestock and other goods while leaving the rightful owners destitute.

By other accounts, the French administration and the fresh energy which Toussaint imported into the region were a shot in the arm for the former Spanish colony, which had languished for a long time in the doldrums. The French general Pamphile de Lacroix claimed that the union of the two territories was of mutual benefit, that it created a commerce in livestock badly needed on the French side which was very profitable to the livestock owners on the Spanish side; moreover, "the black soldiers, subject to an austere discipline, had done only a little damage; and there remained in the country no more than the troops needed to hold garrisons, and these garrisons also helped circulate money."[85] Once in control of Santo Domingo, Toussaint quickly suspended the clear-cutting of the forests, where the Spanish had been frantically harvesting mahogany and other valuable hardwoods as their best way of getting money out of the colony they were about to lose. He began an important road-building program, and according to Lacroix, he trained the Spanish horses to faster gaits than those known to the Spanish horse trainers. "In the final analysis, this invasion of the blacks, though so much feared, right away became a benefit for the nomadic people of the Spanish part."[86]

The benefit was not accepted without some resistance. Don García received Toussaint's ultimatum on January 6, and was able to mobilize some fifteen hundred men toward the border (one of their commanders was Toussaint's old adversary Antoine Chanlatte). Meanwhile, Toussaint had sent two columns into Spanish territory. Three thousand men commanded by Moyse crossed at Ouanaminthe, while forty-five hundred led by Toussaint and Paul Louverture came via Mirebalais. The Spanish defense soon crumpled; Chanlatte was defeated by Paul Louverture at the Nisao River; and Toussaint received a delegation letting him know that since both Chanlatte and the French general Kerverseau had abruptly fled on a boat bound for Venezuela, there would be no further opposition to a peaceful takeover. By that time, Moyse's force was two days' march from Ciudad Santo Domingo, where civilians feared a repetition of Jean-François's massacre at Fort Liberté.

On January 26, Toussaint accepted the keys of Ciudad Santo Domingo from Don García—his former commander in the Spanish service. These two did a little verbal fencing over Toussaint's previous career in the Spanish military, but in the end the settlement was friendly enough. Though Toussaint refused to take a conventional Spanish loyalty oath, he did solemnly swear to amnesty all Spanish colonists who chose to remain and govern them according to their new-found rights as French citizens. A month later Don García took most of the remaining Spanish troops to Cuba.

In accordance with current French law, Toussaint announced the abolition of slavery in formerly Spanish Santo Domingo. The importation of African slaves to the Western Hemisphere had been first conceived and carried out in Hispaniola; now a son of African slaves had put an end to it on the same spot.

Who was the man who had done these things, and what were his ultimate intentions? If Toussaint had meant to declare independence, now would have been the time. Maitland, speaking for Britain, and the John Adams administration in the United States had made it sufficiently clear that they would support an independent Saint Domingue. But Toussaint resisted this temptation. Though he had begun to behave in many ways as the chief of an independent state, he stopped well short of any open declaration. So long as Saint Domingue remained French at least in name, she could better elude complete dominance by either Britain or the United States, whose presence in the region was much more imposing. As François "Papa Doc" Duvalier would do in twentieth-century Haiti, Toussaint was charting a separate course among the much greater powers that surrounded him, careful never to become a satellite of any one of them.

His enemies, of whom there were plenty, saw him as a dictator in the making. It was even rumored that the British had encouraged him to crown himself king. But Toussaint seemed to prefer a republican government, at least in form. To be sure, that was a fledgling system in Saint Domingue, where the vast majority of the population had left slavery less than a decade before. If Toussaint's actual methods of government were a long way from pure democracy, the same could certainly be said of France.

Both his private character and his public style combined elements of ruthlessness and benevolence so extreme that it is hard to imagine just how they could coexist in the same person. His repression of Rigaud's rebellion was at times so merciless that it is difficult to deny a strain of hypocrisy in the public prayers he uttered during the very same period. Nevertheless, some of his actions suggest that he retained the belief that forgiveness and reconciliation always remain possible even in the worst of cases—a Christian tenet underlying all his ceremonial gestures of faith.

If a kindly paternalism was evident in Toussaint's way of ruling, the signs of raw authoritarianism were certainly there too. Wherever it might spring up, rebellion would be crushed. The labor policy was strict and severe, and its enforcement meant increasing intrusion of the military into all areas of civil administration and civil life. Toussaint's Saint Domingue was on a defense footing, and would maintain that stance by whatever means necessary.

The thing to be defended, above all, was the freedom of the former slaves. Thus far, at least, Toussaint's purpose was clear and unwavering. At whatever cost, the flag of universal liberty flew—and would continue to fly—from one end of the island to the other.

FIVE

The Last Campaign

"From the first troubles in Saint Domingue," Toussaint Louverture liked to say to his guests in 1801,

> I felt that I was destined for great things. When I received this divine portent, I was fifty-four years old; I did not know how to read or write; I had a few *portugaises;* I gave them to a junior officer of the Regiment du Cap; and, thanks to him, in a few months I knew how to sign my name and read correctly.
>
> The revolution of Saint Domingue was going its way; I saw that the Whites could not hold out, because they were divided among themselves and crushed by superior numbers; I congratulated myself on being Black.
>
> It was necessary to begin my career; I crossed into the Spanish region, where they had given asylum and protection to the first troops of my color. This asylum and protection ended up nowhere; I was delighted to see Jean-François turn himself into a Spaniard at the moment when the powerful French Republic proclaimed the general freedom of the Blacks. A secret voice said to me: "Since the Blacks are free, they need a chief," and it is I who must be the chief predicted by the Abbé Raynal. I returned, transported by this sentiment,

to the service of France; France and the voice of God have not deceived me.[1]

This self-portrait is touched up here and there, as political self-portraits tend to be. Certainly there are misrepresentations: Toussaint learned how to read and write in childhood, and at the outbreak of the revolution he was worth far more than "a few portugaises." Finessing the point that in 1791 he was a free, prosperous owner of land and slaves, this description implicitly identifies him with the class of *nouveaux libres,* to whose leadership a force larger than himself had pushed him. In its picture of how Toussaint read and reacted to the situation of the early 1790s, this discourse leaves out more than a little, but is probably accurate as far as it goes.

He refers three times to prophecy and supernatural inspiration, whether "divine portent" or "secret voice." Phrased in the elaborate French reported by General Pamphile de Lacroix, these references have a Catholic tone to them. Toussaint means to assume the mantle prepared for him by the Abbé Raynal, a Catholic priest. His devotion to the Catholic religion was always a prominent feature of his public life—in spite of the fact that the Church had been banned by the Jacobin government during the middle phase of the French Revolution and especially during the Terror. When he accepted the keys to Ciudad Santo Domingo in 1801, Toussaint ordered a Te Deum to be sung— a reassuring gesture for the Spanish citizens, who had expected to confront not only a savage African but also an envoy of the godless Jacobins. He celebrated most of the key events of his career with similar Catholic ceremonies. In Port-au-Prince he had climbed into the pulpit of the principal church to warn the colored population, ex cathedra, of the dire consequences of rebellion against his rule. Cynics denounce Toussaint's Catholicism as *tartufferie,* a hypocritical mask for Machiavellian scheming—but he was probably at least as sincere as any of the Borgia popes.

With the help of the Abbé Grégoire in France, Toussaint arranged for four bishoprics to be created in Saint Domingue. Prominent in the French Revolution since 1789, Grégoire had managed to hold on to his prestige through all its various phases, including the most antireligious ones. He was a longtime abolitionist with a special interest in bringing the blacks of Saint Domingue to full status as French citizens, and reform of the Catholic Church in the colony was one means to that end. New clergy came out from France to take over the new positions, but the old colonial priests (some of whom, like Anthéaume, belonged to Toussaint's inner circle) protested vigorously. Toussaint compromised, sending Guillaume Mauviel, the priest who would have become bishop of Le Cap, to a post in the former Spanish Santo Domingo. The Abbé Colin, a veteran of the old colonial clergy, was named to the Le Cap bishopric in his place. At around the same time, Toussaint declared Catholicism to be the sole religion of Saint Domingue.

Complementing his Christian fervor, Toussaint's allusions to a higher power before the 1801 assemblies can be as easily read in a Vodouisant as in a Catholic context, and in that aspect they are quintessentially Haitian. Toussaint meant to signal to his listeners that he was invested with a spiritual force, but not necessarily or exclusively a Christian spirit. Officially, his Catholicism was strict and exclusive, but if he gave orders against the practice of Vodou, that only made him the first of many Haitian heads of state to forbid Vodou publicly while practicing it himself in private. He knew the conspiratorial significance of the ceremony at Bois Caïman, whether or not he had been there in person, and he knew just as well how the flexible network of Vodouisant communities could function as a cellular structure for rebellion and revolution—that was why he had complained to Laveaux about Macaya beating the drum too often.

Toussaint sometimes professed to abhor Vodou, usually when talking to white Europeans, who could be expected to disapprove of and fear such African practices (though some *blanc* colonists dabbled in Vodou themselves). It was a way of renouncing the Devil—and in the religious context of the time, the Devil and his minions were considered to be every bit as real and tangible as God, Christ, and the community of saints. In the eyes of the Church, the pantheon of African spirits appeared as a host of demons. The African slaves of Saint Domingue, meanwhile, combined spirits and saints in unanticipated ways, seeing Legba, the Vodou spirit of gates and crossroads, in the image of Saint Peter with his key, or the warrior spirit Ogoun in the image of the horseman Saint Jacques le Majeur. The colonial priest-hood was an odd bunch, known for the weakness of both its morals and its doctrine (especially after the expulsion of the Jesuits from Santo Domingo). In these circumstances, Catholicism tended to accommo-date African beliefs more than a little, sometimes completely unwit-tingly and sometimes with one eye deliberately closed. To practice Catholicism and Vodou at the same time, to see them as aspects of a single structure of belief, was more the rule than the exception.

Toussaint sometimes said that the nasal tone of his voice was caused by a Vodou curse that had been cast on him. That was a reason for him to dislike Vodou, but it by no means suggested that he didn't believe in it. During the civil war with Rigaud, the *mambo* Mama Boudin and two *houngans* were arrested in Port-au-Prince for conducting a cere-mony meant to inspire a violent rebellion. Up till that time, Toussaint had done no more than discourage Vodou assemblies and ceremonies (and that inconsistently, depending on how they might suit his own needs), but now he prohibited them altogether. He did not want the revolutionary spirits called to Bois Caïman—Ogoun Ferraille and Erzulie Dantor—to be summoned to revolts against his own regime. That Vodou cults differed according to tribe was also a factor. Tous-saint's Arada group was a minority in Saint Domingue, and so too were the Arada spirits.

The apparent contradictions of Toussaint's personality—the extremes of ruthlessness or beneficence he displayed on different occa-sions and under different circumstances—are most easily resolved in the terms of Vodou, where the individual ego can disappear altogether, ceding control of the person and his actions to an angry or a gentle spirit. Toussaint's "secret voice" had something of this quality, and probably there was more than one such voice. Despite a certain grandiosity in this discourse, he knew the spirit he incarnated was something larger than himself. He would invoke it one last time, when he had personally been overthrown, as the spirit of the revolution he had carried well past the point of no return.

In the first months of 1801, Toussaint Louverture was at the apogee of his military and political success; he looked to be invincible. He had, as

Pamphile de Lacroix put it, "the aura of a prince."[2] He held a kind of court in the government buildings of Cap Français and Port-au-Prince, but though his staff, guests, and courtiers wore the most elaborately formal garb, Toussaint himself preferred "simple dress in the midst of brilliant surroundings," either a plain field uniform of his general's rank, or the clothing of a planter at home on his property, "that is to say, white trousers and a white vest of very fine fabric, with a madras around his head."[3] On the other hand, he was usually attended by officers of his honor guard, a group which grew to eighteen hundred strong and was mounted on the colony's best horses. The guardsmen wore silver helmets with an engraved French motto and red crests; Toussaint's formal arrivals were preceded by trumpets. Chosen for their height and good looks among other qualities, this troop included "names distinguished during the ancien régime"[4]—implying that Toussaint trusted some white citizens of his new polity enough to place them in his bodyguard.

Yet he remained extremely cautious, even or especially at this height of his powers. After all, he had narrowly escaped several assassination attempts by ambush within the last year. He continued to ride all over the colony (on a splendid white stallion named Bel Argent) "with the speed of a thunderbolt," making a mystery of his movements, arriving where he was least expected, and "seeing everything for himself."[5] During this period he was constantly purchasing arms from abroad and caching them all over the country. The English had left him nearly sixty thousand muskets. Sonthonax had distributed fifty thousand guns to the *nouveaux libres* and Toussaint imported at least thirty thousand from the United States. Many of his arms deals were kept secret from his own administrators, but he liked to conduct frequent reviews in which the guns and ammunition were produced and inspected, and he liked to brandish a musket before an audience of field hands, exclaiming, "This is your liberty!"[6]

Toussaint slept for no more than two hours a night, and his endurance, both in the saddle and in the office, was astounding to all who encountered it. He exhausted phalanxes of secretaries in dictating replies to as many as three hundred letters a day, with every appearance of enjoyment. "He planned his future actions and reflected on them while he galloped; he reflected still more when he pretended devoutly to pray."[7]

Toussaint understood the dramatic effect of presenting his personal austerity in the midst of turn-of-the-century splendor; he also found his austerity practical. His self-control was absolute, and "he often pushed his sobriety to the point of abstinence."[8] His eating habits were governed in part by his not unreasonable fear of poison. He kept an "old negress" in each of the colony's important towns, whom he trusted to prepare stews for him and to serve him wine, which he would consume in private. Otherwise he could go for twenty-four hours on a glass of water and a cassava pancake, "or if there was no pancake, on one or two bananas, or two or three potatoes."[9]

His standards of decorum were strict to the point of prudery. He liked his lady guests to be dressed as if for church, and on one occasion is supposed to have covered the décolletage of a young beauty with his own handkerchief, rebuking her mother by saying, "Modesty should be the endowment of your sex."[10] He also forbade the easy extramarital relations that had been so common in the colony—between white men and *femmes de couleur* until 1791 and between the black and colored officers and concubines of all descriptions afterward—a measure that resulted in a number of hasty marriages. It was under this pressure that Agent Roume abruptly divorced his wife, Françoise Guillemine Lambert, who was then living apart from him on the island of Trinité; married his long-term mistress, a colored woman named Mariane Elizabeth Rochard; and formally acknowledged his paternity of their ten-year-old son. Idlinger, who upon the death of Julien Raimond had been appointed general administrator of the national domains, divorced his wife to marry Marthe, a "*fille de plaisir* celebrated in Cap,"[11] one of the colored courtesans who had been mistress to several Frenchmen before moving on to Villatte at the period of his greatest influence. When Villatte fell from power, Marthe had taken up with the pirate Moline, and cynics believed that Idlinger (renowned for his corruption) was as much interested in the pirate's gold as in the charms of his new bride.

In his own case, Toussaint made a few exceptions to this policy of strict marital fidelity. When at home, he followed his own rules. During this same period he created a new department in the colony, called the Canton Louverture, which included his and his wife's large plantations in the area of Ennery, the towns of Hinche and Banica on the Central Plateau, and the port of Gonaïves on the west coast. Of course this chunk of territory also embraced all the posts in the mountains of the Cordon de l'Ouest, Toussaint's original power base, now anchored more firmly than ever by permanent access to livestock and supplies from the grasslands of the Central Plateau. At the other end of this line, Gonaïves was being rebuilt and expanded to rival the splendor of Cap Français; Toussaint intended this town to be his capital.

His wife, Suzanne, was not an especially worldly woman, though she did know how to read and write. The high society in which Toussaint had become a central figure did not much appeal to her. She did make visits to Le Cap sometimes (where she had friends and family), but usually preferred to remain at home in Ennery, where she not only took care of the housekeeping but also managed the coffee plantation, sometimes working alongside her hired hands. A Frenchman who visited her at home described her as the fattest woman he had ever seen, yet not at all bad-looking. Her whole establishment "breathed order and decency," while personally "she seemed to have the modesty of a girl of twenty."[12]

Suzanne, apparently, never traveled south of Gonaïves. Toussaint's marital fidelity was stern in the north, but when he went south, it seemed to relax. His Port-au-Prince residence was a bachelor's paradise. An affair with Madame Desdunes, a *femme de couleur* of the Artibonite region, produced children whose descendants survive to this day. Another special favorite was "la Dame Fissour," the mixed-blood wife of a wealthy *blanc* from Léogane, the first important town south of Port-au-Prince. Such was her intimacy with Toussaint that his bodyguards would permit her to enter his private apartments unannounced at any hour of the day or night—an extraordinary privilege for the wary general to grant to anyone.

At the same time he seems to have enjoyed romantic liaisons with some of the most prominent white women still in the colony, judging from a box of souvenirs he kept at Port-au-Prince (where Suzanne would almost certainly never have come across it). The French general

Boudet and his staff found a false bottom in the box, which revealed "locks of hair of all colors, rings, golden hearts pierced with arrows, little keys, nécessaires, souvenirs, and an infinity of love letters which left no doubt of the success in love obtained by the old Toussaint Louverture! Meanwhile he was Black, and had a repulsive physique . . . but he had made himself the dispenser of all fortunes, and at a whim his power could change any condition."[13]

Women of the highest society now competed for Toussaint's attention and favor, not only behind closed doors but also with extravagant public demonstrations. Catherine Viard, described as one of Toussaint's "favorite adulteresses,"[14] invited him to a special mass (a curious combination of his tastes for public piety and private dalliance). Soon after his return from the annexation of Spanish Santo Domingo, the most prominent women of Port-au-Prince (including the wife of General Agé) turned out on horseback to greet him, shading his progress with palm fronds and presenting him an embroidered pennant.

There was a strong paternal flavor to Toussaint's rule—the population was beginning to call him, affectionately, "Papa Toussaint"—and he had a weakness for damsels in distress. A woman who could gain an audience with him stood a good chance of having her problem rapidly solved, whether or not he was interested in her romantic favors. One especially credulous French husband was rumored to stand watch outside the door of Toussaint's private office while his wife and the black general had long, long conferences within.

Across the board, Toussaint showed a remarkable warmth to the old *grand blanc* class, who had been banned as émigrés by representatives of the French Revolution, but strongly encouraged to return to their properties now that no such representatives were present in Saint Domingue. As Toussaint had incorporated everything he found useful in European military strategy into his own, he now meant to incorporate everything he found valuable in European culture—then the culture of the French Enlightenment—into the new society he was building, a society which actually practiced, without regard to race, the values of *liberté, égalité, fraternité.* He spent the evenings following large receptions in *petits cercles,* which were held in an antechamber to his bedroom otherwise used as an office; these were generally attended by the "principal Whites of the country," the priests with whom Toussaint was intimate, and distinguished foreign visitors. Toussaint knew some phrases of Church Latin, which he liked to deploy in these situations, sometimes using them to baffle poorly educated men who sought positions in his administration. He set great store by real education, both religious and secular, and education was an important topic of his *petits cercles.*

A prominent figure among the returning white proprietors was Bayon de Libertat, of whose reception at Toussaint's palace a curious anecdote is told: "He [Bayon] ran there, and wanted to throw himself into the arms of the one who people everywhere said was his benefactor; but this benefactor recoiled, and cried out in a solemn voice, so that all the world could hear him well: Go easy, Monsieur Manager— today there is a greater distance between me and you than there was in the old days between you and me. Return to Habitation Bréda; be firm and just; make the Blacks work well, so that the success of your small interests will add to the general prosperity of the administration of the first of the Blacks, of the General in Chief of Saint Domingue."[15]

Despite its distinctly apocryphal flavor, this tale is interesting, and maybe its most important detail is that Toussaint performed his reaction *for all the world to hear.* That is to say, he publicly distanced himself from Bayon de Libertat—and by implication from the whole white planter class—while at the same time describing plainly for all hearers just what the role of that class was meant to be in the new order of things. The favor Toussaint showed to the *grand blanc* planters had brought him under some suspicion among many of the *nouveaux libres,* but his response to Bayon makes it clear that the *grands blancs* and their interests are now subordinate to the interests not only of "the first of the Blacks" but also of his whole "administration"; that is, a new black ruling class representing the power of the *nouveau libre* majority. Returning whites were the white grains, integrated into inconsequence by a thorough shakeup with the dark corn in the jar. And if Toussaint's economic policies did allow the white planters to pursue their own "small" interests, that was only in service of the larger interest of restoring the colony's prosperity for the benefit of the black administration and a newly constituted black citizenry.

The rebuilding of the colony was proceeding apace. After ten years of war, Saint Domingue enjoyed a season of stability at the turn of the nineteenth century, and damage from the decade of conflict began to be repaired. The Jewel of the Antilles, Cap Français, was rebuilt to an even more sumptuous level than it had known under the ancien régime, featuring elegant new residences for Toussaint and his officers, eminently including the local commander, Henry Christophe. General Dessalines had accomplished something similar in Saint Marc. Many members of Toussaint's officer corps now had the opportunity to grow wealthy by operating plantations whose *grand blanc* owners had fled. This situation produced some tension with the white landowners who accepted Toussaint's invitation to return; their lands were supposed to be under a leaseholding arrangement whose details had become an impractical legalistic tangle since Sonthonax and Polverel first tried to manage things. In practice, the returning white planters often found it quite difficult to reassert control of their property or to extract the compensation to which they were legally entitled.

Toussaint ordered all earnings from the properties of absentee owners to be paid into public treasuries, both to finance his extremely large army and to pay a corps of civil servants which was often accused of the most flagrant corruption. Income from the rental of absentee-owned plantations and town houses was surprisingly large—one observer estimated it at over four million livres in the Western Department alone. Much of this money was spent on arms, and a great deal simply leaked away. The fact that many civil service posts were unpaid encouraged embezzlement, and at the same time Toussaint was assigning more and more civil service tasks to the military, especially collection of import-export duties. White civilians in Toussaint's inner circle, like Bunel, Idlinger, and Allier (the secretary who did most of Toussaint's correspondence with the home government), were rumored to have both hands in the till. The French general d'Hébécourt, whom Toussaint trusted for negotiations with the English and other surrounding powers, had to be bribed before a returning planter could regain control of his land. In the end, however, the turnover of all sequestered properties required Toussaint's own signature. When Toussaint learned that debts were being sold for collection to the military, he put a stop to it.

In the very brief period of peace Toussaint's administration enjoyed in 1800 and 1801, restoration of the plantation economy was a limited success. Saint Domingue had had several cash crops under the ancien régime; in order of importance they were white sugar, brown sugar, coffee, cotton, and indigo. During the ten years of war, production of all these goods had dropped to less than half their former levels. Toussaint's administration could do little to increase production of white sugar, a labor-intensive process requiring considerable technical skill. Indigo was for all practical purposes abandoned. Disenchanted colonists were heard to complain that too many plantations were buried "in grass and vines."[16] However, exports of cotton and brown sugar increased by several percentage points between 1799 and 1801, while the export of coffee, significantly, nearly doubled during the same period.

If the damage to and deterioration of the plantations during the war years was problematic, the stability of the workforce was still more so. The majority of the newly freed slaves had been born in Africa, and once they were relieved of their *grand blanc* masters their natural inclination was to revert to practices of African village life, which was based on subsistence agriculture, not plantation labor. Toussaint Louverture was perturbed by this trend and by the tendency of many *nouveaux libres* (especially those who had come of age since 1791 and so never experienced slave labor) to adopt a wandering manner of life which Toussaint saw as an abuse of freedom and formally denounced as vagabondage.

Toussaint had objected that the labor policy Hédouville pursued was tantamount to slavery, but he himself was as determined to "make the Blacks work well" as he exhorted Bayon de Libertat to be. In October 1800, he decreed a labor policy still more stern than that proposed by Hédouville; it was based on the military model and enforced by the army. This decree was reiterated and reinforced by the constitution Toussaint created for the colony in 1801, which defined the plantation as a "family, whose father is necessarily the owner of the land or his representative."[17] Here was paternalism of the strictest sort: the "father" had unlimited authority to discipline his "family." Cultivators were to all intents and purposes confined to their plantations and subject to severe penalties if they wandered away or slacked in their work—though now they were to be paid for their labors.

"I have never thought liberty to be license," Toussaint pronounced in an 1801 address, "or that men become free can deliver themselves without consequence to sloth and disorder; my most formal intention is that cultivators remain attached to their respective plantations; that they enjoy a quarter of the income; that no one can be unjust to them without consequences; but at the same time I want them to work still more than in the old days; that they should be submissive, that they exactly fulfill their duties; [I am] well resolved to punish severely whomever avoids them."[18] To many so brusquely subjected to it, this regime looked all too much like slavery.

Most of the black army officers (even those who, like Jean-Jacques Dessalines, were hostile to the return of the white planters) embraced the labor policy, which was designed, among other things, to help them enrich themselves. Dessalines, given broad authority to enforce the labor rules in the west and the south, soon made himself notorious as a more rigorous taskmaster than the *grands blancs* of the bad old days. He put his opinion very simply: "Blacks don't know how to work if you don't force them."[19]

The whip, as such, had been abolished, but Dessalines substituted canes. Often he administered the punishment with his own hand: a beating on the buttocks so severe that the victim could not move for several days afterward. Dessalines caned recalcitrant workers without prejudice, and sometimes unproductive overseers were also beaten. White proprietors on underproducing plantations might be flogged as well—to prove that Dessalines had no favoritism for them. When abuse of the cane became widespread, Toussaint issued orders against it. Dessalines switched to a leathery shrub common all over the Artibonite plain: "I beat with *bayahonde*!" he cried. "Oh yes, I beat."[20] He was just as energetic in repressing rebellions against the work policy here and there in the colony, marching into areas of unrest and killing whomever he happened to meet till the trouble stopped. When he learned that the cultivators were distressed at his appointment to command the new Canton Louverture, he said tersely, "That's their business—I've got a bayonet."[21]

Dessalines's enthusiasm for enforcing labor policies was an extreme case, but many members of the black officer corps probably agreed with Toussaint's larger thinking: it was necessary to restore productivity in order to stabilize trade relationships with neighbors like Jamaica and the United States and, still more important, to raise money for the purchase of arms and the maintenance of a large army for the defense of general liberty—the universal goal. But there was at least one officer who did not agree.

Toussaint had an unusually close and personal relationship with General Moyse, whom he had adopted as a nephew during slavery time. Moyse commanded at Fort Liberté and had been instrumental in Hédouville's expulsion. In Moyse's company, Toussaint was less guarded than usual; in October 1800 he declared: "Does Hédouville believe he can scare me? I have been making war for a long time, and if I have to keep on with it, I am ready. I have had business with three nations and I have beaten all three. Also I am calm in the knowledge that my soldiers will always be firm in the defense of their liberty. If France has more people, let her keep them to fight the English—she won't have too many. She has already lost twenty-two thousand men in our country, and if she sends any more they may very well meet the same fate. I don't want to go to war with France. I have saved this country for her up to now, but if she comes to attack me, I will defend myself."[22] It is an exceptionally frank and quite accurate statement of Toussaint's attitude at this time: his preference was to keep the colony under French rule, so long as general liberty for all and his personal position were not threatened—but he was prepared to fight to the bitter end if these conditions were not met.

Moyse, who hated whites even more bitterly than Dessalines, had a still more intransigent attitude. "The French are no good in this country, and there is no one but them who trouble us, but I will do so much to them that I will oblige them all to leave and abandon their properties. If it was in my power, I would soon be rid of them. That would be one less job to do; what one has begun, one must finish. Let France send her forces here, what will they do? Nothing. I wish she would send three, four, or five hundred thousand men; that would be so many more guns and ammunition for our brothers who are not armed. When we first began to fight for our liberty, we had only one gun, then two, three, and we finished by having all the guns of the French who came here."[23]

In the fall of 1801, Moyse became the focal point of a gathering discontent with Toussaint's draconian labor policy and gathering suspicion of his friendliness with the white planter class. As usual, there was tremendous instinctive resistance among the African-born majority of the former slaves to cooperating with the laborious requirements of the French-model society Toussaint and the other Creole black leaders were trying to create. The natural preference of the Africans was to revert to subsistence farming, which was not very demanding in Saint Domingue (one observer calculated that in this fertile zone three months of work would produce the necessities for twelve), and to the manners and mores of African village life—a tendency which would persist in Haiti for the next two hundred years. In 1801 there was plenty of land available for such use, especially on the thinly populated Spanish side. To prevent unauthorized migration into that area, Toussaint had forbidden sales of formerly Spanish land in lots smaller than fifty carreaux (roughly two hundred acres), but this policy was difficult to enforce. The more the military had to force the former slaves to do plantation labor, the more unpopular the army became.

Toussaint had made Moyse commander of all the Northern Department—previously and potentially the most productive region of the colony—but Moyse was not willing to take the extreme and violent measures Dessalines had used to make the south and the west produce. Contrary to Toussaint's program for reestablishing the plantation economy, Moyse was inclined to allow the plantations of the north to be parceled out into small holdings. The new Canton Louverture cut a slice out of Moyse's territory in the north, and Moyse suspected that Toussaint would give this command to Dessalines, rather than to him. Moreover, Moyse felt that the constitution which Toussaint had devised for the colony contained dangerous infringements on general liberty. Julien Raimond's son-in-law Pascal, who had become one of Toussaint's aides after the collapse of the Third Commission, warned his general in chief that Moyse seemed implausibly unconscious of trouble brewing all over the north.

On the night of October 29, a revolt broke out on the Northern Plain in the style of the first rising of 1791—whites were massacred from Fort Liberté to the gates of Cap Français. The new insurrection swept all over the Northern Department within two days, carrying the towns of Dondon, Acul, Plaisance, Port Margot, and Limbé. The war cry of the rebels was "General Moyse is with us—death to all the whites!" Joseph Flaville, the ever-insubordinate commandant of Limbé, slaughtered the last refugees on the waterfront there as they were trying to find boats to escape. Bayon de Libertat, Toussaint's former master and old friend, was counted among the dead. Moyse might have made a point of that. "Whatever my old uncle does," he had said, "I cannot resign myself to be the executioner of my race; he is always chewing me out for the interests of the metropole; but those are the interests of the Whites, and I won't love the Whites until they give me back the eye they made me lose in battle."[24]

The revolt was well and carefully timed, and caught much of the black military leadership off guard, or almost. Dessalines was celebrating his marriage to Marie Claire Heureuse, a *femme de couleur* he had met during the siege of Jacmel, when she persuaded him to allow her to bring medical supplies through his lines to nurse the sick and wounded in the surrounded town. The wedding festivities, which cost 100,000 livres and went on for three days, took place at Petite Rivière, in the Artibonite region. Toussaint joined the celebration, though he had to tear himself away from La Dame Fissour to do so. Moyse, who had other plans, did not attend.

Unfortunately for Moyse's intentions, Henry Christophe also skipped Dessalines's wedding, and was in position to shut down the revolt inside the gates of Cap Français before it was well begun. He arrested a ringleader named Trois Balles and soon extracted enough other names from him to make thirty arrests. Within twenty-four hours, he was able to reassure the American merchants and agents who had fled to their ships at the first signs of trouble that Le Cap had returned to good order.

Next, Christophe subdued Limbé, Port Margot, and Acul, capturing Joseph Flaville in the process. General Vernet soon regained Plaisance. Dessalines, once recovered from his wedding night, was not far behind. On the plantations where white owners had been slain, he simply massacred the entire work gang.

Toussaint himself was so enraged that when he passed through the rebel zone he ordered the mutineer regiments on parade and summoned certain men to step out of the ranks and blow their own brains out. None refused to obey this order. Christophe had brought Joseph Flaville as a prisoner to Le Cap; Toussaint ordered him and several other conspirators to be blown to bits by grapeshot in the Place d'Armes, before the cathedral there. In a similar scene at Fort Liberté, the rebel Captain Hillarion was bayoneted. In the hills above Le Cap, Toussaint slaughtered a hundred-odd cultivators who had joined the rebellion, and he conducted similar exemplary executions all across the Northern Plain. For years afterward, the residents of Trou du Nord pointed out an old caimite tree around whose trunk the rebels of that region had been massacred.

In the case of Moyse himself, Toussaint—most uncharacteristically—seemed to hesitate. At Dondon, the revolt had been subdued by Moyse himself. At Marmelade, the next town west along the Cordon de l'Ouest, Toussaint received Moyse as if his nephew might possibly still be a loyal subordinate commander. "Everything leads me to believe that you are the author of this revolt," he told Moyse. "Everywhere the rebels have been putting it out that they act in your name—your honor depends on your justifying yourself, and the first way to do it is to bring everything back into good order, because if you are guilty your general's rank will not save you—You are coming from Dondon—how many rebels have you punished there? None. How many have you had arrested?—No one. How can it be that you, commander of the Northern Department, come from a quarter where horrible assassinations have been committed and you have not had anyone arrested or punished! Go back to Dondon, have the guilty parties arrested, but don't have anyone shot—let them be brought to me alive and under sure guard."[25]

By the look of these orders, Toussaint was trying to give Moyse an out. If he was doing it for reasons of sentiment, it was a highly unusual move—never before or after did Toussaint leave anyone standing who had threatened him. Agent Roume, whose analysis of the Moyse affair has a distinctly paranoid flavor, suggests that Toussaint might have been behind the Moyse rebellion himself, and that he meant to leave Moyse free and in feigned rebellion against him, so that when a French military expedition arrived in Saint Domingue, Moyse could lead the white soldiers into fatal ambushes. Far-fetched, yes—but as Roume justly points out, it was unlike Toussaint to let Moyse go, and unlike Moyse to put himself back in Toussaint's power without a struggle.

Returning to Dondon, Moyse obeyed Toussaint's orders, up to a point. He arrested twenty-four men, shot thirteen of them, and sent eleven back to Toussaint—but it was the dead men, presumably, who would have implicated him more certainly in the revolt. Nevertheless, Toussaint still left Moyse at large. But Dessalines appeared at Marmelade to let Moyse know he had no business there. Now part of the Canton Louverture, the town was under Dessalines's command. Moyse passed briefly through Le Cap, without finding much of a welcome; when he returned to Dondon the inhabitants shuttered themselves in their houses.

Toussaint may have hoped that Moyse would flee the colony; if so, Moyse was too stubborn to depart. During a conference at Héricourt Plantation, Christophe and Dessalines persuaded the general in chief that Moyse must be disposed of—Dessalines insisted that Toussaint must get rid of him altogether. Toussaint ordered Moyse's arrest and had him confined in the fort of Port de Paix. By that time all of his secretaries, aides, and junior officers had been executed for their part in the revolt—so Moyse was convicted on the testimony of these dead men. Brought before a firing squad, Moyse himself gave the order to fire.

This episode caused the violent deaths of the two men to whom Toussaint had probably been closest: Moyse and Bayon de Libertat. It also left a dangerous fault line in the reconstructed social fabric of the colony. The violence of the repression silenced Moyse's sympathizers, but it did not make them disappear.

Immediately after asserting control over Spanish Santo Domingo, when "from Cap Samana to Cap Tiburon the authority of the chief of the Blacks extended its sovereign power," Toussaint had hastened to secure his position politically by creating a constitution for the colony. In March 1801 a constitutional assembly, composed of representatives elected from the departments of the colony, convened; curiously, this body included no *nouveaux libres*. Moyse was elected, but refused to serve—an early harbinger of his discontent with Toussaint's consolidation of power.

Julien Raimond, experienced in diplomacy from his service on the various commissions and his long effort lobbying for rights for the *gens de couleur,* was a member of the assembly, along with two other colored men; the seven whites came from the *grand blanc* class, chief among them Bernard Borgella, the mayor of Port-au-Prince who had become part of Toussaint's inner circle. By May, the assembly had produced a succinct and lucid document of seventy-seven articles grouped in thirteen sections. The seventy-seventh article authorized Toussaint Louverture to put the constitution into practice right away, pending its approval by the French government.

Article 1, defining the territory of the colony, declares that Saint Domingue is "part of the French empire, but submitted to special laws."[26] The last phrase (aside from its echo of the home government's most recent pronouncement) had a disagreeable resonance; "special laws" in the past had permitted slavery as an exception to the Rights of Man. But Article 3 puts it very plainly: "Slaves cannot exist on this territory; servitude is abolished forever. All men are born, live and die free and French." The article goes on to outlaw racial discrimination of any kind, in terms of employment and under the law. Article 6 declared the "Catholic, Apostolic and Roman religion" to be the only faith recognized in Saint Domingue.

There follow several sections on morals and property rights, and a firm restatement of Toussaint's labor policy. Article 17 states, somewhat euphemistically: "The introduction of cultivators, indispensable to the reestablishment and growth of agriculture, will take place in Saint Domingue; the Constitution charges the governor to take appropriate measures to encourage and favor this augmentation of arms, to stipulate and balance the different interests, to assure and guarantee the respective engagements resulting from this introduction."[27] What "the introduction of cultivators" boiled down to was the importation of slaves. By the terms of Article 3, such arrivals would have to be freed as soon as they reached the colony, but the cloudy language about "engagements" suggests that some form of indentured servitude was being contemplated. Like the early rulers of Haiti who followed him, Toussaint was willing to participate in a one-way version of the slave trade in order to increase his workforce and his army. Perhaps he justified this dubious idea on the grounds that all slaves imported to Saint Domingue would, constitutionally, be freed there. Bunel was dispatched to Jamaica to purchase ten thousand slaves from the English (at the same time that he made sure that the constitution would not disturb Toussaint's arrangements with Maitland), and Corbett, the British agent at Port-au-Prince, was also discussing the importation of slaves with Toussaint.

In Article 28: "The Constitution names as Governor the citizen Toussaint Louverture, General in Chief of the Army of Saint Domingue, and in consideration of the important service he has rendered to the colony in the most critical circumstances of the Revolution, and by the wish of the grateful inhabitants, the reins of government are confided to him for the rest of his glorious life."[28] Article 29 says that future governors would be limited to a five-year term, renewable "by reason of his good administration," but Article 30 awards Toussaint the right to name his successor—in a secret document to be unsealed only "at the unhappy event of his death."[29] This clause looked a lot like a recipe for the foundation of a dynasty, but (since Toussaint's legitimate sons were young and inexperienced, and the older two were hostages in France) it functioned more as an apple of discord among the black officer corps. Toussaint might have chosen Moyse or Maurepas or Charles Belair or Christophe or Dessalines to succeed him; the secrecy of the succession was probably not the stabilizing element it was meant to be. In Article 31, whoever succeeded Toussaint Louverture was required to take an oath to "remain attached to the French government."[30]

It is commonly held that the Constitutional Assembly was no more than a puppet body, and that the constitution of 1801 was a de facto declaration of independence. Yet it seems more likely that the composition of the assembly reflected Toussaint's desire to produce a document that would be palatable not only to France but also to other powers closer by: the English colonies and the United States. Toussaint himself had no direct experience of the world beyond the shores of Hispaniola, but he made sure that the Constitutional Assembly was controlled by men well seasoned in foreign affairs. Despite the frequent insistence on loyalty and subordination to France, the imperial tendency of the document was unmistakable; the constitution gives Toussaint the dubious distinction of inventing the Haitian concept of rulership for life. And yet his counselors may have been sincere in advising him in that direction.

The notion of leadership for life was not so out of tune with the times as it might seem. In France, Napoleon was on a similar course, though he had not yet declared it. It was not so long since the United States had considered crowning George Washington its king. The American Federalist Alexander Hamilton suggested to Toussaint directly that he create "a life-long executive."[31] The civilized world had been deeply dismayed by the catastrophic instability of the various governments-by-committee spawned by the French Revolution; nostalgia for monarchy and/or military dictatorship was in the wind.

But proclaiming the constitution was an exceedingly dangerous move insofar as it concerned Toussaint's relations with France. Colonel Vincent, described by Pamphile de Lacroix as "one of the small number of Frenchmen who, while always faithful to the interests of the nation, had conserved the credibility and capacity to say everything to Toussaint Louverture," tried mightily to dissuade him. "Toussaint Louverture admitted to him that he was not able to reduce the gigantic momentum that had taken him over. A tremendous force seemed to be dragging him, and that force was occult."[32]

Vincent argued that, despite its protestations of fealty to France, the constitution drained all practical authority over Saint Domingue out of the French government. "He replied that the government would send commissioners to confer with him." At this, Vincent burst out, "Say rather that you want them to send you chargés d'affaires and ambassadors, as the Americans, the Spanish and the English will not fail to do." But what truly horrified Vincent was the discovery that Toussaint had already ordered the constitution to be printed and promulgated (according to Article 77) and evidently meant to present it to the French government as a fait accompli. "This conduct is terrible!" Vincent snapped[33]—a bold thing to say to a man who, despite their long friendship, had had him very roughly arrested on occasion and once subjected him to a mock execution.

Whatever spirit possessed Toussaint would not be gainsaid. He appointed Vincent as emissary to present his constitution to France— Vincent reluctantly accepted the mission. From the United States, where he stopped first, Vincent wrote a long letter to Toussaint, repeating several points from their earlier argument. Again he objected to "the proposed mode of government, which gives you for life an indefinite power—power which, contrary to all the principles most recognized by the French, is in some way hereditary in your hands. The choice of a government confided to the colony alone and to its Military officers, the nomination of all posts, civil and Military, given to the General-in-Chief, remain incomprehensible novelties which affect me most painfully; but when after careful study of every article of this astonishing production, I was able to convince myself that there exists for France no advantage over the other maritime nations." Here Vincent came to the point of Toussaint's own dilemma—how to maintain his complex trade agreements with Britain and the United States without fatally offending France by making it appear that France no longer had its customary trade rights in the colony it had created. "So then, Citizen General, you may be able to conceive as a possible thing that the Colony of Saint Domingue will be nothing more today than a colonial market where all the nations, with equal advantage, would exchange the objects of their industry! So then, the Commerce of France, to which immense sums are owed, would see the guarantee of its debt carried off by the Foreigner."

Vincent still hoped to dissuade Toussaint from what he believed to be a suicidal course, and writing from Virginia, he could probably speak more freely than when in Toussaint's presence in Le Cap. "No, Citizen General, you cannot think this way: the abyss which opens in front of you must frighten you; the good and estimable Toussaint, whom I have always cited as such, and who I want still to believe to be so, could never stray so far. He will not make himself the most guilty and ungrateful of men . . . How great and how worthy you still appear to me, my dear General! How much you may still be able to add to your glory! Continue to love your country and to serve it well; you have so often told me that you have no other ambition; it is effectively the only ambition you should have: your country is France, and not the isolated colony of Saint Domingue." In their last interview, Toussaint had reassured Vincent that independence was not his goal, but now Vincent had to warn him that he was making a very different impression in the United States: "They speak of nothing here but your declared independence. They call you, loudly, King of Saint Domingue."

Moreover, Vincent cautioned, the status Toussaint had given to British diplomats in the colony looked very bad from France, especially when Toussaint favored them over the French agent Roume (who at this time was confined in that Dondon chicken house): "Today the most terrible enemies of the Rights of Man and of France have their representatives, under the government of Toussaint, in the French colony where we have established liberty and equality for all men, principles against which they fight before your eyes, right next to you. Today the representative of France, the warmest friend of your rights, is disrespected under the government of Toussaint—what am I saying, 'disrespected'—it's apparent to all that he is under arrest!" If Toussaint was not seeking independence, that point would be difficult to prove, for those who accused him of that ambition could "produce to their advantage the greater part of your proclamations, where France is almost always forgotten; they will produce the greater part of your deeds, which too often disregard the interests of France; finally they will produce this constitution which will have been distributed everywhere . . . before my arrival, and which will be the despair of all those who have loved and courageously defended the oppressed men of Saint Domingue."[34]

Despite all this fervent pleading, Toussaint was set on his course. Instead of countermanding the constitution, he sent a second envoy to France to reinforce it, in case Vincent gave it an unfavorable presentation. If Vincent disliked Toussaint's drift toward military dictatorship, he probably didn't like the military dictatorship forming under Napoleon in France any better. Certainly it made an unfavorable climate for his mission—yet Vincent apparently did his best to put Toussaint's constitution in a positive light. Napoleon heard him out, then exiled him, though briefly, to Elba.

The constitution was a heavy weight to throw into the delicate balance of Napoleon's decision about how to handle the situation in Saint Domingue. By 1801, it was obvious to everyone that Napoleon and Toussaint had become military dictators of their respective countries, and surely they recognized each other as such. If Toussaint hoped that recognition would bring endorsement and support, he was to be disappointed.

Napoleon Bonaparte had come to power at the head of a conservative, though not explicitly royalist, backlash against the most radical extremes of the French Revolution. As a young officer, Napoleon was wont to absent himself without leave from the French army in order to participate in bootless rebellions in his native Corsica. In calmer times he might have been court-martialed and possibly shot for these derelictions, but revolutionary France, at war on practically all of its borders, was in desperate need of capable commanders, and Napoleon was certainly one of the best available. His ambition was also nakedly apparent: in 1791, War Commissioner Simon-Antoine Sucy commented, "I do not see him stopping short of either the throne or the scaffold."[35]

In 1791 the French throne was in serious jeopardy, though it had not yet been abolished. Louis XVI and his family, arrested in their attempt to flee France at Varennes, were now more or less prisoners of the National Assembly, and the cause of a constitutional monarchy was weakened. Napoleon Bonaparte threw his lot in with the republican side, with such fervor that people began to call him "the little Jacobin." The controversy over the fate of the king finally ended with his execution on January 21, 1793; the following month France, already at war with royalist regimes in Austria and Prussia, went to war with England, Holland, and Spain. In Paris, meanwhile, the National Convention (the legislative body which succeeded the National Assembly in September 1792) was in the final throes of a struggle between the comparatively moderate Girondins and the far left Montagnards. In June 1793 the Montagnards, under the leadership of Georges-Jacques Danton and Maximilien de Robespierre, purged the Girondins from the convention. Two months later the Reign of Terror was proclaimed, and the dread Committee of Public Safety, chaired by Robespierre, began sending a stream of suspect civilians to the guillotine.

The Terror was bloody but relatively short-lived; on July 27, 1794, Robespierre himself fell victim to the death machine he had designed. The Committee of Public Safety collapsed, along with the rest of the Terror's apparatus. During this same period, Napoleon Bonaparte, just twenty-five years old in 1794, had advanced in rank from captain to brigadier general. The new constitution of September 1795 replaced the Committee of Public Safety—which had turned into the chief executive organ of government—with a five-member Executive Directory, complemented by the 750-member legislature. On October 3, General Danican attempted a military coup against this fragile new government. General Napoleon Bonaparte, who happened to be in Paris at the time, put himself at the head of troops loyal to the government and repelled the coup. From this event he emerged a hero and won command of the Army of the Interior.

From 1795 to 1799 he led large-scale campaigns outside French borders, first in Italy, then in Egypt. In October 1799 he left his army in Egypt and returned to France. Fresh from a major victory at Aboukir, he was received with huge popular enthusiasm, but his reception by the increasingly shaky Directory was comparatively cool. The French economy was exhausted by a decade of war all over Europe, and the country was being strangled by a British naval blockade. A coalition of six nations threatened the French republic from without, and within there was a plot to overthrow the Directory and restore Louis XVIII to the throne.

In 1791, war minister La Tour du Pin, alarmed by a series of mutinies in the army, had warned against the threat of "this military democracy, a type of political monster that has always devoured the empires that created it." Eight years later, many had begun to believe that a military dictatorship offered the best chance of saving the republic. Napoleon's brother Lucien was a player in the conspiracy that put one in place. On November 9, 1799, Napoleon commenced what turned out to be an essentially bloodless coup (despite a good deal of scuffling and shots fired in the air) by announcing the dissolution of the Directory. The next day, the legislature appointed him as first among a three-member consulate in charge of the provisional government. As first consul, Napoleon Bonaparte became for all practical purposes the military ruler of France.

Napoleon was a self-invented and self-made man, in much the same style as the black general across the Atlantic Ocean in Saint Domingue, whom he was now obliged to study. Perhaps he was not flattered to see a version of himself in blackface there—though the oft-told tale that Toussaint provoked him with a letter addressed "To the First of the Whites from the First of the Blacks" appears to be false; no such document has ever been found. The view that Napoleon took of Toussaint in 1801 was in fact quite similar to the view that Toussaint was apt to take of the men against whom he had to measure himself: analytic, dispassionate, and often utterly ruthless.

In deciding whether to consider Toussaint Louverture as ally or adversary, Napoleon had many reports and opinions to digest. The extremes of the case were represented on the one hand by the French general Kerverseau, one of Toussaint's most hostile critics, and on the other by Colonel Vincent, one of Toussaint's closest white friends and one of his greatest supporters in the French camp. Kerverseau had made his first tour of Saint Domingue in 1796, soon after Toussaint was named lieutenant governor of the colony by Governor General Laveaux. Suspicious of Toussaint's elevation (and perhaps jealous of his status as second in command), in 1799 Kerverseau filed a memo with the French minister of marine, denouncing "the tricky genius, the hypocritical moderation, the real and pretended fanaticism, and the delirious vanity of the general Toussaint." Kerverseau went on to claim that Toussaint "loves mystery, requires a blind obedience, a devout submission to his will. He wants to govern the colony like a Capuchin convent . . . He loves to wrap himself in clouds; he only moves by night."[36]

In 1801, as Napoleon contemplated how best to deal with

Toussaint's ascendancy in Saint Domingue, Kerverseau filed a longer report, claiming that under the old colonial regime Toussaint had been regarded by Africans as a sort of magical being, but by most whites as an "energetic, industrious and honest person"—until the revolution "transported him into another sphere, giving wings to passions thus far enchained, and creating in him a new man." He belittled Toussaint's military ability, claiming that he "prays on the mountain while his soldiers fight on the plain."[37] More damningly, Kerverseau accused Toussaint of disregarding or subverting the authority of representatives of the French government to whom he should have been subordinate, and of making arrangements with the Americans and the British which might have been considered treasonable from the point of view of France. He singled out the better-known compliments of Toussaint's admirers, like Laveaux's hailing him as a "black Spartacus," for a contemptuous debunking. At the same time, Kerverseau could not always restrain himself from a grudging admiration: "in the particular relations I then had with him, I had often occasion to admire the justice of his judgment, the finesse of his repartee, and a combination of ideas truly astonishing to find in a man born and grown old in slavery, whose principal occupation for forty years had been the care of mules and horses, and the whole of whose studies had been limited to learning to read and to sign, but poorly, his name." But a few lines later he reminds himself and his readers that "we cannot forget that he was one of the principal authors of the disasters of the colony and one of the most notable chiefs of those bands of rebel Blacks who, dagger and torch in hand, made of the most opulent country in the universe a wasteland of desolation and grief."[38]

Colonel Vincent had served in Saint Domingue for ten years longer than Kerverseau, arriving as a brigadier general in 1786. Trained as an engineer, he was mainly responsible for the building of fortifications; his marriage to a Creole landowner rooted him in the colony. At an early date he became one of Toussaint's closest white confidants and advisers, and remained so to the bitter end. In 1799 he too had filed a memorandum with the French minister of marine: "The true leader of the colony, divisionary general and chief of all the armed forces, whom I should call to begin with truly illustrious, is Toussaint Louverture, by all measures a truly astonishing man, an unshakeable friend of France . . . the protector of Europeans and of all good men . . . Effectively, all must yield before the rare and healthy intelligence, the indefatigable zeal and the amazing level-headedness of this extraordinary man."[39] By 1801 his opinion of Toussaint had become somewhat more ambivalent, thanks to the arguments he and Toussaint had had over the constitution, but still he did his utmost to dissuade Napoleon from opposing Toussaint by force.

In his final exile on Saint Helena, Napoleon analyzed the matter thus:

> The prosperous situation in which the Republic found itself in the present of 1801, after the Peace of Lunéville, made already foreseeable the moment when England would be obliged to lay down her arms, and when we would be empowered to adopt a definitive policy on Saint Domingue. Two such presented themselves to the meditations of the First Consul: the first to clothe General Toussaint Louverture with civilian and military authority and with the title of Governor-General; to entrust command to the black generals; to consolidate and legalize the work discipline established by Toussaint, which had already been crowned by happy success; to require the black leaseholders* to pay a tax or a rent to the former French proprietors, to conserve for the metropole the exclusive right to trade with the whole colony, by having the coasts patrolled by numerous cruisers. The other policy consisted of reconquering the colony by force of arms, bringing back to France all the blacks who had occupied ranks superior to that of battalion chief, disarming the blacks while assuring them of their civil liberty, and restoring property to the [white] colonists. These projects each had advantages and inconveniences. The advantages of the first were palpable: the Republic would have an army of twenty-five to thirty thou-

---

*Meaning those who were operating the plantations of French colonists who had fled Saint Domingue.

sand blacks, sufficient to make all America tremble; that would be a new element of power and one that would cost no sacrifice, either in men or in money. The former landowners would doubtless lose three quarters of their fortune; but French commerce would lose nothing there, since it always enjoyed the exclusive trade privilege. The second project was more advantageous to the colonial landowners, it was more in line with justice; but it required a war which would bring about the loss of many men and much money, the conflicting pretensions of the blacks, the colored men, and the white landowners would always be an object of discord and an embarrassment to the metropole; Saint Domingue would always rest on a volcano: thus the First Consul was inclined toward the first policy, because that was the one that sound politics seemed to recommend to him—the one that would give more influence to his flag in America. What might he not undertake, with an army of the twenty-five to thirty thousand blacks, in Jamaica, the Antilles, Canada, the United States even, and the Spanish colonies?[40]

The wistful strains of hindsight suffuse these lines. If Napoleon had foreseen just how destructive the policy of retaking Saint Domingue by force of arms would turn out to be, he almost certainly would have adopted the option of conciliating the black leadership. He was too politically astute not to have seen, even as he made the decision to commit himself to the opposite course, what an extraordinary opportunity for expansion was the path of cooperating with Toussaint Louverture and his generals. Though in 1801 Napoleon had not yet crowned himself emperor, he already had an imperial bent, and the possibility of an imposing French empire in the New World was real. The army which Toussaint had forged was certainly the most formidable fighting force in the Caribbean, if not in the whole Western Hemisphere. That army might well have spread the abolition of slavery, under the flag and the liberating rhetoric of the French Revolution, all across the Spanish and French colonies of the Greater and Lesser Antilles and even into

Louisiana, which was then still a French possession. If it had done so, we would be living in a very different world today.

So very delicately balanced, Napoleon's decision finally tipped the wrong way. Many details of Toussaint's conduct in 1801 helped to turn the first consul against him, not to mention the pressure which the vociferous colonial lobby could bring to bear in Paris. Since in hindsight Napoleon saw plainly enough that the colonists were "almost all royalists and sold out to the English," it is something of a mystery how they were able to capture his attention at the time. Though the French Revolution had put him on the road to power, it was power pure and simple that interested Napoleon most of all.

In public he maintained an antislavery position, against the colonial lobby which clamored for the restoration of slavery in the colonies. But his private opinions were probably more ambivalent. Real racial egalitarians like the Abbé Raynal, the Abbé Grégoire, Brissot, and Sonthonax were comparatively rare even in the most left-leaning phases of the French Revolution; Napoleon likely shared the well-established European view of black Africans as something just a little less than human. He was recently married to Josephine Beauharnais, a Creole from Martinique, who had lost her family properties (at least for the moment) to the slave insurrection there. A famous courtesan long before she drew Napoleon into her sphere, Josephine undoubtedly had an unusual degree of influence on the first consul, and her sentiments were naturally in favor of the other dispossessed colonists of the French Caribbean islands.

By the fall of 1801, Napoleon had already been seriously provoked by the leak of Toussaint's treaties with the British and by his taking possession of the Spanish side of the island. In treating with the British Toussaint had usurped French national authority, and in occupying the former Spanish colony he had flouted direct orders from the home government. Napoleon quietly annulled the black occupation of Spanish Santo Domingo almost as soon as he learned of it, and in March 1801, Toussaint Louverture was secretly expunged from the rolls of the French army.

But Vincent's arrival in Paris was the last straw—as Vincent himself had predicted. "He was bearer," Napoleon recalled at Saint Helena, "of the Constitution which Toussaint had adopted on his sole authority, which he had had printed and put into execution and of which he now notified France. Not only the authority, but even the honor and dignity of the Republic were outraged: of all the ways of proclaiming his independence and raising the flag of rebellion, Toussaint L'Ouverture had chosen the most outrageous, the one which the metropole could least tolerate. From that moment on there was nothing more to deliberate; the chiefs of the blacks were ungrateful rebellious Africans, with whom it was impossible to establish a system. The honor, along with the interest of France, required that we make them go back into nothingness."[41]

That, however, was easier said than done.

Toussaint's motives during this period are somewhat obscure, but it seems plain enough that he did not really want to make Saint Domingue independent, for if he had he could well have done so. President John Adams of the United States supported the idea of independence. England, whose unease at the idea of a nation of free Africans so near to Jamaica was overbalanced by the tremendous damage to France that the loss of the colony would entail, would also have supported the move; there were even rumors that England secretly offered to endorse Toussaint's crowning himself king. Toussaint had told Vincent in their last interview, "I know that the English government is the most dangerous to me and the most perfidious to France" but "I need it."[42]

What Toussaint really hoped to achieve was a sort of commonwealth status for Saint Domingue: complete local autonomy combined with the protection of France in foreign affairs. By some analyses the fatal flaw of this conception was simply that it was too far ahead of its time. Toussaint's nearly successful effort to bring it about involved a judicious deployment of carrot and stick. The fat juicy carrot was the prospect he had persuasively demonstrated of restoring the vast prosperity of Saint Domingue for the benefit of France. Toussaint augmented that prospect by taking special pains to create a safe haven in his new society for the white planter class, even at the risk of alienating his black power base. The idea of equalized cooperation among the races, coupled with the prohibition of all racial discrimination in his constitution of 1801, was a good two hundred years ahead of its time.

But if Napoleon chose to decline the carrot, the stick was ready and waiting: an army over twenty thousand strong, backed by a population well armed and thoroughly determined to fight to the death for freedom.

In 1801 the dominoes began to fall in a direction unfavorable to the realization of Toussaint's hopes and dreams. In March of that year, Thomas Jefferson succeeded John Adams as U.S. president. A southern slaveholder, Jefferson was a solid supporter of the U.S. version of the ancien régime. From the very beginning, the liberation of the slaves of Saint Domingue had been a matter of tremendous anxiety for the southern states, whose political interest Jefferson was committed to defend. He must have viewed the meteoric rise of Saint Domingue's blacks to equality with some personal discomfort also. His own colored mistress, Sally Hemings, could obtain freedom only at the pleasure of her master, and under the American system both she and their children together were legally defined as Negroes, since no category for persons of mixed African and European blood officially existed.

In July 1801, President Jefferson let the French know that the United States was opposed to an independent black state in Saint Domingue and that it preferred the restoration of French authority there. Still more critically, peace negotiations that began in October led to an agreement that the British navy would not interfere with a French expedition to Saint Domingue.

Napoleon appointed Emmanuel Leclerc, his sister Pauline's husband, as captain general of the force sent to ensure respect for French authority—21,175 crack veterans from Napoleon's European campaigns. Fascinated by tales of Saint Domingue's wealth, the soldiers whiled away their passage by fashioning money belts to hide all the gold they expected to loot. Some cynics have reasoned that the first consul (who had won power through a military coup) wanted to get rid of these men, or at least prevent them from hanging idly around the capital; in the end most would die in the war against the blacks.

Certainly Napoleon did want to remove his sister Pauline—a famous beauty, adventuress, and all-around troublemaker—as far from Paris as possible. Initially reluctant, Pauline was coaxed with descriptions of how charming and seductive she could make herself appear in the tropical *déshabillé* popular in the colony; she embarked with her toddler son, Dermide, and a considerable entourage of servants and courtiers in a flagship specially refitted for her comfort. The fleet also carried Toussaint Louverture's elder sons, Placide and Isaac, with their tutor (a priest named Coisnon), and a boatload of Toussaint's mulatto adversaries who were returning from exile, including Rigaud, Pétion, and Villatte.

Colonel Vincent did not accompany the expedition. His defense of Toussaint's constitution had put him under a cloud, and he may have worsened his situation by filing a memorandum which argued that to regain control of Saint Domingue would be impossible, or, if by some remote chance it did succeed, not worth the terrible cost. He had no better luck persuading Napoleon to abandon the expedition than he'd had convincing Toussaint to abandon his constitution—though his warnings proved correct in both cases. However, Napoleon did recall Vincent from exile to make use of his very privileged knowledge of the situation in Saint Domingue, where he had for sixteen years been director of fortifications. And his confidential relationship with Toussaint meant that he had all sorts of valuable information about Toussaint's measures for defense.

Once he saw the expedition was inevitable, Vincent did all he could to ensure its success; it's clear that he hoped to regain the favor of the government in the process. He produced a checklist of dozens of men he knew in civil and military posts all over the country, with notes on their rank, their race, their character, and their most likely reaction to the appearance of this large French force. He furnished Captain General Leclerc with annotated maps and copious, detailed advice for his plan of attack. He sent a bundle of letters to men of all stations that he knew in the colony, in hopes of bringing about a peaceful reception for the French.

To Christophe, whom he thought likely to prove loyal to France when the chips came down, he wrote: "We count very much on your

Help, my dear General, for the success of this great enterprise,"[43] and exhorted him particularly to guarantee the security of Cap Français for the French. To Leclerc, Vincent mentioned that Christophe would probably be forced to show any letters he received to both Toussaint and Moyse. In his checklist Vincent described Moyse as "a wicked young man . . . and infinitely dangerous,"[44] but in his letter to him he said, "Let the brave men of Saint Domingue look with pleasure on the arrival of those who have only been sent to assure the rights of all . . . you can do a great deal, Citizen General, with the Spirit of your brothers, and my hope has always been that your conduct will assure the motherland of your obedience."[45] As it happened, Moyse was executed soon after Vincent wrote this letter, and long before it could reach him.

There was no letter for Dessalines, but in his notes Vincent observed that while the extent of that general's power should be greatly reduced, there was no one as efficient as he in getting work out of the blacks, so he ought, one way or another, to be retained in that role. To Pascal, now at the top of Toussaint's secretarial pool, he wrote, "It's up to you, who have the confidence of the General in Chief, to unite yourself with the Citizen Allier, whom I salute, to prevent Toussaint from straying."[46] At around the same time, Allier (another of Toussaint's white secretaries) wrote to his family in France that he was throwing in his lot with Toussaint forever and so must bid them forever adieu.

Because he had so staunchly defended Toussaint's loyalty to France, Vincent had a major personal interest in Toussaint's reaction to the expedition. "Through you," he wrote to the general in chief, "I may become the happiest or most unhappy of men." Before he left Saint Domingue, Vincent had perceived Toussaint to be in the grip of an "occult force"; now he tried addressing himself directly to Toussaint's guardian angel. "Let not your good (but always too defiant) Spirit conceive any anxiety over these great dispositions—they spring from the vast genius of the great man [Napoleon] who is directing everything. His character is to love everything that is great; I am sure that no one esteems you so much as he; he knows that you have done great things, that you have been humane and Generous; the Restorer of a France made larger by his works will never lose sight of one who, without (so to speak) receiving any help from the metropole, has nonetheless known how to chase her most dangerous enemies out of the Colony, and to conserve it for France; he could give you no more certain proof than to send the distinguished General who will command in Saint Domingue; he seems to have sought the surest way to reconcile himself with you in sending General Leclerc to the colony, who brings with him his young Wife, sister of the First Consul."[47]

These assurances were fundamentally false, though Vincent doubtless wanted to believe them. Most likely Toussaint never received this letter.

News of France's maritime peace with England unnerved Toussaint considerably, since it was certain to rattle his delicate balance among England, the United States, and France. When Bunel returned from Jamaica with news of the peace negotiations between France and England, Toussaint stopped Santo Domingo's press from publishing it, on the grounds that the news had not come through official channels. But the rumor spread all over the colony, particularly within the white planter class.

"Ill-wishers are spreading the noise that France is coming with thousands of men to annihilate the colony and liberty," Toussaint announced, rebuking those "who lend to the French government liberticide intentions, who claim that it doesn't want to send me my children because it wants to hold them as hostages." Toussaint refused to believe the rumors, or so he claimed, "but in the case that this injustice should be real, it suffices for me to tell you that there is only one thing left to do for a child whose father and mother are so unnatural as to want to destroy him, and that is to place his vengeance in the hands of God. I am a soldier, I don't fear men, I only fear God—if it is necessary to die, I will die as a soldier of honor who has nothing to reproach himself."[48] His mind was deeply divided in those days, between fading hopes for conciliation and the increasing probability of war.

Since putting down the Moyse rebellion, Toussaint had redoubled his measures to enforce internal security. He ordered investigations of all officers who had seemed sluggish in responding to the revolt. In Toussaint's view, idleness was the mother of rebellious tendencies; thus his work regulations became ever more strict. "As soon as a child is able to walk," he proclaimed, "he should be applied to some useful work proportionate to his strength." Dissipation, too, might foster rebelliousness, and in the same proclamation Toussaint insisted again that "marriage is the most holy of social institutions"[49] and promised to purge the military and civil service of all those who lived with concubines or with more than one woman at the same time. Women were no longer to be permitted in military barracks—a most unpopular edict. In Toussaint's mind, idleness, loose morals, and insubordination were all of a piece. These were the germs of the Moyse rebellion and he was determined to stamp them out.

Despite the catastrophic failure of that rebellion, small revolts continued to crop up among the African-born segment of the *nouveaux libres*. Lamour Dérance, a maroon leader who had never accepted the new national authority Toussaint was constructing, raided the town of Marigot on the south coast, and briefly threatened Jacmel, until Dessalines marched against him from Léogane. Lamour Dérance was driven back to the mountains, but Dessalines failed to capture him or destroy his forces.

On December 8, Toussaint ordered the public execution of twenty-three blacks who had been captured in the midst of Vodou ceremonies; these were always instrumental in stirring up revolutionary sentiment, especially among the African-born. The *houngans* and *mambos* who died had names like Saint Jean Père l'Eternité and Sainte Jésus Maman Bondieu. Dessalines had pushed for the executions, as a way of intimidating the cultivators of the Cul de Sac plain, and he was the one to carry them out. The victims were shot, then decapitated, to make doubly sure they were dead. One Jean Pimon died like a soldier who had nothing with which to reproach himself, remarking to Dessalines as he faced the guns: "Blan weté, Mulatre weté, si lautre weté, patat va abi."[50] This cryptic statement was understood to mean that if everyone turned on the ordinary blacks, the goose of general liberty would be cooked.

With the news of a French-English treaty on the wind, Toussaint was rushing to bring the thirteen demibrigades of his army to full strength at fifteen hundred each. With the addition of his honor guard, his force would reach twenty-five thousand; the military budget was

35 million livres. More field hands were drafted into the army, and some of the guns that had been distributed to civilians were now appropriated for use by the military. Recruits now included boys between the ages of eight and twelve. At Saint Marc, Dessalines shot two children, eight and nine years old, when they resisted this draft.

Toussaint's strategy involved the fortification of the most inaccessible points of the mountainous interior, where European troops would be most challenged, exhausted, and bewildered, and where Toussaint's fusion of conventional European tactics with African-style guerrilla warfare would work to best advantage. He closed off most of the roads and passes into the interior to all but the military, in part to block random migration of fugitive field hands into the formerly Spanish territory but still more to conceal his war preparations from all but his own soldiers. The area of the Cordon de l'Ouest, now reorganized as the Canton Louverture and embracing Toussaint's personal stronghold at Ennery, was sealed in this way, along with another region further to the south, at the end of the Cahos mountain range overlooking the Artibonite River.

Unfortunately for the secrecy of Toussaint's war plan, Colonel Vincent had personally supervised most of the fortifications all over the colony, was well acquainted with the black army's various headquarters and habits of moving between them, and knew Toussaint well enough that he could predict preparations and maneuvers he had not seen with his own eyes. Much of the information he furnished Leclerc was based on direct observation, but a lot of his guesswork also proved accurate.

Vincent foresaw that the most dangerous theater of war would be a very sizable region of the interior whose limits were, to the north, the mountain towns of Vallière, Dondon, and Marmelade; to the east, Hinche on the Central Plateau; to the southeast, Mirebalais; with a line west of Mirebalais along the Artibonite River to the region of Petite Rivière at the westernmost extension of the Cahos mountain range. He knew that Toussaint had secretly built a road for supply wagons from Dondon to several of these other interior points, many of which lay along the original frontier between the French and Spanish colonies. He knew that Toussaint had long maintained a headquarters at Boché

Plantation just outside Marmelade, and he expected—correctly, as it turned out—that the blacks would have cached much of their ammunition there and also along the Ravine à Couleuvre, a long, deep defile which provided a route from Hinche and the Central Plateau to the main road a few miles south of Gonaïves.

The black army would certainly have placed cannon in the forts of this broad area, but Vincent was confident that the cannon would not be very well positioned and that the skills of the artillerymen would be poor. He recommended that the French land in force on the Spanish side of the island, secure Hinche, and use that town as a base for attacking the rest of Toussaint's positions in the interior from the rear. At the same time it would of course be necessary to take the significant ports on the coast, Le Cap, Port-au-Prince, and Gonaïves—but Vincent believed it essential to have a substantial French force already present on the Central Plateau, threatening the whole mountainous region along the old frontier, where Toussaint's army would have planned its retreat from the coasts.

All these measures were to be undertaken if, and only if, diplomacy failed. Vincent had put as much energy into the diplomatic strategy as into the military one.

Toussaint had his own informants in France, and he knew that a fleet was being outfitted for a vast expedition. Even to the last minute he may have hoped that this operation was another decoy, for the last fleet that had set out with published orders for Saint Domingue had sailed instead, on secret orders, for Egypt. It was still just barely possible that the French would accept the nice carrot he was offering, and spare him the necessity of using his stick. Once the fleet had left port, Toussaint had no reliable news of it during the several weeks it took to cross the Atlantic.

Though he had now taken control of Spanish Santo Domingo, his troops there were thinly spread, and this eastern area of Hispaniola remained the most likely point for an invasion. Toussaint embarked on a tour of his positions there, but he had not gone very far before he was overtaken by messengers from General Christophe, warning him that

French warships had been sighted. He hastened to Point Samana, the easternmost extremity of the island, expecting that the fleet would make its first landfall there.

There were sixty-seven ships in all, and when Toussaint got his first sight of them from the rocky heights of Point Samana, he quailed for an instant. "We'll all have to die," he told his officers. "All France has come to Saint Domingue."[51] He may have meant the last part literally. French Saint Domingue was approximately the size of Vermont, and Toussaint, who had spent his whole life on the island, had no way of conceiving just how big France really was. But he had known that the fleet was almost certain to come, and for months he had been making ready to meet it. Within minutes he had recovered his fortitude and was dispatching messengers to activate the defense.

During the Atlantic crossing, the squadrons of the French fleet had been scattered by storms. A couple of these were waiting off Point Samana by the time Leclerc himself arrived there. Though other ships were yet to come, the captain general knew that he must have been observed and did not want to give Toussaint too long to prepare his response. The fleet moved clockwise around the island, detaching forces to occupy various points along the way.

Vincent's extremely detailed campaign plan had less influence than the grand strategy which had been designed in advance by Napoleon: General Kerverseau was to land at Ciudad Santo Domingo, General Darbois on the south coast of the Grande Anse, and General Boudet at Port-au-Prince. On February 2, Leclerc's own squadron appeared at the mouth of the Cap Français harbor. A smaller squadron carrying General Donatien Rochambeau and the troops of his command sailed on to Fort Liberté.

Notwithstanding their reputations for military success, both Napoleon Bonaparte and Toussaint Louverture preferred to settle conflicts by diplomacy if possible; neither liked to spend men and matériel for nothing, and both preached against useless bloodshed (with some real sincerity). Leclerc's instructions were to try the diplomatic route first. He had been furnished with proclamations from Napoleon insisting that the French army had arrived to defend and guarantee the freedom of the blacks—not, as everyone suspected, to restore slavery.

Coisnon, with Isaac and Placide Louverture, was supposed to have been transferred to a small, fast boat that would have put him in Saint Domingue several days ahead of the main fleet. He would have delivered reassuring communications from Napoleon, including a letter from the first consul to Toussaint. Vincent wrote a letter of introduction intended to serve as a safe-conduct for Coisnon anywhere in the colony, addressed to whomever it might concern but full of beguiling references to the general in chief (for Vincent suspected that Coisnon would have trouble meeting in person with Toussaint, who might prefer to deal with him through cat's-paws like Christophe). If possible, the priest was also meant to deliver Vincent's letters to Toussaint, Christophe, Moyse, and the Frenchmen in Toussaint's inner circle. Coisnon had the most delicate task of persuading Toussaint to accept the arrival of Captain General Leclerc without a struggle. In this scenario, Leclerc's role was simply to take over Toussaint's command.

But Toussaint had had no military superior in the colony since Laveaux. Sonthonax, Hédouville, and the almost completely disempowered Roume had played the part of the civilian intendant established in the prerevolutionary colonial structure. Toussaint had known how to outmaneuver all of them. By the end of 1801, the military had completely usurped civilian power in Saint Domingue. The shoes that Toussaint was filling had been left vacant by Galbaud and then by Laveaux. France had given him the rank of general in chief. His own constitution proclaimed him governor for life, and the citizens of Saint Domingue had begun to address him as such (reminded, sometimes, by the flats of his honor guard's swords). Still, it was not much more than a year since he had told Laveaux of his wish for a single European chief in the colony. There was just a chance that he might be persuaded to accept Leclerc as such.

Coisnon had a tricky and dangerous mission, as Vincent could testify from his own recent experience. His best protection would have been the trust and affection of his students, Isaac and Placide, and Toussaint's presumed happiness in seeing his sons again. But as it happened, Coisnon and the young men were not sent in advance of the fleet after all, whether because the rough weather during the crossing prevented it, or because Leclerc was too proud to temporize with the black rebels. The priest and Toussaint's sons were still with Leclerc's squadron when it hove to at the mouth of the Cap Français harbor, and Leclerc seemed in no hurry to send them ashore.

The buoys marking the safe channel through the reefs into the harbor had been removed. Leclerc's admiral, Villaret-Joyeuse, could not bring his warships into port without the help of local pilots. Emissaries landed in a small boat, requesting that the town's commander, General Christophe, assist their landing.

Christophe, like Toussaint, had been a free man before 1791. In his early days he had seen something of the world as the slave of an English sea captain, and he had attended the battle of Savannah with the other French colonial forces there. He had been an important commander in the civil war with Rigaud and the mulattoes, though not quite so important as Dessalines. So long as Moyse enjoyed Toussaint's favor, Christophe's command was limited to the immediate area of Le Cap, but Moyse's death had expanded his power all over the north of the colony.

Both Vincent and Roume (who had recently arrived in the United States and was filing his reports from there) believed that Christophe would be loyal to France rather than Toussaint if it came to a choice between them. According to Roume, Christophe had told him that Toussaint would have to be "not only an atrocious scoundrel, but also stupid or out of his mind if he wanted to betray France to ally himself with England and make himself independent."[52] Roume claimed that Christophe had accepted from Toussaint his promotion to brigadier general only because he thought he would be shot if he refused. To Forfait, the minister of marine, Roume offered to use his own influence to get Christophe to betray Toussaint. Vincent, meanwhile, wrote to Leclerc that "we can count on Christophe at least at the moment of the appearance of our forces; I worked toward that idea for a year before my departure."[53] Apparently Vincent believed he had a secret understanding with Christophe that he would preserve Le Cap and turn it over to the French, if it should come to that. If Coisnon's effort to persuade Toussaint failed, phase two of his mission (more hazardous still) was to turn other black leaders against Toussaint, especially Christophe and perhaps Dessalines.

Coisnon, however, remained shipboard. When other messengers from the fleet reached him, Christophe stalled, replying to Leclerc that he could not receive the French army without instruction from Governor General Toussaint Louverture—who supposedly was nowhere to be found.

Toussaint's movements during these first days of the invasion are occluded. By his own generally disingenuous account written in the Fort de Joux, Le Cap was already burning by the time he got his first glimpse of the situation from the height of Grand Boucan. However, almost a week elapsed between Leclerc's first landfall at Point Samana and his landing in force at Le Cap on February 4, and Toussaint, renowned for the speed of his movement, would hardly have taken so long to cover the distance between those two points. Leclerc's messenger noticed that during their parleys General Christophe stood near the cracked door of an inner office, and suspected that Christophe's responses were controlled by someone on the other side. Vincent had predicted that such would be the case—that Toussaint would try to manipulate Christophe without showing his hand to the French, and that under Toussaint's close surveillance, Christophe would not be able to act freely.

Leclerc sent a testy letter to Christophe (whom the civilian authorities and numerous whites in the town were imploring not to oppose the French landing), advising him that eight thousand men were landing at Port-au-Prince and four thousand at Fort Liberté,* and summoning him to surrender the harbor forts immediately. Christophe's reply was intransigent: "You will not enter the city of Le Cap before it has been reduced to ashes, and even on the ashes I will fight you still."[54]

Rochambeau, an undiplomatic individual whom a later phase of the invasion would prove to be alarmingly sadistic as well as hotheaded,

---

*These numbers were probably exaggerated for effect. Much of Leclerc's army had not yet completed the Atlantic crossing. Rochambeau's force at Fort Liberté, for example, was probably nearer two thousand than four thousand.

forced the issue on February 2 by attacking the harbor posts at Fort Liberté, not troubling himself with any peaceful preliminaries. Toussaint's concluding remark at Point Samana had been "France is deceived; she comes to defend herself and enslave the blacks."[55] In the same spirit, the defenders of Fort Liberté shouted, "Down with the whites! Down with slavery!" The battle was bloody, and cost the life of at least one noble French officer. Rochambeau butchered all the prisoners he took. Once this news reached Le Cap there was no turning back and the war was on.

On February 4, Leclerc sailed with General Hardy and a detachment of troops for a landing at Limbé, west of Morne du Cap on the Baie d'Acul, hoping that a convergence movement on Cap Français might also preserve the rich plantations of the Northern Plain. On the road toward the town this detachment met stubborn resistance, commanded in person, according to one of Hardy's memos, by Toussaint Louverture (whose presence at this place and date suggests that he might well have been in Cap Français earlier, directing Christophe and stalling for time). In town, as the French forced their way ashore, Christophe set an example by setting fire to his own magnificent residence with his own hands. Soon the whole town, so recently restored from the disaster of 1793, was again ablaze. A doleful procession of civilian refugees climbed to the height of Morne Lavigie to watch the conflagration. Christophe did not offer battle on the scale that he had promised, but instead (probably in obedience to Toussaint's recent order and certainly in conformity with Toussaint's overall strategy) preserved his demibrigade by retreating. On February 6, Leclerc's force, marching north from Limbé, joined one of Rochambeau's columns crossing the plain from Fort Liberté, and the next day Leclerc entered Le Cap to find that Christophe had kept the first part of his vow: the town was nothing but a smoldering ruin.

There were others besides Vincent who had tried to dissuade Napoleon from the invasion; a colonist named Page had warned him, "You will throw eight thousand men into Saint Domingue; they will take up their positions; doubtless Louverture will not have the impudence to fight them; he will retreat into the mountains and leave them to be consumed

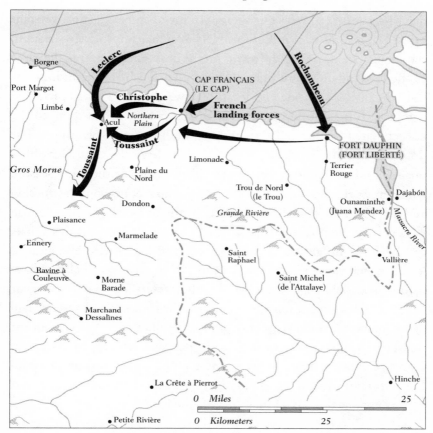

LeClerc's Attack on Cap Français, February 4–6, 1802

by the temperature of the towns and the want of fresh provisions."[56] And in an amiable postmortem talk with Pamphile de Lacroix, Christophe remarked that the black resistance should have "known how to fly when it was best, and cover its retreat with deserts it leaves behind it . . . If instead of fighting, our system of resistance had consisted in running and in alarming the Blacks, you would never have been able to touch us. Old Toussaint never stopped saying so; no one wanted to believe him. We had arms; our pride in using them ruined us."[57]

"Old Toussaint's" strategy for resistance and his explicit orders in the first days of the invasion were close to what Page and Christophe described. Though his army was well-seasoned, determined, and confident, he was indeed wary of risking it in the open field against veterans of the Napoleonic wars in Europe. His preference was to deny terrain to the enemy by destroying the towns on the coast and scorching the earth of the lowlands, then to fight a war of attrition from the mountains until the invasion buckled under its own weight (as Page had predicted it must). Toussaint had seen what the fever season had done to the unacclimated English invaders and had nothing against letting disease do as much of his work as possible. A February 7 letter to Dessalines put it vividly: "Do not forget that while waiting for the rainy season, which must rid us of our enemies, we have no recourse but destruction and fire. Consider that the land bathed with our sweat must not furnish our enemies the least nourishment. Jam up all the roads, throw horses and corpses into all the springs; have everything burned and annihilated, so that those who come to return us to slavery will always have before them the image of the hell that they deserve."[58]

Dessalines was supposed to burn Port-au-Prince, and Toussaint had sent similar orders to his other commanders all over the colony, but the first French movements were so swift, determined, and effective that many of his messengers were intercepted. The courier to Paul Louverture in Ciudad Santo Domingo had actually been given two letters, a false one directing him to receive the French and a true one commanding him to destroy the town and retreat. The French picked off this courier, presented the false letter, and occupied Santo Domingo without firing a shot. In Santiago to the north, the priest Mauviel had been rusticating since Toussaint changed his mind about installing him as bishop of the Le Cap cathedral. He persuaded Santiago's mulatto commander, Clervaux, to yield to the French without a struggle. Thus Toussaint almost immediately lost all the key points he had been at such pains to secure in the Spanish part of the island.

In the west, there were other disasters. Dommage, a trusted commander at Jérémie, failed to receive Toussaint's dispatch. Persuaded by Napoleon's proclamation,* he turned over the town to the French and

---

*"The government sends you the Captain General Leclerc; he brings with him great forces to protect you against your enemies and the enemies of the Republic. If anyone tells you: these forces are destined to ravish away your liberty, reply, the Republic will not suffer that it should be taken from us, *etc.*" (Madiou II, p. 173).

gave them a firm foothold on the Grande Anse. Laplume, who was similarly seduced and may also have been disaffected since the suppression of the Moyse rebellion, disobeyed the order to burn Les Cayes and the surrounding area, and instead offered his services to the French.

When Toussaint launched his couriers from Point Samana, Dessalines was absent from Port-au-Prince. In his place the white General Agé commanded, at least in name—a local cynic reported that Agé was constantly drunk and knew more about houses where he could get free libations than he did about his own officer corps. When General Boudet landed his messengers, Agé secretly let them know that he had no real power in the situation; actual authority lay with his nominal subordinate, the mulatto Lamartinière. It was Lamartinière who arrested Boudet's messengers, who were held as hostages for the next several weeks.

Misled by pride in his arms, Lamartinière thought he could hold the town without burning it. A couple of days' temporizing gave Boudet time to organize a successful attack on February 5, the day after the forced landing at Le Cap. Lamartinière had threatened to massacre the white population if Boudet tried to fight his way ashore, but about half of them hid in their houses and came out later to welcome the French soldiers after Boudet had secured the town. Lamartinière's attempt to blow up the arsenal failed. At Savane Valembrun, on the site where one of "Papa Doc" Duvalier's most notorious prisons would later stand, he executed the whites he had been able to capture, then retreated to Croix des Bouquets.

The first week of hostilities left both sides in a state of shock. The French were stunned by the destruction of Le Cap and by anarchy all over the Northern Plain, where the field hands had uncached their guns and begun to burn, pillage, and slaughter the white population. (Old friend to liberty though he was, the Abbé Delahaye was among the slain.) For his part, Toussaint must have been rattled by the speed and extent of his losses and by the betrayals of so many of his officers. In a week's time the invasion had practically reduced him to his original "arrondissement" in the Cordon de l'Ouest.

Around Port de Paix, on the Atlantic coast west of Le Cap, General

Maurepas was putting up a brilliant resistance to an assault led by the French general Humbert. Port de Paix was so well defended that Vincent had warned Leclerc that it was not worth the danger and difficulty of attacking it and that the artillery defending the harbor was exceptionally well placed. Maurepas, whom Vincent characterized as "extraordinarily hard,"[59] killed a third of Humbert's twelve hundred men before blowing up the forts, setting the town on fire, and retreating up the valley of Trois Rivières with his Ninth Regiment still intact.

But for the moment Toussaint was out of communication with Maurepas. When Leclerc decided to revert to diplomacy, Toussaint was willing to entertain the idea. Belatedly, Coisnon got the chance to try his hand.

Toussaint had gone to ground at Ennery, a secure pocket in the mountains just northeast of Gonaïves where he and his wife owned several plantations. Ennery was a crossroads controlling not only the ways to the Gonaïves port but also the length of the Cordon de l'Ouest via Marmelade to Dondon, the way to Borgne via the heights of Limbé and Port Margot, and the way to Port de Paix via Gros Morne. On the night of February 8, Toussaint's sons, twenty-one-year-old Placide and twenty-year-old Isaac, arrived there with their tutor, Coisnon. It had been almost six years since their parents had seen them; their reunion was a tearful one.

Some effort had been spent on cementing the young men's loyalty to France. Before the fleet sailed, they had been entertained by Napoleon Bonaparte in person: a grand dinner at the Tuileries, where Colonel Vincent, Captain General Leclerc, and other dignitaries were among the guests. After presenting Isaac and Placide with fancy dress uniforms and richly ornamented swords and pistols, Napoleon charged them with a message: "When you arrive in your country, you will make it known to your father that the French government accords him protection, glory and honor, and that it is not sending an army into the country to battle him, but only to make the French name respected against enemies of the country."[60]

Placide, who had not long before been used as a decoy by Napoleon—he had embarked on an Egypt-bound ship to make observers and spies believe the fleet was sailing for Saint Domingue— seems to have taken these instructions with a grain of salt. At Ennery, it was Isaac who presented Napoleon's argument. "While he spoke, Toussaint kept the most profound silence; his features no longer had the expression of a father who listened; they expressed the withdrawal of an impassive Statesman."[61] Whereupon Coisnon presented the letter which Napoleon had written to Toussaint. This missive, both firm and friendly in tone, announced that Captain General Leclerc was to be appointed as "first magistrate" of the country—a position superior to Toussaint's. It reminded the black leader that Leclerc came with "sufficient forces to make the sovereignty of the French people respected." It hoped that "you are going to prove to us the sincerity of the sentiments you have constantly expressed in all the letters which you have written to us." After an equivocal discussion of the Constitution (extremely mild by comparison with Napoleon's real opinion of that document) the letter comes to the point: "What can you desire? The liberty of the blacks? You know that in all the countries we have been, we have given it to the peoples who didn't have it. Consideration, honors and fortune? After all the services you rendered, which you will still render under present circumstances, and with the special feelings we have for you, you should not be uncertain of your consideration, your fortune and the honors that await you."[62]

These honeyed phrases were false to the bone. Napoleon was already resolved to reduce Toussaint and other black leaders "to nothingness." Leclerc had secret orders to arrest and deport the black officers as soon as feasible, and the restoration of slavery in Saint Domingue was part of the hidden agenda.

Toussaint thanked Coisnon for his care of his sons, and told him briefly that he would not treat with Leclerc until the latter had stopped his offensive movements. He spent the rest of the night composing a reply to the captain general, then rode down to Gonaïves to attend mass there, on the morning of February 9. On his return to Ennery he sent Coisnon and his sons back to Le Cap with his reply to Leclerc.

Soon after, his wife arrived in Ennery, with a pack train bearing the treasuries of Arcahaie, Saint Marc, Verrettes, Petite Rivière, and Gonaïves. Toussaint had a plan to combine all the funds of the various towns into a single war chest if an invasion did come, but he was on the wrong side of the island at the critical moment when the fleet arrived, and the speed of their operations allowed the French to capture some of this money right away. In the many areas where the local commanders decided for whatever reason to yield to the French without a fight, the local operating funds were lost.

Toussaint's reply reproached Leclerc for opening hostilities before delivering Napoleon's letter to him; he was already thinking in terms of a subsequent legal defense. Otherwise, he temporized, asking for a truce and for time to reflect and to pray that there would be no more unnecessary "effusion of blood."[63] This letter threw Leclerc into a rage. He denounced Toussaint as a rebel in the presence of Isaac, Placide, and his aides-de-camp. When he had calmed down he drafted a reply offering a two-day armistice, stating that if Toussaint acknowledged his authority Leclerc would accept him as his second in command, but if he had not done so in two days' time he would be declared an outlaw and "devoured by the vengeance of the Republic."[64]

For the third time in as many days, Isaac and Placide crossed the dizzying peaks of the mountains separating Le Cap from Gonaïves; this time Coisnon was too exhausted to accompany them. At the Gonaïves headquarters, Toussaint told his sons what would become the kernel of his defense from the Fort de Joux: "My children, I declare war on General Leclerc but not on France; I want him to respect the Constitution that the people of Saint Domingue have given themselves." Somewhat more recklessly, he added, "I cannot deal with the First Consul, since he has shredded the act which guarantees our liberties"[65]—a statement which shows that Toussaint had plainly detected the attitude Napoleon meant to conceal.

Then he asked his sons to choose a side, promising, "I will use neither ruse nor violence to keep you with me."[66] Isaac, the younger, was the first to reply: "You see in me a faithful servant of France, who could never resolve himself to bear arms against her." Placide, who may or may not have been Toussaint's blood son, said, "I am with you, my father, I fear the future, I fear slavery, I am ready to fight to oppose myself to it, I know nothing more of France."[67] Placide was promptly incorporated into Toussaint's honor guard. Toussaint announced to that elite group and its officers, "He is prepared to die for our cause"—the guardsmen had already declared, "We will all die for liberty."[68] Isaac did not return to Leclerc, but remained with his mother and his younger brother, Saint-Jean; he observed much of what followed as a noncombatant.

On February 17, Leclerc issued a proclamation outlawing the generals Toussaint and Christophe, but not the other black officers or soldiers of Toussaint's army, who were told that they would be incorporated into the French forces if they chose to change sides. A similar amnesty was offered to the revolting field hands; if they laid down their arms they would be treated as "stray children,"[69] and sent back to their plantations. General Leclerc declared that he was entering the campaign in person and that he would not take his boots off until Toussaint had been brought to submission. If he was faithful to this vow, he must have ended—three months later—with a pair of very smelly feet.

Dessalines, whose ability to move men swiftly over difficult terrain was equal to Toussaint's, was at large with his portion of the army in the area surrounding Port-au-Prince. Though he was not able to destroy the capital he kept it in a constant state of alert, while at the same time controlling Saint Marc (where he had built a fine house), threatening Léogane, and terrorizing the plantations in the plain of Cul de Sac. On the Atlantic coast west of Cap Français, Maurepas had regrouped in the hills above Port de Paix and reinforced himself with several thousand armed field hands. He would have retaken the town if a naval cannonade had not turned back his freshened forces.

On February 19, Leclerc launched a three-pronged attack intended either to surround Toussaint at Ennery or to force him out to the coast at Gonaïves. With General Hardy, Leclerc began a march south from Cap Français. Rochambeau was leading a column southwest from Fort Liberté toward Ennery and Gonaïves via Saint Raphaël and the Central Plateau. Boudet marched north from Port-au-Prince.

Leclerc's strategy did not follow Vincent's recommendations in every detail: he had allowed four hundred of Humbert's troops to be killed at Port de Paix, and the remaining eight hundred were tied up in a sideline struggle with Maurepas and the Ninth Regiment. And he had not brought his troops from the Spanish side to occupy Hinche and other key points along the old border where Toussaint's line of retreat could be cut off. Rochambeau's column cut a swath across the Central Plateau, but simply passed over this territory without firmly occupying it.

At this point, however, Toussaint was not contemplating a wholesale retreat to the interior. He was determined to hold Gonaïves, the seaport he felt best able to defend, if at all possible, but at the same time he had to meet the threat from Rochambeau. In these early days of the invasion, Napoleon's crack veterans were living up to their big reputation—moving rapidly, careless of the discouraging terrain, and proving themselves very difficult to stop or slow down. Leclerc's advance put such pressure on Ennery that Toussaint was compelled to send his family to a more secure area south of Gonaïves; nevertheless, Hardy's vanguard captured his youngest son, Saint-Jean, during the family's retreat. Isaac, Suzanne, and a handful of nieces and cousins found shelter at Lacroix Plantation.

Toussaint had arms depots and entrenchments along the Ravine à Couleuvre, which winds from the heights of Morne Barade down to Lacroix and Périsse plantations, on the dry edge of the Savane Désolée some seven miles south of Gonaïves. Barade was a dangerous crossroads for Toussaint—his brother Pierre had been killed there during the trouble with Biassou in 1794—and he was determined to reach it before Rochambeau. The race was a close one, for Vincent had told Leclerc of the importance of this position, and Rochambeau had recruited a traitor from Toussaint's army to guide him.

The relative strength of the forces that met at Ravine à Couleuvre is hard to ascertain. Rochambeau had probably landed about eighteen hundred men at Fort Liberté, but some had been diverted from his march on Gonaïves. By some accounts Toussaint was moving with no more than four hundred men of his guard; others say he had as many as three thousand regular troops. By all accounts there was a larger number of armed cultivators already waiting to support him in the ravine.*

---

*In the Fort de Joux memoir Toussaint claims to have made this march with just three hundred grenadiers and sixty cavalrymen, and to have learned from prisoners that Rochambeau's force was four thousand strong. Both sides, however, were inclined to exaggerate enemy strength and minimize their own in their reporting.

Aside from the urgency of the purely military objective, Toussaint was also under pressure to defend his family, thinly sheltered at Lacroix Plantation just to his rear.

Heavy rain on February 20 slowed the French advance; nevertheless Rochambeau managed to occupy the heights of Morne Barade on the night of February 22, hours or minutes before Toussaint arrived there. The battle began in the darkness; by daybreak the French had forced the defenders out the bottom of the ravine onto the flat ground of Périsse Plantation. Here Toussaint was able to rally his honor guard cavalry and organize a desperate charge which scattered the French and drove Rochambeau's men back into the mouth of Ravine à Couleuvre.

That same morning, General Vernet was retreating, inch by inch, before Leclerc and Hardy's advance on Gonaïves. Toussaint, exhausted and frustrated by the outcome at Ravine à Couleuvre, rode his horse into the town's cathedral and tore down the cross, shouting that he would no longer serve this Jesus who had betrayed him. A more warlike spirit had apparently mounted his head. Gonaïves could not be held, but Leclerc found the town in ashes, as he had found Le Cap. Toussaint, now collapsing with fever as well as exhaustion, rode south to Pont d'Ester, where his family and army were waiting.

Ravine à Couleuvre was a loss for both sides. Toussaint had not been able to hold key terrain, but he had gotten away with his army more or less intact. According to a report Leclerc filed a couple of days later, six hundred of his men had been killed outright and thirty-five hundred wounded. The French were able to win engagements, but establishing real control over the country was a different and much more difficult matter.

For Toussaint, the worst consequence—the one he most feared—of the drawn battle at Ravine à Couleuvre and the loss of Gonaïves was being completely cut off from Maurepas and the Ninth Regiment at Port de Paix. Now Leclerc was able to support Humbert and his detachment (which had been taking a beating from Maurepas since their landing) by sending reinforcements toward Port de Paix via Gros Morne (another route which Vincent had explained to him). At around the same time Maurepas received inaccurate but disheartening news that Toussaint had been completely demolished at Ravine à Couleuvre.

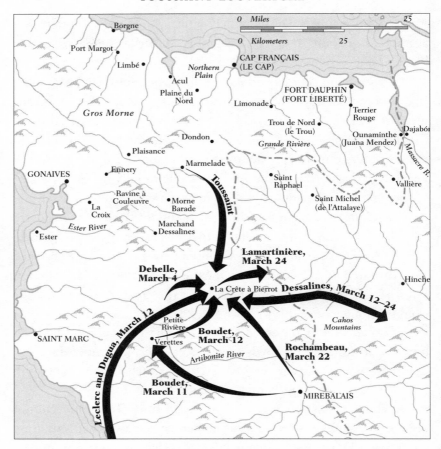

La Crête á Pierrot, March 4–24, 1802

Still worse, a rebel commander of the Ninth, Lubin Golart (who had sided with Rigaud during the mulatto-black civil war), attacked him from the direction of Jean Rabel. Surrounded by three hostile forces and out of communication with his commander, Maurepas surrendered to Leclerc on February 25.

Dessalines, meanwhile, had been playing cat and mouse with Boudet since the latter's landing at Port-au-Prince two weeks earlier. On February 24 he slaughtered all the whites of Saint Marc and set the town afire, beginning with his own opulent residence, as Christophe had done at Le Cap. Boudet rushed to the rescue but arrived too late, and while the French general stared aghast at the hundreds of scorched corpses in the ashes of Saint Marc, Dessalines slipped south to his rear. He would have succeeded in destroying Port-au-Prince this time if Pamphile de Lacroix, commanding during Boudet's absence, had not hastily enlisted the aid of two large maroon bands led by Lafortune and Lamour Dérance, both disaffected by Toussaint's harsh labor policy and the severe repression of the Moyse rebellion. Lamour Dérance, who had been skirmishing with Dessalines before the French invasion, was willing to accept the enemy of his enemy as his friend.

Dessalines doubled back across the plain of Cul de Sac, razing the plantations and rounding up white prisoners. On February 28, he met Toussaint above the town of Petite Rivière, on a hilltop called La Crête à Pierrot. A fort begun there by the British had once been under the command of Blanc Cassenave. Later on, Toussaint had completed the fortifications, with the help of a French engineer. The hilltop, tucked in a bend of the Artibonite River, controlled the passes into the Grand Cahos mountains and access to the Mirebalais area and the Central Plateau from Arcahaie and Saint Marc on the coast. The fort, which was hardly a hundred yards square and armed with only twelve cannon, was the centerpiece of the second phase of Toussaint's defense.

As Cap Français was for the time being uninhabitable, Leclerc established a temporary headquarters in Port-au-Prince. Among the surviving white population, the first flush of enthusiasm for the French arrival was rather quick to fade. Though glad to be relieved of the more tyrannical aspects of Toussaint's rule, the proprietors of Port-au-Prince were concerned that the French army might treat them and their territory not as fellow citizens and French ground to be defended, but as a conquered land to be exploited and looted. Napoleon's armies had formed such habits all over Europe, and stories of their predatory style had already circulated in Saint Domingue.

To a considerable extent, such fears were proved true. Of the 2.5 million livres General Boudet found in the Port-au-Prince treasury, he immediately scattered a million and a half among his troops—nor did he forget himself in this redistribution. The locals accused him of a spirit of pillage. Leclerc had seen some version of Toussaint's tax rolls (the government was supposed to have taken in some 20 million livres during the past year), so he had a notion of how much money he ought to be able to find. When he learned that 1.5 million livres were still in the treasury of Les Cayes, Leclerc dispatched Admiral Latouche Tréville to confiscate it. He arrested Bunel, Toussaint's diplomat and paymaster, and seized a ship bound for the United States with 3 million livres, undoubtedly intended for the purchase of more arms.

Port-au-Prince civilians found themselves under a military rule at least as harsh as Toussaint's had been. Their animals and supplies were requisitioned for the army—but never paid for. As they had feared, the inhabitants were treated as a conquered people. They had to make a full declaration of all their means or be accused of collaboration with the black enemy. Eager to restore sugar and coffee production (for the profit of the army), Leclerc ordered the landowners back to their plantations, accusing them of harboring groundless fears—while he himself went nowhere without a heavy guard. In reality, the outlying areas were far less secure than they had been under Toussaint, and the planters began to recognize that despite his shortcomings, their chances of restoring their fortunes might have been better with him than with Leclerc.

Dessalines had intended to destroy the fortifications at La Crête à Pierrot before pressing further into the interior, but after his conference with Toussaint he ordered the walls to be repaired instead, and hastily had new trenches dug outside of them. The day after Toussaint's departure, March 1, Dessalines executed all the white inhabitants of Petite Rivière and all the white prisoners he had brought there from the plain of Cul de Sac, with the exception of a doctor named Descourtilz and a handful of musicians from a band maintained for Toussaint's formal entertainments. He left these survivors in the fort under guard of Lamartinière and a small garrison, while he himself led a force to the interior with the idea of razing and burning Mirebalais.

Toussaint, so far as the French were concerned, had disappeared. Leclerc, whose boots must have begun to chafe by then, believed that, having been forced south from Ravine à Couleuvre, Toussaint must be somewhere in the area of Petite Rivière. He changed the focus of the

French maneuvers with the idea of trapping him there—a strategy Toussaint had apparently anticipated. A noose was gradually drawing tight on La Crête à Pierrot, but Toussaint himself would not be found there, and the fort on the hill was a death trap—for the French.

Now wandering in the Grand Cahos mountains, Rochambeau's column never found Toussaint, who was by then far north of where he was believed to be, and Rochambeau also failed to engage Dessalines, who eluded him in the mountains on the way to Mirebalais. Rochambeau's men did manage to intercept the pack train carrying the treasuries from the Western Department into the interior; it is likely that the legend of Toussaint's "buried treasure" really ends here. Meanwhile, some divisions of the French army had captured stupendous sums on the coast, and when news of Rochambeau's huge score spread, units that so far had found no plunder grew all the more eager for their opportunity.

On March 4, General Debelle reached Petite Rivière with a force of two thousand men. Outraged by the butchered white bodies strewn over the town, the French grenadiers were easily provoked into charging a skein of black skirmishers outside the walls of the fort on the hill above. By some accounts they were also intoxicated by the illusional prospect of loot. At the last moment the skirmishers dove into trenches just below the walls and the fort's cannon raked the French charge with grapeshot, doing incredible damage. Then a detachment of Toussaint's honor guard cavalry rode out of the woods north of the fort to sweep the field. Lamartinière had a garrison of only three hundred, but this dismal quarter hour cost the French four hundred dead, and Debelle himself was seriously wounded, along with another French general, Devaux.

Dessalines, meanwhile, had been leading Rochambeau on a merry dance through the Grand Cahos mountains, pausing here and there to slaughter white civilians—a task he always undertook with enthusiasm, though sometimes he would spare a few whites whom he found acculturated enough "to eat callaloo." On March 4, a detachment from General Boudet's division found the ruins Dessalines had left at Mirebalais. On March 9, Boudet's main force reached Verrettes, just south of the Artibonite, where eight hundred white civilians lay stiffening in their coagulated blood. Furious at this spectacle, they moved west along the river and forded it during the night of March 11. At first light on March 12, they found black soldiers apparently sleeping outside the wall of the fort at La Crête à Pierrot.

Rochambeau's force was approaching this formidable position as well, but no one wanted to wait for its arrival. The other French generals had all been captivated by the illusion of treasure inside the fort (in fact there was none), and none of them wanted to share it with Rochambeau's unit. General Boudet launched his charge without waiting for support, and the defeat Debelle had suffered during the previous week repeated itself in every detail: hundreds of French grenadiers were slain, and Boudet himself was put out of action by a wound in the heel. Just minutes later, another division commanded by General Dugua fell into the same trap, charging from the town of Petite Rivière. These two efforts cost the French a total of nearly eight hundred casualties, and General Dugua was struck by two balls. Captain General Leclerc, who had accompanied Dugua from Port-au-Prince, was knocked down with a badly bruised groin, and would have been slain by the sabers of the black cavalry if an officer named Dalton had not carried him away from the battle lines on his back. Greed, opined a civilian observer, had made the heroes of Marengo forget the most important military maxim: Never despise one's enemy.

For the moment, Pamphile de Lacroix was the only French general left standing on the field; he paused for a moment to "recognize just how adapted to war the Blacks of Saint Domingue had become."[70] Aside from Toussaint's organized troops, all the French movements were constantly harassed by the armed field hands who sniped at their flanks from cover. "It was obvious that we no longer inspired moral terror," Lacroix brooded, "and that is the worst misfortune that can befall an army."[71]

Dessalines, who never failed to inspire both moral and mortal terror, had returned to the fort on the night of March 11 to exhort the garrison: "I want no one with me but the brave; we will be attacked this morning; let those who want to be slaves of the French leave the fort, but those who are willing to die as free men stand by me."[72] No one accepted the offer to escape. Standing by the door of the powder magazine with a blazing torch, Dessalines promised to blow up the fort if the French managed to enter it, but during Boudet's charge that morning he chose to climb the ramparts bare-chested and lay waste to assaulting Frenchmen with his sword. As previously, the honor guard cavalry led by Monpoint and Morisset rode out from the woods to deliver a coup de grâce. A black militia commander, Gottereau, led a troop of armed cultivators onto the field from the bank of the Artibonite, took a large number of French and slew them with bayonets. That night, packs of dogs came out to eat the corpses that no one could remove from the field. Later on, Pamphile de Lacroix, lacking tools enough to have the rotting bodies buried, ordered them burnt, an attempt that succeeded poorly and created an "odor still more unbearable than the first,"[73] which permeated everyone's wool clothing and suffocated the French camps.

The situation at La Crête à Pierrot devolved into a siege. Following the bloodbath of March 12, Dessalines ordered the fortification of a small rise just to the east above the main fort, then departed in search of fresh munitions from a depot at Plassac which, unfortunately for the black resistance, Boudet's division had blown up a few days before. At Morne Nolo, Dessalines lost an engagement with a French force led by General Hardy, who cut Dessalines's communications with Lamartinière at the fort; Hardy's arrival also forced the honor guard cavalry to retreat from the area, seeking to rejoin either Dessalines or Toussaint.

On March 22, the impetuous Rochambeau appeared on the scene, hastily recalled from the ruins of Mirebalais. André Rigaud had been assigned to Rochambeau's staff. When he saw the situation at La Crête à Pierrot, he feigned illness and excused himself to Port-au-Prince. Rochambeau was not so prudent. Before Leclerc could countermand him, he tried to charge the small redoubt Dessalines had erected before his departure, now occupied by Lamartinière with two hundred men and a few cannon. This futile effort cost him three hundred men. However, General Lacroix managed to establish mortar batteries from which the colored commander Pétion, an experienced artilleryman, was able to drop shells into the main fort. From March 22 to March 24, the bombardment was constant.

Toussaint Louverture, meanwhile, had slipped north through whatever French lines still existed; on March 2 he flushed a light French garrison out of Ennery, set fire to the town, made a feint toward Gonaïves, then began to circle through Saint Raphaël, Saint Michel, Marmelade, and Dondon, raising resistance among the cultivators everywhere he could—as Christophe was doing all over the Northern Plain. Sentiment was not universally in favor of Toussaint in this region, however; the French propaganda in support of general liberty continued to erode his base, and some inhabitants sarcastically suggested, "Let him raise Moyse from the dead to fight the Whites."[74]

Toussaint did not yet know that Maurepas had surrendered, and he hoped to relieve and rejoin Maurepas's Ninth Regiment—but first he had to attack and defeat General Desfourneaux at Plaisance. In the midst of this engagement, to his great dismay, he saw that the French had been reinforced by a portion of Maurepas's regiment now under command of Lubin Golart. Toussaint rode before them, shouting out, "Soldiers of the Ninth, do you dare fire on your general and your brothers?" By the account of Isaac Louverture, "These words had the effect of a thunderbolt on those soldiers; they fell to their knees, and if the European soldiers had not fired on him and pressed forward, all the Ninth Regiment would have gone over to Toussaint Louverture."[75] Unluckily for the black resistance, the French fire was well aimed on this day; a messenger bringing word from Dessalines of the state of siege at La Crête à Pierrot was hit and bled to death in Toussaint's arms.

From the start, Toussaint had devised a strategy of double encirclement. Once Leclerc had been lured to besiege La Crête à Pierrot, Toussaint, reinforced by Maurepas and the Ninth Regiment, would fall on his rear, surround him, arrest him, and deport him to account for himself in France—following the same route taken by Hédouville, Sonthonax, and most other representatives of the home government who had had the bad judgment to antagonize Toussaint Louverture. But the Ninth was lost, and by the time Toussaint (severely battered in his battle with Desfourneaux) could rally men enough to try the plan, it was too late.

On March 24, as he toured his posts, General Lacroix found some of his men flogging an elderly black couple who supposedly had been caught leaving the fort. He rebuked the soldiers and ordered the old people released. Once they had limped to a safe distance, however, they mocked the French soldiers by dancing the chica, then fled with the speed of young antelope. Appalled at his error, Lacroix guessed that they must have been couriers from Toussaint Louverture, who was known to be advancing on Leclerc's rear. In fact, they had come from

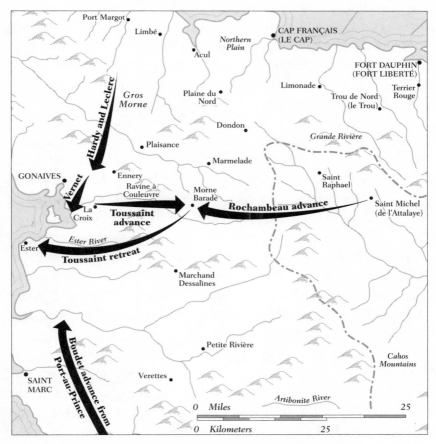

Ravine à Couleuvre, February 22–23, 1802

Dessalines with an order to evacuate the fort. That night, Lamartinière took the survivors of the nine hundred men Dessalines had left him twelve days before and cut his way out through the French siege lines, leaving Lacroix with his jaw dropped: "We surrounded his post with more than twelve thousand men; he got away without losing half of his garrison, and left us nothing but his dead and his wounded."[76] The latter were all butchered on Rochambeau's order when his men entered the fort the next morning.

It was a bitter disappointment for Toussaint to have so nearly missed his quarry. After a doleful meeting with Dessalines on the heights of Morne Calvaire, he retreated to Chassériaux Plantation, near Grands Fonds in the Petit Cahos mountains; his family had already found shelter in that area and his honor guard was waiting for him there. The French, meanwhile, limped back to Port-au-Prince in scarcely a cheerier frame of mind; they had lost two thousand men at La Crête à Pierrot. Pamphile de Lacroix ordered his men to march in squares with empty centers, so that the citizens of the capital would not realize the extent of the French losses.

Like Ravine à Couleuvre, La Crête à Pierrot is best understood as a loss for both sides. The French had technically gained ground, but they had the same difficulty holding it that Napoleon would soon encounter in campaigns against guerrilla resistance in Spain. "This is a war of Arabs," Leclerc wrote to Napoleon. "We have hardly passed through when the blacks occupy the neighboring woods and cut our communications."[77] "Though victorious everywhere," wrote Lieutenant Moreau de Jonnes, "we possessed nothing but our guns. The enemy did not hold anywhere, and yet remained master of the country."[78] Or in the words of a nineteenth-century French historian, Antoine Métral: "Everywhere this ground hid enemies, in a wood, behind a boulder; Liberty gave birth to them."[79]

Also at Toussaint's camp at Grands Fonds were Sabès and Gimont, the two emissaries whom General Boudet had sent ashore at Port-au-Prince before forcing his landing there. Since Lamartinière had taken them prisoner, they had been dragged all over the country, and narrowly missed being slain with the other white captives by Dessalines at Petite

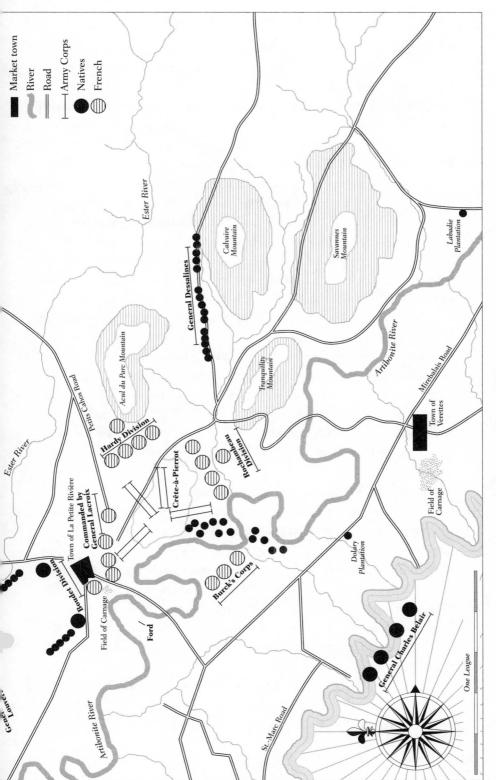

Legend

- Market town
- River
- Road
- Army Corps
- Natives ●
- French

Ester River

Calvaire Mountain

General Dessalines

Savannes Mountain

Labadie Plantation

Acul du Parc Mountain

Petits Cahos Road

Hardy Division

Tranquility Mountain

Rochambeau Division

Crête-à-Pierrot

Artibonite River

Michelais Road

Town of Verettes

Field of Carnage

Town of La Petite Rivière **Commanded by General Lacroix**

Bourdet Division

Burck's Corps

Dolary Plantation

Field of Carnage

Ford

General Louverture

Artibonite River

General Charles Belair

St-Marc Road

One League

The French Army's Siege of La Crête-à-Pierrot

Rivière. Now Toussaint summoned them into his presence, debated with them the legitimacy of Leclerc's actions versus his own, then sent them under safe-conduct back to General Boudet, with a note suggesting that his nephew Chancy, captured while carrying dispatches to Dommage several weeks previously, might be released in exchange.

By some accounts, Toussaint also sent a letter to Napoleon for Boudet to transmit. Though this document has never been definitively identified, a version which circulated at the time fits well enough with the rest of Toussaint's correspondence to be credible. "The high post I occupy is not my own choice, imperious circumstances placed me there against my will . . . I saw this unfortunate isle a prey to the fury of factions. My reputation and my color gave me a certain influence on the people who live here; and I was called to authority with almost a unanimous voice."[80]

"Adulation has ruined Toussaint," Colonel Vincent had written to a friend just before the expedition sailed.[81] If authentic, Toussaint's words do suggest that he was at least a little intoxicated by the power which he had obtained by a considerably more circuitous route than what he describes. His next claims, though, are hard to dispute: "I stifled sedition, calmed revolt, established tranquility; I replaced anarchy with good order; finally I gave the people both peace and a constitution. Citizen Consul, are your own pretensions founded on any more legitimate titles?"[82]

This question, if audacious, was a fair one.

"You offer liberty to the blacks," Toussaint goes on, "saying that wherever you have been you have given it to those who did not have it. I have only an imperfect knowledge of events which have recently taken place in Europe, but the reports that have reached me do not agree with that assertion. The liberty which one may enjoy in France, in Belgium, in Switzerland, or in the Batavian, Ligurian and Cisalpine republics would never satisfy the people of Saint Domingue. We are a long way from aspiring to an independence like that."[83]

The statement is so startling as to throw the authenticity of the entire letter into doubt. Never before had Toussaint openly raised the issue of independence—but circumstances had changed drastically since the French invasion began. To say that what the French called liberty was not good enough for the people of Saint Domingue was a slap in Napoleon's face. Why would Toussaint risk such a provocation?

Maybe Napoleon, who would not receive the letter for two months at least (supposing he ever received it at all), was not the intended audience. Toussaint knew something about propaganda, and he had reason to hope that such a message would feed doubt among the French officers and even their troops. Most of the French soldiers had begun their careers during the revolution. They did see themselves as liberators, and some already wondered exactly why they had been sent to suppress a revolution that claimed the same ideas—liberty, fraternity, equality—as their own. During the siege of La Crête à Pierrot, the white soldiers heard the black soldiers inside the walls singing their own revolutionary anthem, "The Marseillaise." Doubt crept in. Later in the struggle, a good number of soldiers from Polish regiments actually did change sides. If Toussaint really did write the letter, he meant for his critique of Napoleon to play on the French officers' suspicions of the first consul's imperial ambitions.

Whether this letter to Napoleon was authentic or not, Toussaint was definitely trying to establish a new diplomatic channel with Boudet—a loop that excluded Captain General Leclerc. However, Sabès and Gimont had barely departed on their mission to Boudet when word came to Toussaint's camp that General Hardy had swept across Toussaint's property at La Coupe à l'Inde, taking numerous prisoners and, most importantly, Toussaint's favorite horse, the white stallion Bel Argent. Furious, Toussaint set off in pursuit. On March 29, Hardy was caught between Toussaint's men and Christophe's at Dondon and forced to beat a hasty retreat to Cap Français. Though Bel Argent was not recovered, this victory was a terrific boost to the morale of the black resistance.

Immediately following the evacuation of La Crête à Pierrot, Toussaint had sent word north that Leclerc's forces had been annihilated there. This message wasn't as true as he wished it were; though noticeably limping, the French army was not crippled yet. But his master strategy had been successful in luring practically all the French troops into the Artibonite Valley toward La Crête à Pierrot. Leclerc had left Le Cap defended by a mere four hundred soldiers under the mulatto General Boyer, supported by twelve hundred sailors from the fleet moored in the harbor. During the siege at La Crête à Pierrot, Toussaint had been very successful in whipping up guerrilla resistance along the Cordon de l'Ouest, led by maroon chieftains like Sylla, Romain, and Macaya (he who beat the drum too often). Troops from Toussaint's regular army were also operating all over the Northern Department, under Christophe and Colonel Jean-Baptiste Sans-Souci, who commanded at Grande Rivière and proved especially expert in combining conventional and guerrilla tactics.

During the month of March, these guerrilla leaders, working in coordination, cut French communications between the Northern Department and the rest of the country, raised rebellion at Borgne, Port Français, and Morne Rouge, burned Limbé, and isolated Cap Français, leaving the town open to an assault by Sans-Souci from Grande Rivière. Seriously unnerved, Admiral Villaret-Joyeuse reported to Napoleon that San-Souci's attack had carried terribly close to Le Cap; "if they had felt their own strength as well as knowing our weakness, the idea of what could have happened makes one shudder."[84] The battle in which Toussaint and Christophe routed Hardy actually went on for several days and alarmed Villaret-Joyeuse still further. Hardy had lost four or five hundred men in his flight, and the whole Northern Plain had been set afire (one more time), to the effect that "at midnight and in the middle of the harbor one could read by the light of the flames."[85]

Hardy's return, which coincided with the arrival at Le Cap of fresh troops from France, moved Sans-Souci to retire. He delivered about a hundred prisoners to Toussaint, who had returned to his headquarters at Marmelade. At this point Toussaint had recovered control over all of his original power base, the Cordon de l'Ouest. Leclerc dared not cross the territory he had supposedly just conquered, but had to rush back to Cap Français by boat. On April 1, he wrote to Napoleon that he had only seven thousand fit men in the field; five thousand of his troops were in the hospital. Another five thousand were already dead, though Leclerc did not mention it.

The French forces of invasion had expected a swift and total victory. As it turned out, that's what they absolutely needed. Though they were able to win many engagements with startling speed, their successes were never complete. Unacclimated European troops could not sustain the rigors of a campaign in this country over the long haul. Well aware of this difficulty, Vincent had urged the use of as many acclimated Spanish Creole troops as possible, but no one heeded this advice.

The terrain was difficult, not to say impossible. In the effort to explain the problem to superiors in France, one young lieutenant flung a crumpled ball of paper on the table, declaring bitterly that Saint Domingue looked like that. To this day one of Haiti's most telling proverbs is *Deyè mòn gegne mòn* (Behind the mountains are more mountains). By day the French troops labored through staggering heat on forced marches, suffocating in their sweat-drenched wool uniforms. At night it was surprisingly cold on the heights and often they'd be drenched by torrential evening rains, so pneumonia joined dysentery and the mosquito-borne fevers which afflicted them. Unreliable supply lines often left them poorly fed. And a great many more than their officers would admit had simply been killed outright in battle.

The men of Toussaint's regular army (not to mention the flocks of field hands who were turning into paramilitary groups to resist the invasion), liked bread and salt meat if they could get it, but if not they got by very well on the cassava and fruit that were everywhere available to them. They liked uniforms and boots if they could get them, but if not they fought just as well half-naked and could move barefoot over the most horrendous terrain with the speed and agility of goats. Little settlements all over the mountains provided them with food and shelter. If these men had trouble standing up to the French military on conventional open battlefields, guerrilla tactics suited them down to the ground, and they could hold out forever in these mountains.

What followed has mystified many observers. With Toussaint as strong as he was in the north, and Dessalines threatening the French all over the Western Department, the black resistance had a winning edge over the invasion. Perhaps (as Villaret-Joyeuse so frantically hoped) the leaders simply did not know it.

The prisoners whom Sans-Souci brought to Toussaint at Marmelade made a great impression. Toussaint treated them well, and even had a beef killed in their honor; he was generally humane to prisoners under his direct control, though he was often accused of tacitly suggesting massacres by his subordinates. These veterans of European wars were redoubtable; Morisset, a commander of Toussaint's honor guard, reported that "none of us can run through the woods or climb mountains and rocks any faster than them";[86] he also claimed to have seen them pull down wild horses by the ears.

The prisoners at Marmelade let Toussaint know that they had landed at Le Cap from a Dutch port just five days before they were captured, and Toussaint also learned around the same time that the Peace of Amiens had been confirmed by the signing of a treaty between England and France. The knowledge that no British blockade would dam a steady stream of such fearsome warriors flowing from France may have disheartened him. He could not have known that Leclerc was writing desperate pleas for reinforcements that were not in fact forthcoming, or that the first signs of a yellow fever epidemic had already appeared among the French at Cap Français.

On April 26, General Henry Christophe, who was said to be "tired of living in the woods like a brigand,"[87] submitted to the authority of Captain General Leclerc, on the condition that he retain his rank in the French army. He turned over some twelve hundred regular black troops, along with the towns of Acul, Boucan, Cardinaux, Saint Suzanne, Port Français, Mornet, Grande Rivière, and Dondon—practically all the points of entry between the mountains and the Northern Plain. The loss of these posts seriously weakened the defense of Toussaint's position in the Cordon de l'Ouest—the distance between Dondon and his Marmelade headquarters was alarmingly short—and brought about his own offer to surrender on May 1.

Whether Christophe's submission was an outright betrayal of Toussaint has been much debated. Vincent had predicted that Christophe would prove loyal to France if forced to a choice, but instead he had burned Le Cap and followed Toussaint in fighting the invasion. Roume believed that Christophe was ready to turn on Toussaint. Yet shortly before he did change sides, when the French camp suggested that he capture Toussaint by treachery and turn him in, Christophe rejected the proposition with huge indignation and also showed the letters to Toussaint. The theory that Christophe was acting under Toussaint's secret direction when he surrendered to Leclerc is strange but not inconceivable—it is consistent with the idea that Toussaint used Christophe as a cat's-paw when Leclerc first appeared outside the harbor of Le Cap. Certainly, he never liked to let his own hand show openly in such maneuvers.

From one point of view, it is incredible that Christophe should have accepted terms with the French without Toussaint's tacit consent and encouragement. On the other hand, other generals had done so while out of communication with their chief commander and had come to no harm. Some members of Toussaint's officer cadre may have begun to feel that they would prosper better if Toussaint were out of the picture—as Toussaint had once felt about Jean-François, Biassou, Blanc Cassenave, Dieudonné, Villatte, Rigaud, Sonthonax, and Hédouville.

Toussaint had taken care to open a separate line of communication with Boudet a month earlier, so the idea of coming to terms with the French must have been on his mind for some time. On the heels of Christophe's submission, when his own security at Marmelade was imminently threatened from Dondon, he wrote to Leclerc a generally conciliatory letter, which ended with a caution: "whatever the resources of the French army might be, he would always be strong and powerful enough to burn, ravage, and sell dearly a life which had also sometimes been useful to the mother country."[88] Pamphile de Lacroix seconded this opinion: "however feeble he might have become, he would not cease to be redoubtable, entrenched in the heart of the colony, in the middle of inaccessible mountains, whence he could come out to carry ravage and sedition all around him."[89]

The French estimated that Toussaint still had some four thousand troops at his disposal, as well as the larger numbers of armed cultivators he might raise. Leclerc wrote to the minister of marine on April 21 that "it will be impossible for me to enter into campaign again before having received the twelve thousand men for which I have asked you."[90] The surrender of Christophe a few days later must have encouraged the captain general, who hoped in the same letter to exploit "dissensions" rumored among the black chiefs. However, Leclerc was already becoming dangerously dependent on "colonial troops"—that is to say, black rebel units that had quite recently changed sides with their officers.

During the last week of April, Toussaint (whose own communications had been much interrupted) learned of his brother Paul Louverture's submission at Ciudad Santo Domingo. The fact that so many black generals—Paul Louverture, Maurepas, Clervaux, and now Christophe—had been maintained in their French military ranks after capitulation lent credence to the Napoleonic propaganda that the French army was committed to the defense of general liberty. The fact that, even at this point, Toussaint was unwilling to pronounce the magic word that would have rallied more of the population to his cause suggested that independence from France had never been his goal. At the moment that he began to treat with Leclerc, he must have felt both isolated and surrounded—and under immediate threat of an assault on Marmelade from Dondon which, if it failed to capture him, would have put him desperately on the run.

Dessalines was difficult to persuade, and probably was never entirely persuaded. "Listen well," he told his men. "If Dessalines surrenders to them a hundred times, he will betray them a hundred times."[91] More than likely Toussaint felt the same; characteristically he betrayed nothing of the thought.

"He never showed anything," wrote the daughter of one of Toussaint's numerous white secretaries. "My father often told us the impression he had from these private meetings. By the doubtful light of a little lamp, the somber face was still more black. When he scrutinized you, he was like a lynx. But when he was observed, he withdrew into himself, masked his regard. Raising his eyes to heaven, he hid his pupil beneath his thick eyelid, letting nothing show but the white. So, he became hideous. My father, as young and brave as he was, could not face this demonic visage."[92]

Filter out the antique racism and a rather disconcerting picture of Toussaint still remains. In hypnosis, such eye movement is a symptom of trance. In Vodou it is a sign of possession. To most people the alien is frightening; no wonder the young Frenchman read a "demonic visage" into Toussaint's entranced expression. No doubt Toussaint really was communing with his spirits when in these late-night meditations he struggled to choose the right word, or phrase, or action. In the close of his supposed letter to Napoleon, Toussaint turned again to the Christian God: "Let him decide between me and my enemies, between those who have violated his teachings and abjured his holy name, and the man who has never ceased to adore him."[93]

On May 6, Toussaint Louverture rode into Cap Français in the midst of three hundred horsemen of his honor guard. Leclerc, who was dining shipboard with the naval officers, seemed to be taken by surprise. By the time he hastened back to shore, Toussaint's guard had occupied the government palace, and by one (perhaps exaggerated) account, his men were stalking the grounds with their sabers drawn. Jacques de Norvins, a young French officer, described the scene: Toussaint Louverture "had followed Leclerc into his salon where they sat down on a couch facing the door. I was not much reassured by this interview, nor by the haughty manner of Toussaint's numerous guards who, leaning on their sabers, filled the surroundings, the courtyard and the apartments of the residence, while others guarded their horses, and while Toussaint also leaned on his saber, which he held upright between his legs . . . Any bad sign on the part of Toussaint," Norvins concluded, and "at any moment the sabers of those black dragoons could have come out of their scabbards."[94]

In this crackling atmosphere, it was Toussaint who seemed to dictate terms to Leclerc. The black generals still in rebellion—Vernet, Charles Belair, and Dessalines—would be retained in their ranks in the French army, despite the fact that, when reproached by Leclerc for the massacres in which some three thousand civilians had died, Toussaint replied flatly, "It was Dessalines." When Leclerc insisted that Toussaint himself continue service as his "lieutenant," Toussaint demurred: "My general, I am too old and too ill; I need rest and to live in the country. I can no longer serve the Republic. I want to go with my children to my plantation at Ennery."[95] Undoubtedly he strongly suspected that Leclerc meant to have him arrested and did not mean to give him the least opportunity.

The tension was diffused, somewhat, by a banquet, but Toussaint was not in a festive mood. "He said he was sick," Norvins reports, "and did not even eat any soup; no more did he want to drink any wine. Only, at dessert, I offered him some Gruyère cheese; he took the plate and cut out a square piece, from which he removed a big enough thickness from all four sides, took in his fingers what remained from this singular operation, ate it without bread, and drank a glass of water from a carafe broached since the dinner began; it was thus that he did honor to the General in Chief's table."[96]

Following this austere celebration, Toussaint rode out, still surrounded by the men of his guard (which, two thousand strong, would "retire" with him at Ennery). On the public square at Marmelade he bade farewell to his assembled troops, then continued toward his Ennery plantations. En route, legend has it, he was hailed by someone who asked, "General, have you abandoned us?" and Toussaint replied, "No, my children, all your brothers are under arms, and all the officers conserve their ranks."[97]

It was not only in the ranks of the French army that the blacks of Saint Domingue remained under arms. Even after Toussaint's surrender, resistance never completely stopped—nor did Toussaint stop tacitly encouraging it. A general effort to disarm the population soon proved almost completely futile. Sans-Souci, who was even more enraged than Toussaint at the way Christophe's surrender had cut him off at the knees, began organizing for a fresh rebellion almost immediately. The guerrilla leader Sylla was actively resisting at Mapou, a point between Ennery and Plaisance, at the time of Toussaint's retirement to Ennery, and Sylla's presence helped secure Toussaint there. It took a major assault to dislodge Sylla from that position, and even then neither he nor his men could be captured.

Suspicion of Toussaint's secret involvement in such eruptions was constant. Makajoux, a commander in the neighboring town of Pilate, wrote to his French superior, "Toussaint and the other chiefs have surrendered only in appearance, and have only sought to give their troops an entry among you in order to surprise you at the first possible moment."[98] Leclerc himself had the same attitude: "That ambitious man, from the moment that I pardoned him, has not ceased to secretly

conspire . . . He has tried to organize an insurrection among the cultivators to make them rise en masse. The reports that have come to me
from all the generals, even General Dessalines, on the conduct he has
maintained since his submission leave me in no doubt in that regard. I
have intercepted letters which he wrote to a so-called Fontaine who is
his agent in Le Cap. These letters prove that he has been conspiring and
desiring to regain his old influence in the colony. He has been waiting
for the effects of diseases on the army."[99]

Those effects were already rampant. In a separate letter of the same
date, Leclerc put it bluntly: "If the First Consul wants to have an army
in Saint Domingue in the month of October, he will need to send it
from the ports of France, for the ravages of disease here are beyond all
description."[100] And yet, reinforcements were practically useless; so
severe was the fever season of 1802 that troops were said to march from
the ships directly into the grave.

It was not yet known in the early 1800s that malaria and yellow
fever were mosquito-borne illnesses, but the military did understand
that the mountains were healthier than the ports—which may have
provided a pretext for sending large numbers of troops into the region
of Plaisance and Ennery during the first week of June 1802. "Toussaint
is of bad faith," Leclerc wrote on June 6, "as I very well expected of him,
but I have gained from his submission the goal which I hoped, which
was to detach Dessalines and Christophe from him, with their troops. I
will order his arrest, and I believe I can count on Dessalines, whose
spirit I have mastered, enough to charge him to go arrest Toussaint."[101]
Events would soon prove that Leclerc had not mastered Dessalines's
spirit in the slightest, but probably he would not have dared arrest
Toussaint without some assurance from the black generals that the
move would not provoke a revolt on their part.

Toussaint's behavior during this fatal period has puzzled most
observers, who find it difficult to understand why he walked into the
fairly obvious trap which Leclerc had prepared for him. The bait was a
pair of letters, one from the regional commander, General Brunet, the
other from Leclerc himself: "Since you persist in thinking that the large
number of troops found at Plaisance frightens the cultivators there, I

charge General Brunet to concert himself with you concerning the placement of a part of these troops." Brunet followed up in silkier tones: "We have, my dear general, some arrangements to make together which it is impossible to discuss by letter, but which a conference of one hour would settle."[102]

Toussaint clung to these two letters till his last days as a prisoner in France. It seems almost impossible that he did not see through them, though Pamphile de Lacroix argues that he was simply duped. "He cried out when he received General Brunet's letter, 'You see these Whites, they don't suspect anything, they know everything—and still they have to come consult old Toussaint.' "[103] In this version, vanity, and a susceptibility to flattery which nothing else in his whole career suggests, were the weaknesses whereby Toussaint let himself be lured out of his stronghold at Ennery, where it would have been much more difficult if not impossible to capture him, to a meeting with Brunet at Georges Plantation. There the small escort which Toussaint had brought with him was overpowered, and Toussaint was seized, rushed the short distance to Gonaïves, and hustled aboard *La Créole,* which sailed to the harbor of Le Cap, where he was transferred to *L'Héros* for deportation to France.

But never in his whole life had Toussaint shown himself to be so gullible. More plausible is the idea that his last moves were forced—or that, through the same sort of small miscalculations that had moved him to surrender a month before, he believed they were forced. In fact, the displacement of Sylla from Mapou had seriously weakened his position in Ennery. French troops were moving in force into Ennery as well as Plaisance and getting into contentions with the local "cultivators," many of whom were actually members of Toussaint's honor guard. If he did nothing to stop this buildup, he would soon be outnumbered and overpowered at his last retreat. Therefore, in hope of a diplomatic solution, he took the calculated risk of going to meet Brunet, after Brunet, pleading his own ill health, had declined to come to meet him at Ennery. Events proved his calculation to be mistaken.

It is argued by some, most notably the Caribbean commentator Aimé Césaire, that Toussaint's apparently blind cooperation in his own arrest was an intentional sacrifice, meant to separate the momentum of the Haitian Revolution from depending on himself as an individual, or on any other particular person. In this interpretation, Toussaint's decision to accept Brunet's invitation to Georges Plantation amounts to a deliberate choice of martyrdom. The last letters Toussaint wrote from prison do suggest that some such idea may have entered his mind, but however fervent his Catholicism, it seems doubtful that he would have wanted to push the imitation of Christ quite so far. And although he was certainly able to put the welfare of his people ahead of his own, it was rare for him to lose sight of his personal interests so completely. It's more likely that, under the extreme pressure of his situation, he gambled and lost.

And yet his arrest did prove that the Haitian Revolution could now get along very well without him. At the moment of his deportation, Toussaint understood that perfectly. "In overthrowing me," he said as he boarded *L'Héros,* "you have only cut down the trunk of the tree of liberty of the Blacks in Saint Domingue: it will spring back from the roots, for they are numerous and deep."[104]

Not very long afterward, Leclerc was forced to agree, writing first, "It is not everything to have removed Toussaint, there are two thousand other chiefs here to have taken away," and then, still more hopelessly, "Here is my opinion of this country. It is necessary to destroy all the negroes of the mountains, men and women, sparing only children under the age of twelve, and destroy half of those of the plain, without leaving a single colored man in the colony who has ever worn an epaulette. Without that, the colony will never be at peace."[105] As much as to admit outright that by Toussaint's agency the spirit of revolution had been so thoroughly diffused among the blacks of Saint Domingue that his own or anyone's personal leadership no longer mattered.

SIX

Toussaint in Chains

During the ten years of his ascendancy, Toussaint preserved Bréda Plantation and its white managers from the bloody slave rebellion that broke out all over the Northern Plain in the summer of 1791, then joined the rebel slaves in the fall of that year. Next, along with many of the rebel slaves of the region, he became part of the Spanish colonial army and began to do battle with French Revolutionary forces in Saint Domingue on behalf of pan-European royalism. In 1794 he changed his name from Toussaint Bréda to Toussaint Louverture and flabbergasted all observers by suddenly switching the four thousand men he now commanded from the Spanish to the French Revolutionary side of the conflict. France abolished slavery in 1794, and Toussaint permanently cast his lot with the French. As a brigadier general, fighting on several fronts at once, he expelled the Spanish and the British from Saint Domingue. As governor general of the colony, he won an ugly civil war with the mulatto faction, then took over the Spanish side of Hispaniola in the name of France. By 1801 he had emerged as the de facto ruler of the entire island. He had either militarily defeated or politically outmaneuvered all the great powers of Europe that meant to claim this rich prize for themselves. In the first months of 1802 he had fought an invasion force sent from France to a draw, and then retired with full honors from the army and the government. In the summer of that year he was arrested by the French and shipped to a prison in the heart of France, from which he would never return.

Only one other man of that time could rival Toussaint's meteoric trajectory, with its dizzying climb and precipitous fall: Napoleon Bonaparte, who in so many ways resembled the black leader whose nemesis he became.

"If I wanted to count all the services of all kinds that I have rendered to the government," Toussaint Louverture dictated in his prison cell at the Fort de Joux, "I would need several volumes, and still I wouldn't finish it all. And to compensate me for all these services, they arrested me arbitrarily in Saint Domingue; they choked me and dragged me on board like a criminal, without any decorum and without regard for my rank. Is that the recompense due to my work? Should my conduct make me expect such treatment?"[1]

These lines are drawn from a seventy-five-page memoir which Toussaint composed, with the help of a French secretary, in the prison cell where he was doomed eventually to die without ever hearing any reply to any of his arguments. The Fort de Joux was a dismal place, at least from the point of view of the black general. High in the Jura mountains, in the region of Franche-Comté, near the French town of Pontarlier in one direction and the Swiss frontier in another, the ninth-century château is about as remote as one can get from ports and the ocean while remaining on French territory—a feature of real importance to Toussaint's captors. The man who had ordered his deportation from Saint Domingue, Bonaparte's brother-in-law Captain General Emmanuel Leclerc, wrote to the home government not long after: "You cannot possibly keep Toussaint at too great a distance from the sea, nor put him in a prison too sure; that man has fanaticized this country to such a point that his presence here would set it on fire all over again."[2]

The mountains surrounding the Fort de Joux are capped with snow eight months out of twelve. The fortress has a well over five hundred feet deep, intended for use during sieges; most of the serfs who were forced to cut the shaft through the solid rock died somewhere down in those depths, never allowed to return to the surface. One of the château's medieval masters returned from a Crusade to find his seventeen-year-old wife, Berthe de Joux, engaged in a love affair. He locked her into a three-by-three-by-four-foot cavity, where somehow she survived for ten years. She did not have space to stand erect but she could look out through two sets of bars to see the corpse, then the skeleton of her lover, hanging from a gallows on the opposite cliff.

By the time Toussaint arrived there, the defenses of the Fort de Joux had been evolving for nearly eight centuries. The fortress was ringed by five concentric walls and three moats, each with its own drawbridge. Toussaint was imprisoned in the oldest and innermost enclosure, behind five heavy double doors at the end of a long vaulted corridor. His cell was also a low barrel vault, built with colossal blocks of Jura limestone. The floor measured twenty feet by twelve. The window embrasure, at the opposite end of the cell from the door, had been bricked in for greater security; a narrow space at the top of the brickwork admitted a little daylight through a grille beyond. Toussaint, who had been carried across France in a closed coach with a large military escort from the ship that had taken him from Saint Domingue, was brought to a prison in nearby Besançon sometime during the night of August 22, 1802, then transferred to the Fort de Joux dungeon at two in the morning of August 23. He would never leave his cell.

"When I got down from the ship," he wrote, "they made me climb into a coach. I hoped then that they would bring me before a tribunal, there to make an account of my conduct, and there to be judged. But far from that; without giving me an instant of repose, they took me, to a fort on the frontiers of the Republic, where they have shut me into a terrible cell."[3] At times, Toussaint's plaints in his memoir strike a tragic note: "They have sent me to France naked as a worm; they have seized my property and my papers; they have spread the most atrocious calumnies on my account. Is this not to cut off someone's legs and order him to walk? Is it not to cut out his tongue and tell him to talk? Is it not to bury a man alive?"[4]

First Consul Napoleon Bonaparte made no direct reply to any of these messages. At the same time he was receiving frequent letters, with a weirdly similar tone, from Captain General Leclerc, whose ostensible mission had been to relieve Toussaint Louverture of his post as governor general of Saint Domingue, and who had done so at the cost of most of the men in his very large command, not to mention the ruin of his own health. "As for myself," wrote Leclerc,

> I have always served you with devotion; I will continue, I will execute all your orders to the letter. I will justify the good opinion that you have of me, but I cannot resign myself to stay on here next summer. Since I have been here I have had nothing but the spectacle of fires, insurrections, assassinations, the dead and the dying. My soul is shriveled, no mirthful idea can make me forget these hideous scenes. I struggle here against the blacks, against the whites, against poverty and penuriousness in money, against my discouraged army. When I have spent another six months in this style, I will have the right to claim repose. As for Madame Leclerc, she is ill, and a model of courage; she is very much worthy to be your sister.
>
> Let me know, I beg you, what measures you have taken to come to my rescue; but do not send me my army in pieces; send me some good corps and no more debris like the greater part of the battalions I have so far received.[5]

Dated October 7, 1802, this letter was Leclerc's last. By the time it reached France, he was already dead—along with some fifty thousand of the eighty thousand troops who had been sent to subdue the Negro rebellion in Saint Domingue. Though outmaneuvered by his enemy, Toussaint Louverture managed to outlive him, hanging on in his frigid cell till April 1803.

What Toussaint wanted and, in his prison, did his best to lobby for, was Napoleon's judgment of the case between himself and Leclerc. Sometimes he put the request with a naïve simplicity that may have been feigned: "If two children fight each other, shouldn't their father or mother stop them from doing so, find out which is the aggressor, punish that one or punish them both, in the case that both of them are wrong? By the same token, General Leclerc had no right to have me arrested. The government alone could have had us both arrested, could have heard and judged us. Meanwhile General Leclerc enjoys liberty, while here I am at the bottom of this cell!"[6]

Though Napoleon declined to render any judgment of the case that Toussaint was trying to construct between himself and Leclerc, he did finally admit, in the memoir written at Saint Helena after his definitive fall from power, that he had been wrong to oppose the revolution in Saint Domingue: "I have to reproach myself for the attempt at the colony during the Consulate; it was a great mistake to have wanted to subdue it by force; I should have contented myself to govern it through the intermediary of Toussaint."[7] And he went on to say that he had all the more reason to regret the error because he saw it even at the time, and acted "against his own inclination." He "did nothing but yield to the opinions of his State council and his ministers, dragged along by the howling of the colonists, who formed a large party in Paris and who moreover were almost all royalists and sold out to the English faction."[8] The extent of his error may have begun to dawn on him in the summer and fall of 1802, but that did not influence him to show mercy to his prisoner, Toussaint Louverture.

If Napoleon's descriptions of his judgments and misjudgments regarding Toussaint and Saint Domingue come across as a little queasy, Toussaint confronted an even trickier task as he set about constructing his Fort de Joux memoir as a brief for the military trial he hoped would be held. Somehow he had to make it plausible that a war which had devastated the colony from one end to the other and already caused some twenty thousand deaths had all been brought about by errors of protocol on the part of Captain General Leclerc. A big challenge certainly, but he gave it his best shot.

"It is my duty," he began, "to render to the French government an exact account of my conduct; I will recount the facts with all the innocence and frankness of an old soldier, adding such reflections as naturally present themselves. Finally, I will tell the truth, if it be against myself."[9]

This opening sally is rhetorically impressive without being especially credible; Toussaint, far from being a simple old soldier, possessed such sharp political acumen that he might well have given lessons to Machiavelli.

"The colony of Saint-Domingue, of which I was commander, enjoyed the greatest possible tranquility; agriculture and commerce were flourishing there. The island had reached a degree of splendor never before seen. And all that—I dare to say it—was my doing."[10]

This paragraph is really the cornerstone of Toussaint's whole defense. He could claim with perfect justice that he had restored the colony from the ruins of the early 1790s to something approaching, if not actually exceeding, its magnificent prosperity before war and revolution ravaged it. Moreover, he had reason to believe that Napoleon was aware and at least to some extent appreciative of this achievement. The difficulty lay in finessing the fact that everything Toussaint rebuilt he later, and just as deliberately, tore down.

"However, since we were on a war footing, the commission had rendered a decree which ordered me to take all necessary measures to prevent the enemies of the Republic from penetrating into the island. In consequence, I had given the order to all the commanders of the seaports not to allow any warships to enter any harbor if they were not recognized by me and had not obtained my permission. Be it a fleet of whatever nation, it was absolutely forbidden to enter the port or even the anchorage, unless I had recognized for myself where it came from and what port it had sailed from."[11]

Regarding this "decree," it should be noted that the remnants of the civil commission in question were completely under Toussaint's thumb at this time. Roume, the last French representative still on the island, had been released from his Dondon chicken house just shortly before the decree was issued. Toussaint's strategy, however, is to argue that his resistance to the landing of Captain General Leclerc and his army derived from orders he had received from the French government itself.

The French fleet made its first landfall off Point Samana, at the easternmost extremity of the island. It is likely that Toussaint got his first glimpse of the warships there, though in his memoir he does not admit it. Instead he claims that he was on an agricultural tour in the interior of what had been until quite recently the Spanish region of the island—Toussaint had occupied it for France just a year before—and that the first news he had of the fleet's arrival was the dispatch from General Henry Christophe at Cap Français.

Toussaint's movements during the next couple of days are open to question; no one can prove with certainty just where he was. In the memoir he claims that "I hastened to render myself to Cap, in spite of the flooding of the river at Hinche, hoping to have pleasure of embracing my brothers in arms from Europe, and at the same time to receive orders from the French government."[12] En route he encountered General Jean-Jacques Dessalines, who told him that more ships had appeared before the port of Saint Marc. These had been detached from the French fleet, but in the memoir Toussaint pretends to believe that they might have constituted some foreign invasion force. He continued on his way toward Cap Français, until from an observation post on the height of a mountain called Grand Boucan he saw—to his shock and horror!—that the city had been set on fire.

In his memoir, Toussaint argues that Christophe was forced to resist the French landing and burn down the town because "if the commander of the fleet had really had peaceful intentions, he would have waited for me."[13] Now that the French had landed in force, Toussaint, according to his memoir, approached their line with the idea "to have a conference" but "they fired on us at twenty-five paces from the gate. My horse was pierced with a ball; another bullet tore off the hat of one of my officers. This unforeseen circumstance forced me to abandon the high road, to cross the savannah and the forests in order to reach Héricourt plantation, where I waited three days for news from the commander of the fleet, but always uselessly."[14]

In fact, Toussaint's army was by then resisting Leclerc's multi-pronged invasion with all its power. Full-scale war had broken out, and Toussaint in his memoir does his very best to blame Leclerc for all the hostilities: "if the intentions of the government had been good and peaceful with respect to me and with respect to all those who had contributed to the happiness which the colony then enjoyed, General Leclerc would surely not have followed or executed the orders he had received, for he debarked in the island as an enemy, doing evil for the pleasure of doing it, without addressing himself to the commander [Toussaint himself] and without communicating his powers to him."[15]

Toussaint's interview with Leclerc's envoy the Abbé Coisnon should have resolved the question of Leclerc's authority, but Toussaint's description of their conversation explains why it didn't:

> After the conduct of this general, I could have no confidence in him, that he had landed as an enemy, that in spite of that I had believed that it was my duty to go before him in order to hinder the progress of evil, but that then he had caused me to be fired on, that I had run the greatest dangers, that finally, if his intentions were as pure as those of the government that sent him, he would have taken the trouble to write me to inform me of his mission; that he should have sent me a fast boat ahead of the fleet, with you, sir [Coisnon], and my children, as it is ordinarily done, to announce his arrival to me and make me party to his powers, that since he had not fulfilled any of these formalities, the evil was done and that thus I definitively refused to seek him out; that however, to prove my attachment and my submission to the French government, I consented to write a letter to the General Leclerc.[16]

Toussaint also wrote a reply directly to Napoleon, requesting that Leclerc be recalled and reprimanded—a futile effort since there was no one but Leclerc himself to forward this message to the first consul. Diplomacy failed and the war went on. With three French columns advancing on him from different directions, Toussaint could easily recognize a plan to encircle him on his plantations at Ennery and, if he could not be trapped and captured there, force him down to the coast at Gonaïves.

"These new hostilities brought me new reflections," he wrote from the Fort de Joux. "I thought that the conduct of General Leclerc was very much contrary to the intentions of the government, since the First Consul, in his letter, promised peace, while he, Leclerc, made war. I saw that instead of trying to stop the evil, he did nothing but augment it.

'Does he not fear,' I said to myself, 'in persisting in such conduct, to be blamed by his government? Can he possibly hope to win the approval of the First Consul, of that great man whose equity and impartiality are so well known, while I myself shall be condemned?' So I took the course of defending myself in case of attack, and in spite of the fact that I had few troops, I made my dispositions accordingly."[17]

Toussaint next mentions, rather casually, "I ordered the town of Gonaïves to be burned, and marched at the head of the column directed toward Pont-de-l'Ester."[18] What follows is a brief but essentially accurate report of what had turned into an all-out war which lasted three months and which ended only when both sides were depleted and exhausted, whereupon negotiations were opened by Leclerc's and Toussaint's subordinates.

"General Christophe, upon his return, brought me back a letter from General Leclerc, which said that it would be a beautiful day for him if he could convince me to cooperate with him and to submit myself to the orders of the Republic. I replied right away that I had always been obedient to the French government, since I had constantly borne arms for it; that if, according to principle, they had comported themselves with me as they should have done, there would never have been a single shot fired; that peace would never even have been troubled in the island, and that the intentions of the government would have been fulfilled."[19] This passage is the closing argument of the least plausible phase of Toussaint's defense: the idea that in battling the French expedition tooth and nail, until he had exhausted every resource in his reach, he actually believed himself to be enacting the intentions of the French government.

Thereafter he is on much firmer ground, for the peace settlement he reached with Leclerc included a complete amnesty for all events of the bloody conflict that had just ended. In his Fort de Joux cell, Toussaint quotes Leclerc's proffer from memory, which proves that his memory was a good one, for though he does not recall the original document verbatim, all the essential points are preserved: "Never fear, you nor the generals under your orders, and the inhabitants who are with you, that I will pursue anyone for his past conduct; I shall draw the veil of oblivion over the events which have taken place in Saint Domingue. In that I imi-

tate the example which the First Consul gave to France on 18 Brumaire.*
In the future, I desire to see nothing but good citizens on this island. You
ask for repose; when one has commanded as you have, and supported
for so long the burden of government, repose is your due. But I hope
that during your retirement, you will, in your moments of leisure, share
your enlightenment with me, for the prosperity of Saint Domingue."[20]

By the terms of this arrangement, all hostilities officially ceased.
Toussaint retired to his plantations at Ennery; his officers retained their
rank and were incorporated, along with their men, into Leclerc's force.
Leclerc needed them desperately by then, for more than half the soldiers he'd brought from France were dead, and his officer corps had
been decimated. There was more fighting to be done, for all hostilities
had not in fact ceased. Guerrilla bands who'd never been wholly under
Toussaint's control were still resisting in the mountains, and the French
suspected that Toussaint might secretly be controlling some of them.

However, there was no proof at all of those suspicions, and so the
complaints in Toussaint's memoir about the manner of his arrest seem
extremely well justified. The fact of the matter is that, from the start,
Leclerc carried secret orders from Napoleon to arrest all the senior black
officers and deport them to France. These were difficult to carry out,
however, even after the war had supposedly ended. Once Leclerc had
merged the black army with his own drastically weakened force, he
didn't dare arrest any black general. Toussaint had been allowed to take
some two thousand men of his honor guard into retirement with him;
these men had supposedly laid down their swords and taken up imple-
ments of agriculture, but an attempt on Toussaint in his stronghold at
Ennery seemed a poor risk.

So Toussaint was invited to "share his enlightenment" with General
Brunet on a nearby plantation. Just why he chose to stick his head into
this trap has mystified most students of his story, but whatever his
motives, he was easily made prisoner there, while a simultaneous raid
on Ennery captured his family. The arrest really was a treacherous ploy,
as well as a clear violation of the terms for peace that had been agreed,
and Toussaint's exclamations of shock and dismay have a more sincere

*November 9, 1799, by the French Revolutionary calendar, the date of the bloodless coup that
elevated Napoleon to the consulate.

ring than many other protestations in his memoir. He was especially offended at being treated as a common criminal and denied the respect to which, as a general in the French army, he clearly was entitled.

> If you had no more need of my services and if you wanted to replace me, shouldn't you have behaved with me as you always behave with regard to white French generals? You warn them before divesting them of their authority; you send a person charged with making them aware of the order to turn over command to this one or that; in the case that they refuse to obey, then you take extreme measures against them, then you can justly treat them as rebels and ship them to France . . . Shouldn't General Leclerc have sent for me and warned me himself that people had made this or that report to him, true or not, against me? Shouldn't he have said to me: 'I have given you my word and promised you the protection of the government; today, since you have made yourself culpable, I am going to send you before that government, to make an account of your conduct.' Or else: 'The government orders you to place yourself before it; I transmit that order to you.' But nothing of the sort; on the contrary he acted toward me with means one has never employed even with respect to the worst criminals. No doubt I owe this treatment to my color; but my color . . . has my color ever hindered me from serving my country with fidelity and zeal? Does the color of my body tarnish my honor and my courage?[21]

With that, Toussaint had struck into the heart of the matter.

Well before the Leclerc expedition, proofs of the honor and courage of his service to France were written all over his body: "I have spilled my blood for my country; I took a bullet in the right hip, which I have still in my body, I had a violent contusion to the head, occasioned by a cannonball; it rattled my jaw so severely that the greater part of my teeth fell out and those that are left to me are still very loose. Finally, I have received on different occasions seventeen wounds whose honorable scars remain to me."[22] Toussaint's self-description as a naïvely frank old soldier may have been difficult to take at face value, but the service record his scars could show was much, much more convincing.

On September 15, 1802, one General Caffarelli appeared at the Fort de Joux. Napoleon considered Caffarelli to be one of his very most skillful interrogators, a man from whom nothing could finally be withheld. Caffarelli grilled Toussaint for twelve days and learned practically nothing at all.

"I committed myself to fulfill this mission," Caffarelli wrote to Napoleon,

> in such a manner as to attain the goal that you desire, and if I have not arrived at that goal, it is because this profoundly double-dealing and deceptive man, master of himself, precise and adroit, had his theme well prepared in advance and said nothing except what he wanted to say.
>
> From the first day he broached a conversation during which he treated me to a very long narrative about what had happened in Saint Domingue. This conversation, which lasted a long time, ended up nowhere and taught me nothing. I left him, putting him on notice that I would return the next day to know if he didn't have anything else to tell me.[23]

Napoleon, who had absolutely no interest in judging the dispute that Toussaint presented between himself and Leclerc, had instructed Caffarelli to question him closely on three points: "what treaties he had made with the agents of England," "his political views," and "information about his treasure."[24] A rumor had traveled from the colony to Paris that Toussaint, shortly before he settled the peace with Leclerc, had buried a fortune in gold on one of his properties at Ennery, then, in classic pirate style, murdered the men who had done the digging. In two hundred years no evidence to support this legend has ever turned up.

However, Toussaint avows in his memoir that at the opening of the French Revolution he was worth 648,000 francs. This very substantial value would have put him on par with the *grands blancs* of Saint

Domingue in all respects save the all-important racial one. Napoleon, whose government was as usual strapped for cash, was very interested to know what had happened to this money and if it could possibly be recovered.

Caffarelli got nowhere with this line of questioning. Toussaint had introduced the sum of his worth into the memoir as a prelude to saying that he had invested most of the money in wartime efforts, especially against the English invaders. His memoir insists that while he had found the public treasuries empty when he was first appointed as governor general, he had done much to fill them during his tenure. However, the Leclerc expedition had the good luck to get control of most of this money in the early days of the invasion. An unnamed *homme de couleur,* entrusted with the treasury of the Northern Department at Cap Français, turned it over to Leclerc when the French general occupied the ruins of the town. The treasury kept at Gonaïves, probably comprising all revenues from the Artibonite region if not the whole Western Department, was intercepted in the Cahos mountains by Rochambeau's division when it crossed diagonally from Fort Liberté to Gonaïves. Toussaint told Caffarelli that his and his wife's combined resources amounted to 250,000 francs at the time of the French landing (thus greatly depleted from ten years before) and that part of these private funds had been kept with the Gonaïves treasury, the other part with the treasury of Le Cap, and so had been lost to the French with the rest.

When Caffarelli quizzed him on the tale that six men sent to bury Toussaint's treasure before Rochambeau crossed the Grand Cahos had been "massacred upon their return," Toussaint protested that it was "an atrocious calumny invented by his enemies"[25] and insisted that as soon as the rumor began to spread he had produced, alive and well, the guards who were supposed to have been slain.

Toussaint and Suzanne were rich in land, not money, or at least they had been reduced to such a situation after the French invasion and Toussaint's retirement. Their holdings were large, and probably included more than those Toussaint admitted to Caffarelli: Héricourt, the sugar plantation in the Northern Plain; three contiguous plantations at Ennery, and sizable tracts across the Spanish border on the Central Plateau, which were used for raising cattle and horses. Some of these lands Toussaint had certainly bought before the revolution; others, like Héricourt, which had been owned by the comte de Noé, and the Central Plateau ranches, which were outside French Saint Domingue's territorial limits until 1801, he must have annexed sometime after 1791. As for any liquid capital, he gave no answer to any of Caffarelli's questions but the one already recorded in his memoir: he had spent his last sou in defense of the colony. The story is likely to be true, considering the heavy traffic Toussaint had with arms merchants in the United States throughout the months preceding Leclerc's invasion.

Napoleon was just as acutely interested in Toussaint's dealings with the English who had invaded Saint Domingue in 1793. After many extremely costly battles, most in the area of the port of Saint Marc, Toussaint had managed to engineer their final departure by diplomatic means. The fact that he had signed treaties with a foreign power without full authorization of the French government could be interpreted as treasonable—there were rumors too that the English might have lured Toussaint in the direction of independence.

Again, Caffarelli's interrogation could get no traction on this subject. Toussaint admitted only to two treaties concluded with General Maitland, one of which simply settled the British evacuation of the couple of points on the island they still occupied at the end of 1798. The second treaty covered British trade privileges with Saint Domingue, along with the nonaggression pact: Maitland promised not to interfere with Saint Domingue's shipping in Caribbean waters, Toussaint undertook not to attack Jamaica. This last commitment was a special nuisance for Napoleon, who had been entertaining a plan to use Saint Domingue as a base for just such an attack.

Caffarelli probed Toussaint concerning the suspicion that Toussaint had somehow "sold" himself to the English, but Toussaint insisted that he had received nothing from them other than a saddle and trappings for his horse, which he at first refused but was persuaded to accept as a personal gesture from General Maitland, and twenty barrels of gunpowder which Maitland also offered him. Otherwise he had no supplies or guns or munitions from the English; his war matériel was purchased from the United States or (quite frequently) captured from his enemies.

Between September 15 and September 24, Caffarelli interviewed Toussaint seven times. Of their second encounter, Caffarelli reported, "I found him trembling with cold, and sick, he was suffering a lot and could hardly speak."[26] The climate of the high and frosty Jura mountains could hardly be expected to suit an elderly man with many war wounds, who had spent his whole life in the tropics. In lieu of conversation Toussaint offered Caffarelli the document he had dictated. "I shut myself up to read this memoir right away," said the interrogator; "it was not difficult for me to recognize that the conversation of the previous day was nothing but an abridgment of this writing, on which he had built his whole defense."[27] In the subsequent interviews, Caffarelli could not get Toussaint to deviate by a hair from the defensive strategy which his memoir rehearsed. Despite his weakness, illness, and all the pressure Caffarelli could bring to bear on him, Toussaint said "nothing except what he wanted to say."

Caffarelli was worth his salt as an investigator, and after several days of being stonewalled he shifted his own tactics, with the idea of "exciting his amour propre . . . I told him that everything he had declared up to the present was beneath a man like himself, who was the first man of his color, who had won glory as a soldier, who had governed for a long time, who actually fallen low, unfortunate, and without hope of raising himself back up, he could win a kind of glory heretofore unknown to him, but which could be useful to him, and which would consist of having the courage to break out of the circle of denial in which he had shut himself, to declare nobly that he had driven off the agents of the Republic, because they were an obstacle to his designs, that he had organized an army, an administration, had accumulated treasuries, filled the arsenals and warehouses to assure his independence. That by going in this direction he would win the kind of glory which suited his real courage, and could get himself pardoned for many faults."[28]

This gambit was a cunning one, and suggests that Caffarelli had been able to discern aspects of Toussaint's character (pride in his achievements, outrage at the sorry way they'd been received) which

Toussaint during their interviews was doing his best to conceal. If Toussaint had taken the bait, Caffarelli might have tempted him to confess a plan to make Saint Domingue independent of France—a fault which certainly would not have been pardoned. Toussaint was impressed, but only into silence. When he spoke again, it was on the same lines as before.

"I saw him show spirit," Caffarelli concluded, "on just two occasions.

"The one, when they brought him the clothing and underwear which they had prepared for him." According to the program of small deprivations and humiliations designed by Napoleon for his prisoner, Toussaint was divested of his uniform and given clothing such as an ordinary peasant would wear; he was not insensible to the insult.

"The second, when they asked him to give up his razor. He said that the men who took that instrument from him must be very small-minded, since they suspected he lacked the necessary courage to bear his misfortune, that he had a family and that moreover his religion forbade him any attempt on his own life."[29]

There for once, however briefly, Toussaint did show a flash of his true colors, those which Caffarelli had tried unsuccessfully to expose. Caffarelli, though frustrated as ever, was also grudgingly impressed. "He seemed to me, in his prison, patient, resigned, and expecting from the First Consul all the justice which he believes he deserves." It's not far to the very last line of Caffarelli's report: "His prison is cold, sound, and very secure. He communicates with no one."[30]

Caffarelli's report does not go into Toussaint's "political views" in very general terms, though some specifics of his political dealings with the English are covered, and Toussaint gave the interrogator a fairly detailed report on the capacities and sentiments of many men in his officer corps who were still in Saint Domingue. So his overall political attitude must be deduced from what he said, and what he wrote, and from his actions. These show that he believed in the Rights of Man and of Citizen, as the French Revolution had proclaimed them not so very long before. And that he himself, regardless of race, was entitled to the rights and prerogatives of a French citizen and to those of a high-ranking officer in the French army. Therefore he believed with his whole being that he was entitled to his day in court. He could not have been fool enough to be certain that a trial would vindicate him, but he believed that a trial would give him a fair chance. He had composed the best defense he could, and he believed that he had an absolute right to present it, whatever the outcome might be.

In the silence following Caffarelli's departure, winter settled over the Fort de Joux. Naturally, Toussaint's health began to worsen, in that extreme cold and at that unaccustomed altitude; no one could have expected any different. No word came of any trial; no reply to Toussaint's memoir arrived from the first consul. In the last weeks and months of 1802, Toussaint must have begun to suspect that Napoleon did intend to bury him alive.

SEVEN

Scattering the Bones

Written without benefit of a secretary, and thus in a roughly phonetic French, Toussaint's last letters to Napoleon strike a note of pathos: "I beg you in the name of God in the name of humanity to cast a favorable glance upon my claim, on my position and my family . . . I have worked for a long time to acquire honor and glory from my government and to attract the esteem of my fellow citizens, and I am today crowned with thorns and with the most marked ingratitude for recompense."[1]

As for his position in his prison, he had described it earlier in his official memoir: "Is it not to cut off someone's legs and order him to walk? Is it not to cut out his tongue and tell him to talk? Is it not to bury a man alive?"[2] A draft of these poignant lines, written in Toussaint's phonetic French, was found after his death in the folds of the head cloth he always wore as a talisman of the spirits that walked with him. The last document he was able to conceal from his jailers, it meant so much to him that during the last days of his life he kept it bound to the bones of his head. To place it so was a magical act: a plea to the unseen world for justice.

To bury Toussaint Louverture alive seems to have been Napoleon Bonaparte's exact intention. To make a martyr of the black leader would be as dangerous as to allow him to return to Saint Domingue.

There had never been any intention to offer him the stage which a military trial would have afforded. He remained in his dungeon—in the innermost circle of five enclosures, defended by its rings of moats and drawbridges. As the winter months wore on, a series of small humiliations, all ordered from Paris, harried him in the direction of anonymity. His watch was taken from him, and his last correspondence, including the letters from Leclerc and Brunet which had betrayed him into arrest. For his general's uniform had been substituted the rough woolen clothing of an ordinary French mountain peasant. "I presume," wrote the minister of marine, "that you have removed from him everything that might have any rapport with a uniform, Toussaint is his name; that is the sole appellation which should be given him."[3]

The minister ordered that Toussaint should receive "appropriate treatment, that he should be sufficiently clothed and warmed."[4] Exactly what that meant in practice can be deduced from the result. Although the records of the fortress show that more was spent on Toussaint's maintenance than on many other prisoners there, his situation was not a healthy one for an elderly man who had never before left the tropics, and it was not intended to be. Though Toussaint was not absolutely starved to death, his rations left him undernourished. Though he was not absolutely left to die of exposure, he was given meager fuel for his fire.

At the end of January 1803, he began to complain of illness, but was never treated by a doctor. On April 7, he was found dead in his chair by the hearth of his cell. An autopsy revealed signs of a fatal respiratory infection, encouraged by malnutrition and the bitter mountain cold, and probably given an initial foothold by the old wounds to his head. His body was interred in an unmarked grave in a sort of potter's field for old soldiers at the Fort de Joux. There was to be no martyrdom for Toussaint Louverture, and there would be no relics either.

These very systematic efforts to erase the existence of Toussaint Louverture proved to be completely futile. Months before Toussaint drew his last breath, Captain General Leclerc expired in Saint Domingue of yellow fever. Most of his enormous army followed him into the grave, casualties of either disease or the combat which had reopened on a grand scale in July 1802, when news arrived in Saint Domingue of the restoration of slavery in Guadeloupe. What Toussaint had predicted on the deck of *L'Héros* about the depth, extension, and tenacity of the roots of the tree of black liberty in Saint Domingue proved to be absolutely true. It was not enough to have removed Toussaint, as Leclerc had woefully reported. To regain mastery of Saint Domingue really would have required the extermination of most of the black population, and if the French were willing to undertake just that, in the end they were not able.

Certainly Toussaint had foreseen this outcome, and it is possible that in permitting himself to be arrested, he had intentionally sacrificed his personal career to it. That argument is undermined by all the evidence of intelligent self-interest throughout Toussaint's history—but in the end one can hardly dispute Aimé Césaire's contention that "Toussaint had the tragic sense of life: on the one hand he was a Christian, sincerely and not as a feint as some have insinuated; and on the other hand, a contemporary of the French Revolution, he saw, like so many others among its contemporaries, the modern form of destiny. To die like Brissot. Like Robespierre. For a long time, he had prepared himself for that eventuality. Still more, he knew it was inevitable."[5]

During this time, Napoleon Bonaparte also seemed to be governed by a strange fatality. On May 20, 1802, he had proclaimed a law which made his intentions regarding slavery quite unmistakable: according to Article 3, "The trade in blacks and their importation into the said colonies will take place in conformity with the law and rules existing before the said époque of 1789."[6] By this clause the status quo before the French Revolution was to be restored, so far as the colonies were concerned.

Resistance had never completely stopped among leaders like Sylla and Sans-Souci, but when news of the restoration of slavery in Guadeloupe reached Saint Domingue, the rest of the officer cadre built by Toussaint began to desert French ranks and raise rebellion: Charles Belair, Clervaux, Christophe, and finally Dessalines. The blow to the French, already drastically weakened by the fever season and further compromised by near-total dependence on "colonial troops" (that is to say, the black troops of Toussaint's army), was fatal. A couple of weeks after Dessalines turned on him, Leclerc was dead of the fever.

The extravagant cruelties of his successor in command, General Donatien Rochambeau, were futile, except to inspire reprisals in kind. Rochambeau had black prisoners torn apart by dogs in the public squares, as if in a Roman amphitheater, and held a macabre ball for the *femmes de couleur,* at whose climax the fresh-slain corpses of their male relations were unveiled to them. If this kind of atrocity was meant to terrify the black and colored revolutionaries into submission, it had the opposite effect. In May 1803, when England declared war on France again, the position of the French in Saint Domingue became absolutely hopeless. Once it was clear that Dessalines would capture Cap Français, Rochambeau wisely put to sea, with the last remnant of an army that had once numbered eighty thousand, and let himself be captured by the British fleet.

On January 1, 1804, the independence of Haiti was declared. Later in 1804, Dessalines became emperor of Haiti. During the same year, on Dessalines's order, and mostly under his personal supervision, the slaughter of the surviving *grands blancs* of the old colony began.

A French survivor, Pierre Chazotte, describes Dessalines's tour of the killing grounds at Jérémie: "When they entered the prisons, they viewed many corpses, besmeared with gore; in every apartment the floor was two inches deep, encrusted with coagulated blood; the walls were dark crimsoned with the gushes of human blood, suddenly rushing from inflicted wounds. Having viewed this slaughterhouse of human bodies, they again mounted their horses, and rode to the place on the Western road, where upwards of 1,400 corpses lay, heaped one upon another, and formed two very high mounts. The blood flowing beneath had made an issue crossing the road, and formed a bar of coagulated blood 40 feet wide. The negroes from the country would not stamp their feet on that blood; they had practised a bypath, reaching the blockhouses on the southern hill, and thereby manifested their horror at Dessalines's deeds."[7]

Two hundred years later a Haitian friend told me, with a matter-of-fact solemnity, that there are certain injuries—it was understood that the abuse of slavery was definitely among them—which can be washed away only by blood.

Appalling as it may have been, Dessalines's course of action was nothing if not logical. When Toussaint had tried to incorporate the white property owners into his vision of a new reformed society founded on universal recognition of the Rights of Man, the whites had done nothing but betray him. By comparison with Toussaint, Dessalines has often been denounced as a savage. Where the concilia-tory Toussaint liked to say, *"Dousman alé lwen,"* (The gentlest way goes furthest), Dessalines snarled a harsher order: *"Koupé têt, boulé kay!"* (Cut off their heads and burn their houses!).

Severe as it was, Dessalines's consolidation of power contained an extraordinary progressive element. The massacres of 1804 were atro-cious, but in fact not all the whites were slaughtered. The death sentence was mainly restricted to those associated with the old *grand blanc* slave-owning class. Others who Dessalines thought might be useful to a new Haitian society—doctors, clerks, merchants, a whole Polish regiment that had switched from the French to the Haitian side—he preserved by the simple expedient of redefining them as black. Henceforward, Haiti would be an independent black nation, and to be both white and Haitian would be a contradiction in terms. This radical measure became a matter of law in the constitution of 1805, whereby all citizens of Haiti, regardless of their pigmentation, are defined as *nèg*. To this day, all for-eigners in Haiti, regardless of their pigmentation, are called *blancs*.

On the road from Port-au-Prince to Léogane there is a *hounfor,* or Vodou temple, arranged as many of them are to confront the outside world with the powers of both the right and the left hand. As in many spiritual traditions, in Vodou the work of the left hand is considered to be sinister, while the work of the right is beneficent and healing. The average *houngan,* or Vodou priest, is obliged, for the usual reasons, to "work with both hands."

In this particular *hounfor,* if one stands in the center and faces the courtyard, the road, and the world to which the road leads, one has the Chanm Ginen (chamber of the pacific mysteries of Africa) on one's right hand. The motto above the door reads *Dieu qui donne et Dieu qui fait* (God who gives and God who makes), a phrase which recalls Toussaint's favorite proverb, *Dousman alé lwen.* On the left hand is a more dangerous room with the motto *Fok nan pwen,* which means "There would have not to be any for me not to get some."

The qualities invoked by these mottoes are found together— though not mixed in our common understanding of a mixture—in most Haitians, and can be sharply polarized according to the need of an occasion. Certainly they were sharply polarized from time to time, and according to need, in the personality of Toussaint Louverture. Like most Haitians, he served more than a single spirit: Bondyé or Gran Mêt, analogous with God the Father and Creator in the Christian faith; and various *lwa* imported from Africa, some beneficent, some less so. A powerful strain of charismatic Christianity, completely compatible with the pacific, benevolent Esprit Ginen, runs through his career almost from the start. In the summer of 1793 he expressed his preference of the power of love to the power of force: "we receive everyone with humanity, and brotherhood, even our most Cruel enemies, and we pardon them wholeheartedly, and it is with gentleness that we coax them back from their errors." Nine years later in the Fort de Joux, his sense of the tragedy of his own situation moved him to evoke Christ's crown of thorns.

Toussaint's Christianity, though perhaps inconstant, was not feigned. The record shows that very often he was animated, powerfully, by a Christian spirit. Still, while one considers the forbearance and moderation he mainly exercised, one must also recall that many of the atrocities Dessalines committed under Toussaint's rule were probably done with Toussaint's tacit approval, if not on his secret order.

For a citizen of what we are pleased to call the First World, the apparent contradictions of Toussaint's personality can be difficult to resolve. Within Haitian culture, there are no such contradictions, but simply the actions of different spirits which may possess one's being under different circumstances and in response to vastly different needs. There is no doubt that from time to time Toussaint Louverture made room in himself for angry, vengeful spirits, as well as the more beneficent *lwa.*

The name which he chose for himself, Louverture, implies that his being was ordered by Attibon Legba, the Hermes-like figure who keeps the gates and crossroads. But Legba has his sinister analogue, an inverted reflection called Maît' Kalfou—Master of Crossroads—who has a great capacity for violence and betrayal. Through Maît' Kalfou, Legba is akin to Ghede, the spirit of death, and of sex, and of the appetites. During all of his extraordinary career, Toussaint operated along the spectrum of these spirits and the attributes they represent. In their peculiarly inverted twinship, Attibon Legba and Maît' Kalfou negotiate the no-man's-land between the spirit of *Fok nan pwen* and that of *Dieu qui donne et Dieu qui fait*—between *Dousman alé lwen* and *Koupé têt, boulé kay.*

According to the principles of Vodou, which has remained the actual religion of Haiti from Toussaint's time into ours (though it was not officially recognized until the 1990s, under the presidency of Jean-Bertrand Aristide), no one ever really dies. The death of the body is understood as a transition of state. In contrast to the Judeo-Christian scheme of things, the souls of the Haitian dead do not depart to any distant afterworld, but remain in invisible but close proximity to the world of the living. In aggregate they form a vast spiritual reservoir, called *Les Invisibles* or *Les Morts et les Mystères*—a well of energy available on the other side of any mirror or beneath the surface of any pool.

This near presence of the spirits of the dead foreshortens the Haitian sense of history, so that the events of the Haitian Revolution, though two hundred years in the past, may seem to have happened only yesterday. It is as if for two hundred years the Haitian Revolution has been sleeping very close to the surface, sometimes stirring to press against the fragile membrane that separates it from the world of the present day. Particular *lwa* express themselves from the reservoir of *Les Morts et les Mystères,* and show their power to govern the actions and the policies of the living. The Duvalier regime, which ruled Haiti from 1957 to 1986, particularly associated itself with the spirit of Jean-Jacques Dessalines—the spirit of *Koupé têt, boulé kay,* which rules by force and by terror, which could wash away racism, but only in blood.

In 1990, a democratic revolution brought a gentler, more accommodating spirit to life in the land. In 2004, Haiti's bicentennial year, this second revolution seemed to fail.

The magical work of Vodou is often done by the creation of a *pwen,* an object with a spiritual force bound up in it. In the opinion of some seers, the violence of Haitian history for the past two centuries is explained by the unfortunate fact that the *pwen* for the revolution was made on the element of fire. In 2004, the revolutionary *pwen* was supposed to be done over again, on water. If the effort succeeded, the result remains to be seen.

But Haiti's history since 1804 is scarcely more violent or more troubled than that of the world at large. In the last years of the twentieth century, a priest of Borgne said to me that what Haiti needed to find a way out of its difficulties was the spirit of Toussaint Louverture. At the opening of the twenty-first century, the United States and the rest of the world could use that spirit too.

Afterword

The Image of Toussaint

In December 1861, on the eve of the American Civil War, the abolitionist and justly renowned orator Wendell Phillips delivered a speech on
Toussaint Louverture in New York and Boston. As part of his perora-
tion he drove home this point: "If I stood here tonight to tell the story
of Napoleon, I should take it from the lips of Frenchmen, who find no
language rich enough to paint the great captain of the nineteenth century. Were I here to tell you the story of Washington, I should take it
directly from your hearts—you, who think no marble white enough on
which to carve the name of the Father of his Country. I am about to tell
you the story of a negro who has left hardly one written line. I am to
glean it from the reluctant testimony of Britons, Frenchmen,
Spaniards—men who despised him as a negro and a slave, and hated
him because he had beaten them in many a battle. All the materials
from his biography are from the lips of his enemies."[1]

   This passage is as subtle as it is splendid: the deft insertion of
Toussaint into the peerage of the great white national heroes of his time
is accomplished almost by sleight of hand. At the same time, like much
of the most inspired political rhetoric, it is no better than half true.
Toussaint left a considerable written record (though Phillips likely
knew nothing of it): not only a copious correspondence but also

the memoir he drafted in the Fort de Joux. Moreover, he has been described, from his own time into ours, by friends and admirers as often as by foes and detractors. Yet Phillips is right enough to say that practically all firsthand reports on Toussaint come from the white, European milieu; precious few comments from his black and colored contemporaries have survived. It's also true that very few accounts of Toussaint's life and work have been nonpartisan. He is almost always depicted as absolutely a devil or absolutely a saint.

Portraits of Toussaint from his own time are reminiscent of drawings of American buffalo by European artists working from descriptions and without ever having seen a buffalo. Many of these images seem to be no more than sketches of generic African features, sometimes exaggerated into grotesque caricature. A study by Haitian scholar Fritz Daguillard suggests that two of the early portraits are at least reasonably faithful to their subject. The first, a full profile view, was probably done from life as a watercolor by Nicolas Eustache Maurin. Later rendered as an engraving by Delpech, this portrait became a model for many later artists who transported the basic image of Toussaint's profile into various other contexts. Toussaint liked the original well enough to present it as a gift to the French agent Roume, whose family preserved it. He wears full dress uniform for the occasion: a general's bicorne hat, decorated with red and white feathers and the red, white, and blue French Revolutionary cockade, a high tight neck cloth and a high-collared uniform coat, heavy with gold braid. The features in this image agree with eyewitness descriptions of the time: Toussaint is just slightly pop-eyed, his profile marked by a prominent, underslung lower jaw.

The second portrait, a three-quarter view, was singled out by Toussaint's son Isaac as the only image in which he found his father recognizable. At a glance this second portrait (by M. de Montfayon, who had served under Toussaint as an engineer) does not look much like the first. Toussaint wears a similar coat as in the Maurin portrait, with gold braid, his general's epaulettes, his right hand clasping a spyglass against a ceremonial sash. In this image he is bareheaded, his remaining hair gathered in a queue at the back, and we see that his forehead is very high, and his cranium remarkably large. In the Montfayon image, Toussaint's features look more delicate, less typically African, than in the other; perhaps they were slightly idealized by the artist. If Montfayon makes the jaw less prominent, the difference can be accounted for by the angle of view. The more one looks at the two portraits together, the more reasonable it seems that they represent the same person, though in two different frames of mind. The full profile suggests a head-on belligerence; the three-quarter view presents a wary, intelligent observer. History has shown that Toussaint Louverture possessed both of these qualities, in abundance.

Twentieth-century biographer Pierre Pluchon declares that "Toussaint was in no way a handsome man. On the contrary, his physique was graceless and puny."[2] To be sure, Pluchon is one of Toussaint's demonizers, but even the friendly observers agree that Louverture was, well, funny-looking, though by the time his name became known, most people had learned not to laugh at him. He was short and slight, with a head disproportionately large for the body. Most descriptions report him to have been bowlegged, and in general he seems to have had a jockey's build—and was indeed a famous horseman. His physical capacities, even when he was in his fifties (an ancient age for a slave in a French sugar colony), were very far from "puny." According to the French general Pamphile de Lacroix, who knew Toussaint late in his career, "His body of iron received its vigor only from the tempering of his soul, and being master of his soul, he became master of his body."[3]

The contradictory reports on Toussaint prepared for the French home government by General Kerverseau (his dedicated enemy) and by Colonel Vincent (his determined friend) represent a polarization of opinion that has endured for two centuries. In 1802, as Napoleon prepared the military expedition intended to repress the slave rebellion in Saint Domingue and to humiliate its leader, a couple of propaganda pamphlets were published by Dubroca and by Cousin d'Avallon, who denounced Toussaint in much the same style as Kerverseau had done: "All his acts are covered by a veil of hypocrisy so profound that, although his whole life is a story of perfidy and betrayal, he still has the art to deceive anyone who approaches him about the purity of his sentiments . . . His character is a terrible mélange of fanaticism and atrocious penchants; he passes coolly from the altar to carnage, and from prayer into dark schemes of perfidy . . . For the rest, all his shell of devoutness is nothing but a mask he thought necessary to cover up the depraved sentiments of his heart, to command with a greater success the blind credulity of the Blacks . . . There is no doubt that with the high idea which the Blacks have of him, seconded by the priests who surround him, he has managed to make himself be seen as one inspired, and to order the worst crimes in the name of heaven . . . He has abused the confidence of his first benefactors, he has betrayed the Spanish, England, France under the government of kings, Republican France, his own blood, his fatherland, and the religion which he pretends to respect: such is the portrait of Toussaint Louverture, whose life will be a striking example of the crimes to which ambition may lead, when honesty, education and honor fail to control its excesses."[4]

Wendell Phillips was referring to writers like these when he said that Toussaint's story had been told only by his enemies; yet the black general's adulators were just as numerous. After his overthrow by Napoleon, his imprisonment in the Jura Mountains inspired a sonnet by William Wordsworth:

> Toussaint, the most unhappy Man of Men!
> Whether the whistling Rustic tend his plough
> Within thy hearing, or thy head be now
> Pillowed in some deep dungeon's earless den—
> O miserable Chieftain! Where and when
> Wilt thou find patience? Yet die not, do thou
> Wear rather in thy bonds a cheerful brow;
> Though fallen Thyself, never to rise again,
> Live and take comfort. Thou has left behind
> Powers that will work for thee; air, earth and skie;
> There's not a breathing of the common wind
> That will forget thee; thou has great allies;
> Thy friends are exultations, agonies,
> And love, and Man's unconquerable mind.

Meanwhile, Alphonse de Lamartine, as illustrious a poet in the French tradition as Wordsworth in the English, celebrated and reinforced the legend of Toussaint with a verse play named after its hero. Produced for the first time in 1850, just two years after France had permanently abolished the slavery which Napoleon had restored in 1802, the play was quite popular with the public; the critical response, however, revealed reactionary attitudes. Charles Bercelièvre gave his review the sarcastic title "Blacks are more worthy than whites."

"Can one believe," he went on to say, "that in the nineteenth century, in a country that speaks of nothing but its nationalism and its patriotism, a man would be bold enough to present, in a French theater, a black tragi-comedy in which our compatriots are treated as cowards, as despots, as scoundrels, as thieves, and called by other more or less gracious epithets; in which one hears at every moment: Death to the French! Shame on the French! Do let's massacre the French! . . . That *Toussaint Louverture* should have success among negroes—we understand that much without difficulty, but that this anti-national, anti-patriotic work, fruit of an insane, sick brain, should be produced and accepted on a French stage—that we will never understand."[5]

From this inflamed passage it is very plain not only that the violent loss of Saint Domingue to its former slaves remained a very sore spot in France, even a half century after the fact, but also that despite the final end of slavery in French possessions, the assumption of black racial inferiority, which the ideology of slavery very much required, had scarcely been weakened among Frenchmen. With this play, Lamartine made an argument for the equality of the races which anticipated the black pride movements of the Caribbean basin by nearly a hundred years. He offended his contemporary critics by providing his Toussaint with linguistic powers and a rhetorical style that would have been natural to a white French hero of the theater. From the modern point of view, it seems impossible that Toussaint could be made to speak in elegant Alexandrian rhyming couplets without a very great distortion of his personality, his thought, and his actual mode of expression—yet Lamartine is sometimes ingenious in adapting statements Toussaint was known to have made to the very rigid requirements of the verse form:

Ma double autorité tient tout en équilibre:*
Gouverneur pour le blanc, Spartacus pour le libre,
Tout cède et réussit sous mon règne incertain,
Je demeure indécis ainsi que le destin,
Sûr que la liberté, germant sur ces ruines
Enfonce en attendant d'immortelles racines.[6]

The Haitian people, as they named themselves, were the first to put an end to slavery in the New World, with their definitive defeat of the French in 1803 and their declaration of independence in 1804. In the course of the next half century, the "peculiar institution" died, by slow and miserable degrees or in great spasms of violence, the last of which was the American Civil War. The story of Toussaint Louverture was adopted by the nineteenth-century abolitionists, not only Wendell Phillips but also Englishmen like M. D. Stephens and James Beard, and Frenchmen including Lamartine, Victor Schoelcher, and Gragnon Lacoste, who burnished and enshrined it in legend.

Since Phillips was not constrained by a verse form or by tight theatrical unities, his Toussaint is somewhat truer to life than Lamartine's, though the American orator permits himself many small distortions of fact, and embraces apocryphal details most warmly. For Phillips, as for Lamartine, the career of Toussaint was proof of the argument—as counterintuitive in 1861 as it was in 1850—that black men were as good as white:

> Now, blue-eyed Saxons, proud of your race, go back with me to the commencement of the century, and select what statesman you please. Let him be either European or American; let him have a brain the result of six generations of culture; let him have the ripest training of university routine; let him add

*My double authority holds everything in balance:
 Governor for the white, Spartacus for the freedman,
 All yields and flourishes under my uncertain reign.
 I remain as undecided as destiny
 Sure that liberty, seeding itself in these ruins
 Furrows, while waiting, its immortal roots.

to it the better education of practical life, crown his temples with the silver of seventy years; and show me the man of Saxon Lineage for whom his most sanguine admirer will wreathe a laurel rich as embittered foes have placed on the brow of this negro—rare military skill, profound knowledge of human nature, content to blot out all party distinctions, and trust a state to the blood of its sons— . . . this is the record which the history of rival states makes up for this inspired black of St. Domingo.[7]

When he generalized the concept, Phillips grew more stark. "Some doubt the courage of the negro. Go to Hayti, and stand on those fifty thousand graves of the best soldiers France ever had, and ask them what they think of the negro's sword."[8]

Emerging from the success of the Haitian Revolution, the *gens de couleur,* few in number as they were, enjoyed significant advantages of wealth and education over the vast black majority. The first Haitian historians—Beaubrun Ardouin, Céligny Ardouin, Saint Rémy, Thomas Madiou—came from this class, as did Toussaint's first Haitian biographer, Pauléus Sannon, who served as Haiti's foreign minister during the World War I era. The colored historians who wrote in the early nineteenth century had a rather ambivalent attitude toward Toussaint, whose army had won a fairly well-deserved reputation for brutality during the vicious civil war which pitted the newly freed blacks against the *gens de couleur* and which ended in 1800 with the colored party's being crushed. Though Toussaint's importance to the overthrow of slavery and the independence of Haiti was incontestable, Madiou and the other mulatto historians could hardly help seeing him, and portraying him, as an oppressor of their tribe; Sannon, with a century's distance from the events, described the black general with a greater objectivity and with less strangled rancor.

In the twentieth century, the story of Toussaint was taken up by the writers of Négritude, a pan-Caribbean movement of black cultural pride. The Martinican writer Edouard Glissant, who hails from another former French sugar colony, wrote a play called *Monsieur Toussaint,* which situates the black general in a newly evolving Caribbean literary tradition rather more securely than Lamartine had managed to locate him in the French. Aimé Césaire, best known for his poetry, wrote a book which is part biography, part political analysis, mythologizing Toussaint in a somewhat different way—as the first person to embody a solution to the problem of colonialism. *The Black Jacobins,* by a historian from Trinidad, C. L. R. James, was until recently the standard work on the Haitian Revolution; James, writing in the late 1930s, has the attitudes of a fairly dogmatic Marxist, yet the avowed Marxist disbelief in the power of "extraordinary men" to influence history simply evaporates in James's portrait of Toussaint Louverture.

The Duvalier dynasty in Haiti, the most stable and also the most thoroughly repressive government Haiti has known since independence, associated itself with the violent authoritarianism of Jean-Jacques Dessalines. When Jean-Bertrand Aristide came to Haiti's presidency in 1990, on the crest of a wave of democratizing populism that many Haitians called the "Second Revolution," he seemed to want to identify himself with the more conciliatory figure of Toussaint Louverture. In the beginning, the implied Aristide-Louverture comparison was subliminally subtle, but during the Haitian Revolution's bicentennial year of 2004, when Aristide was forced from office and the country by a United States–assisted coup d'état, he quoted—verbatim—the words Toussaint had famously spoken when he was arrested and deported by the French in 1802.

For two centuries, historians, biographers, playwrights, novelists, and even politicians have constructed whatever Toussaint Louverture they require. Almost always it is an extreme Toussaint: either a vicious, duplicitous, Machiavellian figure who not only destroyed France's richest colony in an (inevitable) regression to African savagery but also laid the foundation of the most authoritarian and repressive elements in the Haitian state which came after him, or a military and political genius, autodidact and self-made man, a wise and good humanitarian who not only led his people to freedom but also envisioned and briefly created a society based on racial harmony, at least two hundred years ahead of its time. The latter figure is found in twentieth-century English biographies by Ralph Korngold and Wenda Parkinson, who, like Colonel Vincent two centuries previously, admire, defend, and advocate for Toussaint. By the usual extreme contrast, the oft-revised and updated biography by the French scholar Pierre Pluchon, while almost certainly the best-documented work of its kind, seems to take its attitude toward Toussaint unadulterated from the hostile, cynical report of General Kerverseau.

To pierce this cloud of contradictions one would like to return to the man himself, but it is difficult to do. Famously elusive in real life, Toussaint Louverture is no less elusive to the historian and biographer. The fictionalizing of his character is encouraged by the fact that during the first fifty years of his life, Toussaint walked so very softly that he left next to no visible tracks at all.

Notes

EPIGRAPH

1. Lacroix, p. 244.
2. Scharon, vol. 2, p. 102.

PREFACE

1. Phillips, p. 21.

ONE
Opening the Gate

1. Schoelcher, p. 94; Dubois, p. 176.
2. Schoelcher, p. 389.
3. Private collection of Gérard Barthélemy.
4. Private collection of Gérard Barthélemy: letter from Toussaint to Don García, 20 March 1794.
5. Private collection of Gérard Barthélemy.
6. Yves Benot, "Sources et documents sur l'insurrection des esclaves

de Saint Domingue," *Annales historique de la révolution Française,* no. 339 (January–March 2005).

7. Fick, p. 113.
8. Dubois, p. 126.
9. Pélage-Marie Duboys, vol. 1, p. 62.
10. Gros, p. 40.
11. Gros, p. 44.
12. Gros, p. 47.
13. Gros, p. 45.
14. Gros, p. 46.
15. Dorsinville, p. 44.
16. Dorsinville, p. 44.
17. Private collection of Gérard Barthélemy.
18. Pluchon, *Un révolutionnaire noir,* p. 77.
19. Laurent, pp. 68–72.
20. Dubois, p. 142.
21. Dubois, p. 144.
22. Pluchon, *Un révolutionnaire noir,* p. 79.
23. Stein, p. 70.
24. Stein, p. 75.
25. Pélage-Marie Duboys, p. 108.
26. Dubois, p. 160.
27. Parkinson, p. 70.
28. Schoelcher, p. 93.

TWO
Before the Storm

1. Métral, p. 325.
2. Métral, p. 326.
3. Sannon, vol. 1, p. 1.
4. Métral, p. 326.
5. Dubois, p. 57.
6. Schoelcher, p. 388.
7. Private collection of Gérard Barthélemy.

8. Barthélemy, "Qui êtes-vous," p. 1.

9. Barthélemy, "Qui êtes-vous," p. 2.

10. Moreau de Saint-Méry, *Description topographique, physique, civile, politique et historique de la partie française de l'île Saint-Domingue* (Paris: Société Française d'Histoire d'Outre-Mer, 1984), vol. 2, p. 580.

11. Private collection of Gérard Barthélemy: Bayon de Libertat to Comte de Bréda, 6 August 1773.

12. Private collection of Gérard Barthélemy: Bayon to Bréda, 18 August 1773.

13. Private collection of Gérard Barthélemy: Delribal to Bréda, 18 October 1773.

14. Private collection of Gérard Barthélemy: Delribal to Bréda, 18 October 1773.

15. Private collection of Gérard Barthélemy: Bayon to Bréda, 23 February 1774.

16. Private collection of Gérard Barthélemy: Bayon to Bréda, 23 November 1773.

17. Barthélemy, "Qui êtes-vous"; Schoelcher, p. 391.

18. Saint-Rémy p. 90.

19. Fouchard, Debien, and Menier, p. 68.

20. Fouchard, Debien, and Menier, p. 79.

21. Barthélemy, "Noirs libres," p. 1.

22. Barthélemy, "Noirs libres," p. 23.

23. Cauna, p. 189.

24. Private collection of Gérard Barthélemy: Bayon to Bréda, 28 May 1794.

25. Cauna, p. 191.

26. Cauna, p. 191.

27. Pluchon, *Un révolutionnaire noir,* p. 203.

28. Cauna, p. 194.

29. Cauna, p. 195.

30. Cauna, p. 196.

31. Pluchon, *Toussaint Louverture d'après le général,* p. 20.

THREE
Turning the Tide

1. Pluchon, *Un révolutionnaire noir,* p. 94.
2. Pluchon, *Un révolutionnaire noir,* p. 95.
3. Pluchon, *Un révolutionnaire noir,* p. 95.
4. Private collection of Gérard Barthélemy; Laurent, p. 95.
5. Bibliothèque Nationale de France, Paris, Fonds Français 1204, vol. 3, piece 458.
6. Métral, p. 328.
7. Métral, p. 331.
8. Métral, p. 331.
9. Schoelcher, p. 93.
10. Madiou, vol. 1, p. 182.
11. Schoelcher, p. 97.
12. Geggus, *Slavery, War and Revolution,* p. 108.
13. Lacroix, p. 188.
14. Madiou, vol. 1, p. 255.
15. Dubois, p. 170.
16. Pluchon, *Un révolutionnaire noir,* p. 105.
17. Sannon, vol. 1, p. 138; Arch. Nat. #124.
18. Sannon, vol. 1, p. 139.
19. Geggus, *Haitian Revolutionary Studies,* p. 121.
20. Pluchon, *Un révolutionnaire noir,* p. 103.
21. Pélage-Marie Duboys, vol. 1, p. 155.
22. Geggus, *Haitian Revolutionary Studies,* p. 136.
23. Geggus, *Haitian Revolutionary Studies,* p. 136.
24. Laurent, p. 105.
25. Laurent, p. 113.
26. Laurent, p. 114.
27. Laurent, p. 119.
28. Laurent, p. 120.
29. Laurent, p. 123.
30. Laurent, p. 131.
31. Laurent, p. 134.
32. Laurent, p. 134.

33. Laurent, p. 135.
34. Laurent, p. 135.
35. Laurent, p. 138.
36. Laurent, p. 138.
37. Ott, p. 84.
38. Schoelcher, p. 144.
39. Laurent, p. 253.
40. Laurent, p. 254.
41. Laurent, p. 163.
42. Schoelcher, p. 137.
43. Schoelcher, p. 138.
44. Madiou, vol. 1, p. 244.
45. Laurent, p. 310.
46. Laurent, p. 311.
47. Laurent, p. 313.
48. Laurent, p. 314.
49. Laurent, p. 315.
50. Laurent, p. 315.
51. Laurent, p. 316.
52. Laurent, p. 316.
53. Laurent, p. 317.
54. Laurent, p. 317.
55. Laurent, p. 319.
56. Laurent, p. 320.
57. Laurent, p. 323.
58. Laurent, p. 323.
59. Laurent, p. 324.
60. Laurent, p. 324.
61. Laurent, p. 325.
62. Bibliothèque Nationale de France, Paris, Fonds Français 1204, vol. 3, piece 86 (22 February 1796).
63. Bibliothèque Nationale de France, Paris, Fonds Français 1204, vol. 3, piece 86 (22 February 1796); Laurent, p. 334.
64. Laurent, p. 307.
65. Pélage-Marie Duboys, p. 215.
66. Pélage-Marie Duboys, p. 232.

67. Schoelcher, p. 172.
68. Schoelcher, p. 171.
69. Schoelcher, p. 172.

FOUR
Closing the Circle

1. Schoelcher, p. 172.
2. Stein, p. 133.
3. Laurent, p. 185.
4. Laurent, pp. 380–81.
5. Pélage-Marie Duboys, vol. 1, p. 227.
6. Laurent, p. 382.
7. Stein, p. 159.
8. Laurent, p. 394.
9. Madiou, vol. 1, p. 317.
10. Madiou, vol. 1, p. 317.
11. Madiou, vol. 1, p. 360.
12. Schoelcher, p. 219.
13. Laurent, p. 423.
14. Stein, p. 162.
15. Stein, p. 162.
16. Pélage-Marie Duboys, vol. 1, p. 281.
17. Pélage-Marie Duboys, vol. 1, p. 285.
18. Private collection of Gérard Barthélemy.
19. Scharon, vol. 2, p. 94.
20. Scharon, vol. 2, p. 95.
21. Scharon, vol. 2, p. 97.
22. Scharon, vol. 2, p. 100.
23. Pluchon, *Toussaint Louverture d'après le général,* p. 26.
24. Pluchon, *Un révolutionnaire noir,* p. 193.
25. Pluchon, *Un révolutionnaire noir,* p. 203.
26. Pluchon, *Un révolutionnaire noir,* p. 180.
27. Pluchon, *Un révolutionnaire noir,* p. 178.
28. Pluchon, *Un révolutionnaire noir,* p. 181.

29. Scharon, vol. 2, p. 202.
30. Laurent, p. 442.
31. Pluchon, *Un révolutionnaire noir,* p. 202.
32. Césaire, p. 249.
33. Pluchon, *Un révolutionnaire noir,* p. 213.
34. Pélage-Marie Duboys, vol. 1, p. 317.
35. James, p. 205; Schoelcher, p. 229.
36. Pélage-Marie Duboys, vol. 1, p. 320.
37. Pélage-Marie Duboys, vol. 2, p. 19.
38. Pélage-Marie Duboys, vol. 2, p. 22.
39. Lacroix, p. 210.
40. Lacroix, p. 210.
41. Lacroix, p. 216.
42. Pluchon, *Un révolutionnaire noir,* p. 227.
43. Pélage-Marie Duboys, vol. 2, p. 30.
44. Schoelcher, p. 382.
45. Dubois, p. 225.
46. Schoelcher, p. 239.
47. Laurent, p. 456.
48. Laurent, p. 461.
49. Pélage-Marie Duboys, vol. 2, p. 170.
50. Brown, p. 129.
51. Archives Nationales de France, Colonies F3 59, pp. 205ff. (Vincent, "Notes sur un grand nombre d'hommes civils et militaires, actuellement dans la colonie de St-Domingue").
52. Brown, p. 137.
53. Brown, p. 141.
54. Brown, p. 138.
55. Brown, p. 148.
56. Pélage-Marie Duboys, vol. 2, p. 59.
57. Pélage-Marie Duboys, vol. 2, p. 68.
58. Pélage-Marie Duboys, vol. 2, p. 80.
59. Pélage-Marie Duboys, vol. 2, p. 71.
60. Pélage-Marie Duboys, vol. 2, p. 87.
61. Pélage-Marie Duboys, vol. 2, p. 113.
62. Pélage-Marie Duboys, vol. 2, p. 113.

63. Pélage-Marie Duboys, vol. 2, p. 101.
64. Pélage-Marie Duboys, vol. 2, p. 104.
65. Pélage-Marie Duboys, vol. 2, p. 128.
66. Private collection of Gérard Barthélemy.
67. Private collection of Gérard Barthélemy.
68. Pélage-Marie Duboys, vol. 2, p. 150.
69. Pélage-Marie Duboys, vol. 2, p. 152.
70. Archives Nationales de France, Colonies F3 59 pp. 183ff. (Vincent to Leclerc, 27 Brumaire, year 10).
71. Pluchon, *Un révolutionnaire noir*, p. 323.
72. Lacroix, p. 238.
73. Lacroix, p. 217.
74. Césaire, p. 262.
75. Lacroix, p. 217.
76. Archives Nationales de France, Colonies F3 59 pp. 183ff. (Vincent to Leclerc, 27 Brumaire, year 10).
77. Pélage-Marie Duboys, vol. 2, p. 172.
78. Pluchon, *Un révolutionnaire noir*, p. 614.
79. Pluchon, *Un révolutionnaire noir*, p. 289.
80. Pluchon, *Un révolutionnaire noir*, p. 263.
81. Private collection of Gérard Barthélemy.
82. Private collection of Gérard Barthélemy.
83. Private collection of Gérard Barthélemy.
84. Pluchon, *Un révolutionnaire noir*, p. 293.
85. Lacroix, p. 259.
86. Lacroix, p. 259.

FIVE

The Last Campaign

1. Lacroix, p. 243.
2. Lacroix, p. 243.
3. Lacroix, p. 242.
4. Lacroix, p. 238.

5. Lacroix, p. 245.
6. Lacroix, p. 245; James, p. 262.
7. Lacroix, p. 245.
8. Lacroix, p. 246.
9. Lacroix, p. 243.
10. Lacroix, p. 237.
11. Pélage-Marie Duboys, vol. 2, p. 228.
12. Schoelcher, p. 387.
13. Lacroix, p. 304.
14. Pélage-Marie Duboys, vol. 2, p. 127.
15. Lacroix, p. 240.
16. Pluchon, *Un révolutionnaire noir*, p. 419.
17. Moïse, p. 74.
18. Moïse, p. 46.
19. Pélage-Marie Duboys, vol. 2, p. 104.
20. Pélage-Marie Duboys, vol. 2, p. 214.
21. Pélage-Marie Duboys, vol. 2, p. 214.
22. Pluchon, *Un révolutionnaire noir*, p. 241.
23. Pluchon, *Un révolutionnaire noir*, p. 253.
24. Moïse, p. 49.
25. Pélage-Marie Duboys, vol. 2, p. 218.
26. Moïse, p. 72.
27. Moïse, p. 74.
28. Moïse, p. 76.
29. Moise, p. 77.
30. Moïse, p. 77.
31. Dubois, p. 242.
32. Lacroix, p. 260.
33. Lacroix, p. 261.
34. Archives Nationales de France, Colonies F3 59, p. 161 (Vincent letter to Toussaint, 19 Thermidor, year 9).
35. Asprey, p. 45.
36. Asprey, p. 45.
37. Pluchon, *Un révolutionnaire noir*, p. 347.
38. Pluchon, *Toussaint Louverture d'après le général*, pp. 26–27.

39. Pluchon, *Un révolutionnaire noir,* p. 353.
40. Saint-Rémy, p. 120.
41. Saint-Rémy, p. 122.
42. Lacroix, p. 261.
43. Archives Nationales de France, Colonies F3 59, p. 169 (Vincent to Christophe, 15 Brumaire, year 10).
44. Archives Nationales de France, Colonies F3 59, pp. 205ff.
45. Archives Nationales de France, Colonies F3 59, p. 167 (Vincent to Moyse, 15 Brumaire, year 10).
46. Archives Nationales de France, Colonies F3 59, p. 170 (Vincent to Pascal, 15 Brumaire, year 10).
47. Archives Nationales de France, Colonies F3 59, p. 166 (Vincent to Toussaint, 15 Brumaire, year 10).
48. Pélage-Marie Duboys, vol. 2, p. 229.
49. Pélage-Marie Duboys, vol. 2, p. 223.
50. Pélage-Marie Duboys, vol. 2, p. 227.
51. Lacroix, p. 283.
52. Private collection of Gérard Barthélemy: Roume to Forfait, 1 December 1801.
53. Archives Nationales de France, Colonies F3 59 (Vincent to Leclerc, 29 Brumaire, year 10).
54. Madiou, vol. 2, p. 172.
55. Lacroix, p. 283.
56. Pluchon, *Un révolutionnaire noir,* p. 462.
57. Lacroix, p. 366.
58. Pluchon, *Un révolutionnaire noir,* p. 481.
59. Archives Nationales de France, Colonies F3 59, pp. 205ff.
60. Madiou, vol. 2, p. 165.
61. Schoelcher, p. 326.
62. Madiou, vol. 2, pp. 209–10.
63. Madiou, vol. 2, p. 213.
64. Madiou, vol. 2, p. 213.
65. Madiou, vol. 2, p. 213.
66. Madiou, vol. 2, p. 213.
67. Schoelcher, p. 329.

68. Madiou, vol. 2, p. 214.
69. Schoelcher, p. 331.
70. Lacroix, p. 331.
71. Lacroix, p. 332.
72. Madiou, vol. 2, p. 266.
73. Lacroix, p. 332.
74. Madiou, vol. 2, p. 272.
75. Métral, p. 259.
76. Lacroix, p. 335.
77. Auguste, p. 146.
78. Pluchon, *Un révolutionnaire noir,* p. 487.
79. Métral, p. 83.
80. Private collection of Gérard Barthélemy.
81. Private collection of Gérard Barthélemy.
82. Private collection of Gérard Barthélemy.
83. Private collection of Gérard Barthélemy.
84. Auguste, p. 145.
85. Auguste, p. 147.
86. Métral, p. 265.
87. Auguste, p. 153.
88. Madiou, vol. 2, p. 304.
89. Lacroix, p. 344.
90. Roussier, p. 131.
91. Pluchon, *Un révolutionnaire noir,* p. 490.
92. Private collection of Gérard Barthélemy; Mme de Michelet, *Histoire de mon père.*
93. Private collection of Gérard Barthélemy.
94. Auguste, pp. 154–55.
95. Pluchon, *Un révolutionnaire noir,* p. 494.
96. Pluchon, *Un révolutionnaire noir,* p. 495.
97. Césaire, p. 307.
98. Auguste, p. 161.
99. Roussier, p. 168.
100. Roussier, p. 166.
101. Roussier, p. 161.

102. Nemours, *Histoire de la captivité,* p. 31.
103. Lacroix, p. 354.
104. Lacroix, p. 354.
105. Roussier, p. 256.

SIX

Toussaint in Chains

1. Saint-Rémy, p. 94.
2. Roussier, p. 183.
3. Saint-Rémy, p. 95.
4. Saint-Rémy, p. 86.
5. Roussier, pp. 259–60.
6. Saint-Rémy, pp. 88–89.
7. Saint-Rémy, p. 123.
8. Saint-Rémy, p. 123.
9. Saint-Rémy, p. 29.
10. Saint-Rémy, p. 29.
11. Saint-Rémy, p. 30.
12. Saint-Rémy, p. 34.
13. Saint-Rémy, p. 36.
14. Saint-Rémy, p. 38.
15. Saint-Rémy, p. 44.
16. Saint-Rémy, pp. 44–45.
17. Saint-Rémy, p. 48.
18. Saint-Rémy, p. 49.
19. Saint-Rémy, p. 67.
20. Saint-Rémy, p. 69.
21. Saint-Rémy, pp. 84–85.
22. Saint-Rémy, p. 94.
23. Nemours, *Histoire de la captivité,* p. 241.
24. Nemours, *Histoire de la captivité,* p. 241.
25. Nemours, *Histoire de la captivité,* p. 246.
26. Nemours, *Histoire de la captivité,* p. 242.
27. Nemours, *Histoire de la captivité,* p. 242.

28. Nemours, *Histoire de la captivité,* p. 247.
29. Nemours, *Histoire de la captivité,* p. 248.
30. Nemours, *Histoire de la captivité,* p. 249.

SEVEN
Scattering the Bones

1. Pluchon, *Un révolutionnaire noir,* p. 527.
2. Saint-Rémy, p. 86.
3. Pluchon, *Un révolutionnaire noir,* p. 532.
4. Roland Lambalot, *Toussaint Louverture au Fort de Joux* (Pontarlier: Office de Tourisme, 1989), p. 19.
5. Césaire, p. 311.
6. Césaire, p. 322.
7. Chazotte, p. 52.

AFTERWORD
The Image of Toussaint

1. Phillips, p. 33.
2. Pluchon, *Un révolutionnaire noir,* p. 59.
3. Lacroix, p. 243.
4. Pluchon, *Un révolutionnaire noir,* pp. 471–72.
5. Lamartine, p. xxvii.
6. Lamartine, p. 35.
7. Phillips, p. 42.
8. Phillips, p. 54.

Bibliography

Asprey, Robert. *The Rise of Napoleon Bonaparte*. New York: Basic Books, 2000.

Auguste, Claude B. and Marcel B. *L'Expédition Leclerc, 1801–1803*. Port-au-Prince: Henri Deschamps, 1985.

Barthélemy, Gérard. "De la Spécificité des noirs libres (affranchis noirs) de Saint-Domingue." Unpublished essay.

———. "Qui êtes-vous Monsieur Toussaint?" Unpublished article.

Brown, Gordon S. *Toussaint's Clause: The Founding Fathers and the Haitian Revolution*. Jackson: University Press of Mississippi, 2005.

Cabon, Père Adolphe. *Histoire d'Haïti*. Port-au-Prince: Petit Séminaire Collège Saint-Martial, 1937.

Cauna, Jacques de, ed. *Toussaint Louverture et l'indépendance d'Haïti*. Paris: Karthala, 2004.

Césaire, Aimé. *Toussaint Louverture: La révolution française et le problème colonial*. Paris: Présence Africaine, 1981.

Chazotte, Peter S. *Historical Sketches of the Revolutions and the Foreign and Civil Wars in the Island of St. Domingo, with a Narrative of the Entire Massacre of the White Population of the Island*. New York: W. M. Applegate, 1840.

Daguillard, Fritz. "The True Likeness of Toussaint Louverture," *Americas,* English edition. July 2003.

Dorsinville, Roger. *De Fatras-Bâton à Toussaint Louverture.* Alger: Entreprise National du Livre, 1980.

Dubois, Laurent. *Avengers of the New World: The Story of the Haitian Revolution.* Cambridge: Belknap Press of Harvard University Press, 2004.

Fick, Carolyn E. *The Making of Haiti: The Saint Domingue Revolution from Below.* Knoxville: University of Tennessee Press, 1990.

Fouchard, Jean, Gabriel Debien, and Marie Antoinette Menier. "Toussaint-Louverture avant 1789: Légendes et Réalités," *Conjonctions: Revue Franco-Haïtienne,* no. 134 (June–July 1977).

Geggus, David Patrick. *Haitian Revolutionary Studies.* Bloomington: Indiana University Press, 2002.

———. *Slavery, War and Revolution: The British Occupation of Saint Domingue, 1793–1798.* Oxford: Clarendon Press, 1982.

Gros. *Récit historique sur les événements qui se sont succédés dans les camps de la Grande Rivière, du Dondon, de Saint Suzanne et autres.* Baltimore: S. & J. Adams, 1793.

Heinl, Robert Debs, and Nancy Gordon Heinl. *Written in Blood: The Story of the Haitian People, 1492–1995.* 2nd ed. Rev. and expanded by Michael Heinl. Lanham, Md.: University Press of America, 1996.

Hurbon, Laënnec. *Religions et lien social: L'église et l'état moderne en Haïti.* Paris: Les Editions du Cerf, 2004.

James, C. L. R. *The Black Jacobins: Toussaint L'Ouverture and the San Domingo Revolution.* London: Allison & Busby, 1980.

King, Stewart R. *Blue Coat or Powdered Wig: Free People of Color in Pre-Revolutionary Saint Domingue.* Athens: University of Georgia Press, 2001.

Korngold, Ralph. *Citizen Toussaint.* New York: Hill and Wang, 1944.

Lacroix, General Pamphile de. *La Révolution d'Haïti.* Paris: Karthala, 1995.

Lamartine, Alphonse de. *Toussaint Louverture,* ed. Léon-François Hoffmann. Exeter: University of Exeter Press, 1998.

Laurent, Gérard M. *Toussaint Louverture à travers sa correspondance.* Madrid: Industrias Gráficas España, 1953.

Madiou, Thomas. *Histoire d'Haïti*. 2 vols. Port-au-Prince: Editions Henri Deschamps, 1989.

Métral, Antoine. *Histoire de l'expédition des Français à Saint-Domingue, Suivie des mémoires et notes d'Isaac Louverture*. Paris: Karthala, 1985.

Moïse, Claude. *Le Projet national de Toussaint Louverture et la constitution de 1801*. Port-au-Prince: Editions Mémoire, 2001.

Nemours, Colonel Alfred. *Histoire de la captivité et la mort de Toussaint-Louverture*. Paris: Editions Berger Levrault, 1929.

———. *Toussaint Louverture fond à Saint-Domingue la liberté et l'égalité*. Port-au-Prince: Editions Fardin, 1945.

O'Brien, Conor Cruise. *The Long Affair: Thomas Jefferson and the French Revolution, 1785–1800*. Chicago: University of Chicago Press, 1996.

Ott, Thomas O. *The Haitian Revolution, 1789–1804*. Knoxville: University of Tennessee Press, 1973.

Parkinson, Wenda. *"This Gilded African": Toussaint L'Ouverture*. London: Quartet Books, 1980.

Pélage-Marie Duboys. *Précis historique des annals de la colonie française de Saint-Domingue depuis 1789*. 2 vols. Manuscript. Paris: Bibliothèque Nationale.

Phillips, Wendell. "Toussaint L'Ouverture." Address delivered in New York and Boston, December 1861.

Pluchon, Pierre. *Toussaint Louverture: Un révolutionnaire noir d'Ancien Régime*. Paris: Fayard, 1989.

———. *Toussaint Louverture d'après le général de Kerverseau*. Port-au-Prince: Editions le Natal, 1987.

Roussier, Paul, ed. *Lettres du Général Leclerc, Commandant en Chef de l'Armée de Saint-Domingue en 1802*. Paris: Ernest Leroux & Société des Colonies Françaises, 1937.

Saint-Rémy, ed. *Mémoires du Général Toussaint-L'Ouverture écrits par lui-même, pouvant servir à l'histoire de sa vie*. Paris: Pagnerre, 1853.

Sannon, H. Pauléus. *Histoire de Toussaint-Louverture*. 3 vols. Port-au-Prince: Heraux, 1933.

Scharon, Faine. *Toussaint Louverture et la révolution de St-Domingue*. 2 vols. Port-au-Prince: Imprimerie de l'État, 1959.

Bibliography

Schoelcher, Victor. *Vie de Toussaint Louverture.* Paris: Karthala, 1982.

Stein, Robert Louis. *Léger Félicité Sonthonax: The Lost Sentinel of the Republic.* Cranbury, N.J.: Associated University Presses, 1985.

Trouillot, Michel Rolph. *Silencing the Past: Power and the Production of History.* Boston: Beacon Press, 1995.

Index

Adams, John, 169–71, 173, 191, 222, 223
Affiba, 59
affranchis (freedmen), 11, 73, 75, 82, 103
African slaves, 6–11, 58, 75, 83–5, 191; abuse of, 15, 68; annual importation of, 16; at Bréda Plantation, 65–70; emancipation of, 19, 54–6, 70, 95, 98, 100–4, 108, 111, 117, 132, 136, 174, 191 (*see also affranchis; anciens libres; nouveaux libres*); French Revolution and, 29; herbal medicine of, 24, 65; insurrection of, 20–45, 50–1, 53–6, 63–4, 75, 78–83, 85, 87, 185; manumission of, 73; life expectancy for, 15–16, 60; religion of, 20, 21 (*see also* Vodou); runaway, *see marronage*

Agé, General Pierre, 153, 182, 188, 200, 237
Ailhaud, Jean-Antoine, 46, 47, 49, 50, 53
Allemand (French commander), 54
Allier, Citizen, 202, 225
American Revolution, 5, 11–12, 30, 31, 41–2, 48, 200
Amiens, Peace of, 258
Amis des Noirs, Les, 38, 46
ancien libres (long-term free blacks), 56, 73, 97, 112, 117*n*, 118, 131, 136, 140, 146, 149
Andro Plantation, 121, 122, 126, 129
Anthéaume, Père, 164, 195
Antilles, 220

ABOUT THE AUTHOR

Madison Smartt Bell is the author of twelve novels and two collections of stories. *All Souls' Rising* was a finalist for the National Book Award and the PEN/Faulkner Award for Fiction. A professor of English and director of the Kratz Center for Creative Writing at Goucher College, he lives in Baltimore, Maryland, with his family.

A NOTE ON THE TYPE

This book was set in Adobe Garamond. Designed for the Adobe Corporation by Robert Slimbach, the fonts are based on types first cut by Claude Garamond (c. 1480–1561). Garamond was a pupil of Geoffroy Tory and is believed to have followed the Venetian models, although he introduced a number of important differences, and it is to him that we owe the letter we now know as "old style." He gave to his letters a certain elegance and feeling of movement that won their creator an immediate reputation and the patronage of Francis I of France.

Composed by North Market Street Graphics,
Lancaster, Pennsylvania